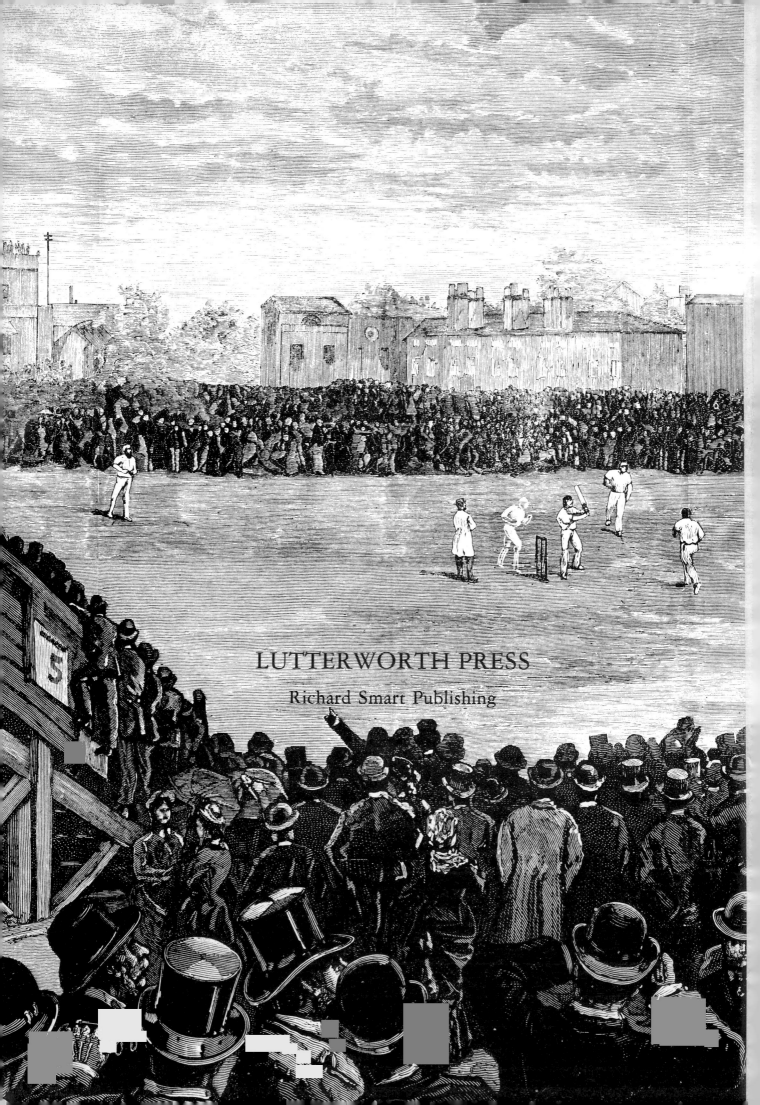

LUTTERWORTH PRESS

Richard Smart Publishing

ENGLAND *versus* AUSTRALIA

A pictorial history of the Test matches since 1877

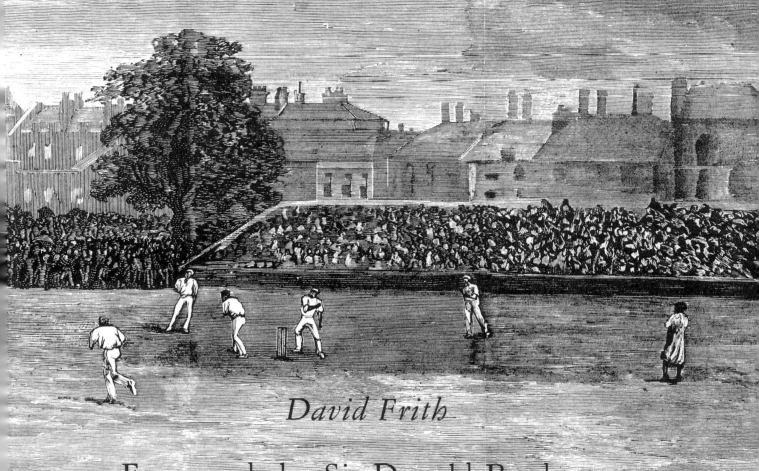

David Frith

Forewords by Sir Donald Bradman and Sir Leonard Hutton

First published 1977

796.35865

H1184488

Published by Lutterworth Press
Luke House, Farnham Road, Guildford, Surrey
and Richard Smart Publishing

ISBN 0 7188 7012 3

Printed by Jolly & Barber Limited
Rugby, Warwickshire

CONTENTS

Sir Leonard Hutton and Sir Donald Bradman meet at a Lord's Taverners function in London in 1974. David Frith (right) absorbs the reminiscences

FOREWORD BY SIR DONALD BRADMAN

In acceding to a request that I write a foreword to this unique pictorial history commemorating the centenary of Anglo-Australian Test cricket, I do so with mixed feelings. First, there is the wistful recollection that my own participation in these games dates back to 1928, so that I have been a witness, as it were, to the grand panorama for almost half the entire period of Test matches and I must be approaching the end of my innings! Second, there is a pride in that I made a contribution – and I like to think an honourable one – to the hundred years now being celebrated. Third, there is a deep humility that I cannot hope to do justice to a sport which, in my opinion, has had a more beneficial influence on the British people than any other. Neither can I adequately portray in words the immortal stories of those wonderful players who paved the way and made this historic record possible.

What a memorable day it must have been at the Melbourne Cricket Ground when, on March 15, 1877, Charles Bannerman of Australia took strike to the first ball ever bowled in Test cricket! Fitting it surely was that he went on to register the first Test century (the only one he ever made in a Test match) and, strangely, became the first man to conclude his innings 'retired hurt'. A grateful public subscribed £1 for every run he made (165) and if one equates the worth of an Australian £1 in 1877 with its current debased value, Charles Bannerman must have been catapulted by that innings into a state of relative affluence.

The drama began to unfold even before the first ball was bowled. Australia's finest bowler of that era, Spofforth, refused to play because the wicketkeeper he favoured (Murdoch) was not chosen. It is noteworthy also that Midwinter played for Australia. In 1881–82 he changed sides, played for England against Australia, and then (with apologies to Ripley) in 1882–83 back again for Australia against England. He remains the only man to have this unique distinction.

A final comment on the first Test is that the over consisted of four balls. I mention this because the scores credit Shaw with bowling 89 overs, of which 50 were maidens – an obviously misleading comparison with modern statistics. This highlights my personal opinion that any reference to maiden overs has long since become anachronistic and serves no useful purpose.

The stage having been set and the curtain having risen, spectators have been entertained, enthralled, exasperated; indeed have passed through almost every known emotion as subsequent kaleidoscopic events unfolded. Some of us were privileged to see cricket of almost indescribable skill and beauty, my outstanding memory being Stan McCabe's unforgettable 232 at Nottingham in 1938. In the concluding stages, he and Fleetwood-Smith put on 77 for the tenth wicket in 28 minutes. McCabe's contribution was 72, and Sir Neville Cardus highlighted the situation by saying: 'Fleetwood-Smith was almost as much a spectator as I was!' We are fortunate that McCabe's innings is enshrined for all time per medium of the pen of Sir Neville, whose contribution to the game of cricket through his unrivalled production of cricket literature will be a source of pleasure to cricket-lovers for generations to come.

One can find many examples of outstanding individual performances, not only of skill and artistry, but also of incredible determination and courage; for success in this great game frequently demands more than just natural ability. The intangible qualities of temperament and judgment are essential, but there is no line in the scorebook to record them.

I look back on my 50 years' association with first-class cricket with gratitude, despite some

traumatic periods, notably the 1932–33 Bodyline series of Tests in which I was quite innocently a central figure.

I prefer to forget moments of disappointment, such as the occasions when, as a selector, I could not persuade my colleagues to my way of thinking.

As an administrator, I have fought hard, but unsuccessfully, against certain Law changes which I remain convinced are not in the best interests of the game.

But transcending these things are the memories of, and friendships with, those wonderful people who have contributed so magnificently to cricket's history, many of them just lovers and supporters who made up for their lack of playing ability by a fanatical devotion to the sport.

Inevitably, of course, the performers get the limelight – though I'm not sure their respective contributions are correctly proportioned. In saying this, I include among 'performers' the umpires who exert such tremendous influence on the conduct of cricket, but seldom receive just praise. How can one measure, for instance, the impact of Frank Chester, who, in my early Test years, was undoubtedly the best umpire under whose adjudication I played, and who stamped his authority on the conduct of play during the '20s and '30s.

I have no intention of attempting to compile a glossary of the greatest players of my time; however, I may be excused the liberty of referring to certain ones who coloured my thinking or gave me the greatest joy. My boyhood hero was not one of the truly 'greats' – he was J.M. (Johnny) Taylor. Somehow or other, his style of batting, his superb outfielding and innate modesty made a deep impression on me. From the day I saw him play on the Sydney Cricket Ground in 1921, I sought to emulate his example.

Maybe it was my youthful and impressionable mind in 1921 that causes me still to regard McDonald and Gregory as the most lethal and devastating opening attack in history. They were closely rivalled, but not, in my view, excelled, by the Lindwall-Miller and the Lillee-Thomson combinations.

Explosive opening bowlers have always captured the imagination of the 'blood and thunder' spectators. One cannot help admiring them, and it would be churlish to deny their crucial part in deciding Test rubbers. Yet, for the connoisseur with less ebullient feelings, there has, I believe, been greater and more lasting pleasure in watching the subtle skills of such twins as Grimmett and O'Reilly, or Laker and Lock.

What cricket-lover could fail to be impressed by the unhurried technical batting skill of Sir Jack Hobbs and Sir Leonard Hutton; the unpredictable and exciting genius of Denis Compton; the grace and elegance of Frank Woolley; and the sheer majestic grandeur of Wally Hammond?

Who could hope to see wicketkeeping better than Oldfield, Tallon or Evans at their best? Fieldsmen like A.P.F. Chapman and Lock were electrifying; medium-pace bowling beyond compare was shown by Tate and Bedser.

I have only touched the fringe of the great names which adorn the pages of *Wisden* and which have contributed to a sporting literature unrivalled by any other sport.

To do justice to the game and its players in a foreword of this length is obviously impossible, and so I make no apology for the inadequacy of my references; though I do seek understanding for the omission of names and events more than worthy of mention. This book will be unique in that it will portray in pictures some of the people, places and events in a glorious one hundred years. My great hope is that the traditions of the past may prove an inspiration to coming generations, and that when the history of the next century comes to be written, it will be no less enthralling than the one just ended.

Adelaide, 1976   DON BRADMAN

FOREWORD BY SIR LEONARD HUTTON

One hundred years of fighting for the Ashes, and the tradition still survives, strong and healthy after many rumblings and minor tremors. The glorious uncertainty of the game marches on to its double-century.

No-one can help but admire and congratulate Australia on her overall success, of which, quite rightly, Australians are immensely proud. Australia is a huge continent with a population lost in it. It is too big, but it is this bigness that has, I think, something to do with their great sporting record.

'Play them at their own game' was the advice I was given when I first came to grips with the men from 'down under'. This I found most difficult to do, as we are all victims of our environment. Climate plays a great part in our sporting lives. There is such variety in Britain, particularly among people and wickets. The Englishman plays differently to the Australian because of the conditions in which we learn the game. To pull and to cut is dangerous for the Englishman in Australia; the Australian batsman in England has no such problems, and I would certainly say that I would prefer to bat on an English Test wicket than I would on what was described to me when I was a boy as 'a shirt-front' Australian pitch. Times have changed. Just about all that remains of the first England v Australia Test is the length of the pitch.

I once asked Sir Stanley Jackson who was the fastest bowler he had played against. He mentioned a man called Jones, an Australian. 'On one occasion', said Sir Stanley, 'I was batting with WG, and Jones made a ball go through the old man's beard.' So fast bowlers were fast then, and I dare say spin bowlers spun the ball sharply enough too.

I have been privileged to see Woodfull, Kippax, Hobbs, to talk to Macartney, Warwick Armstrong, Oldfield, to play against Rhodes, S.F. Barnes, Larwood, Tate, Bradman and O'Reilly, to play with and against Woolley, Sutcliffe, Hammond, Compton, Evans, Statham, Tyson, Trueman, Lindwall and Miller, and many others who were boyhood heroes of mine.

Shall we see the like of these men in the future? To see Bradman at close quarters was a revelation to me; his pull shot was a model of perfection. 'The Don' was the perfect run-making machine.

I shared several good partnerships in Test cricket with Walter Hammond. It was a wonderful experience. Hammond's authority at the wicket was outstanding.

Players such as these two come perhaps only once in a hundred years, as do bowlers of the class of S.F. Barnes and Bill O'Reilly. Both these bowlers had one thing in common: they had excellent direction and could bowl to their field.

I would like to give a thought to those who blazed the trail so long ago. W.G. Grace, Bobby Peel, George Hirst, Wilfred Rhodes. I knew all except WG, and became very close to George Hirst as a schoolboy. George said to me when I was 15 or 16: 'Whatever you do don't get like that Victor Trumper.' This remark concerning the great Australian rather staggered me. I asked George why and he replied: 'Victor Trumper was so superstitious that he made his life a misery!'

A final word on the administration of those fights for the Ashes. We here in England have been very fortunate through the decades in having the MCC at the helm. Their wisdom I am sure has done much to further the game in its best interest between the two countries.

Kingston Hill, 1976   LEN HUTTON

INTRODUCTION

The twenty-two combatants in the first Test match (though it was not then referred to as such), in March 1877 at the tree-fringed Melbourne Cricket Ground, can have had scant notion of how public curiosity in England v Australia matches would swell in the years ahead. Within twenty years the series was firmly established and enticing spectators from all corners of both countries. It was to become a bond of Empire, a focal point of fervid speculation and, at the same time, of reminiscence, compounded as the decades advanced. As the passenger ships made their leisurely way to and fro with their cabinloads of international cricketers, one Test rubber after another extended the saga. Global war twice caused suspensions. Otherwise, the exchanges have been regular and almost frequent enough. Means of communication, crowd expression and other associated phenomena have adjusted to the times: teams are now transported by air in a matter of hours; 'live' pictures of play are transmitted to millions through television; the fabricated radio commentaries of the 1930s have long since been superseded by instantaneous broadcasts.

Charles Bannerman made the first run for Australia on that opening day in 1877; ninety-eight years later Doug Walters made the 100,000th. The cavalcade of great players in between is awe-inspiring, and an imposing crop of tour books and brochures has sprung from their deeds. Charles Pardon, Ranjitsinhji, P.F. Warner, Frank Laver, Philip Trevor, J.B. Hobbs, E.H.D. Sewell, P.G.H. Fender, Sydney Smith, M.A. Noble, A.E.R. Gilligan, Bruce Harris, D.R. Jardine, Arthur Mailey, William Pollock, Neville Cardus, Denzil Batchelor, Clif Cary, J.H. Fingleton, W.J. O'Reilly, John Arlott, E.W. Swanton, A.G. Moyes, E.M. Wellings, Alan Ross, Rex Alston, Peter West, R.S. Whitington – each with his own approach, be it witty, acerbate, penetrative, or happily superficial, with or without a collaborator – these are the authors whose battle dispatches have carried the story through to the present generation. As for newspaper columnage allotted to the Tests, who could possibly calculate it, even to within a thousand yards?

Yet, with all that has gone before, this volume concentrates on the picture, which is said to paint a thousand words. Cardus, each one of whose numerous essays is cherished, may have written of Grimmett as a 'miser' with 'rubbered boots' and 'an arm as low as my grandfather's', but a photograph of the slight spin bowler, cap peak over eyebrows, standing unobtrusively at the end of his little follow-through, having bowled Hobbs, says it another way, and unequivocally. Words may portray the movement, the spirit, and the effect, but the photograph preserves almost perfectly faithfully the outline of the fleeting reality – undiminished and unembellished truth, in all its immediacy; the cruel, unyielding passage of Time cheated for a hundredth of a second.

Cricket as a passion is distinctly contagious. I have often mused over the hour of my own enslavement. On warm, dusty, summer evenings in a quiet Sydney suburb I was Len Hutton, striving to play masterfully forward to the lad across the road's Ian Johnson, turning his off-breaks nastily off the dry grass. It was a relaxation between schooltime and homework, nothing more. In boyhood I had listened with mild interest to the wireless bulletins from Australia during the 1946–47 series, and watched the fuzzy picture on a neighbour's television set during 1948 (when, impressionable child, taking inspiration from the Olympic Games, I ran up and down the street with a cocoa-tin stuffed with smouldering cotton wool, declared our own Games open, and smartly incorporated cricket into our programme). In early youth, in Australia, when school holidays were heavy with boredom, I mounted a

radio vigil while the tense first and second Tests of the 1950–51 series were played out. Then one night Keith's grandfather tottered onto the verandah and asked if I'd like to go with them next day to the Test match. Why not? I would be in good company. The ancient man with the yellowed glasses and his tall, white-haired friend and neighbour were forever talking cricket. Their reminiscences – always of Bardsley, Trumper, Hill and Mailey, Macartney, Andrews, Taylor and Armstrong – rendered them, if anything, better guides and mentors than younger, thrill-seeking companions. Keith scratched in the dust a plan of the Sydney Cricket Ground. The M.A. Noble Stand is here; the Sheridan Stand there; and the pavilion there; this is the Hill; this is the Brewongle Stand: areas and edifices to become quite as familiar to me as my parents' faces.

We set out on that shimmering morning, the fine, old, upright Mr Cooper at the wheel of the venerable, canvas-hooded Chev, wizened Mr Sullings beside him, Keith and I rocking in the back as we rattled up Princes Highway and hit the tramlines in Newtown. Through the old parts of South Sydney – factories, stray Europeans, and imitation-English terraced houses – and into the openness of Moore Park and the expanse of trampled grass now giving best to all shapes and sizes of motor car. Through the turnstile, into a new world. Past the Victor Trumper memorial plaque, into the sunlight, play already in progress, along the crescent at the base of the formidable Hill, onto a wooden seat side-on to the pitch.

A young, square-shouldered fieldsman was poised on the boundary in front of us. Years later he became Bishop of Liverpool. Now he was substituting for one of England's injured players, and the bowling toil befell three valiant men, Bedser, Brown, and Warr. Closing my eyes, I can see again Loxton's clout to midwicket and hear the smack as Bedser's huge hands absorbed the ball. I can still visualise some of Miller's noble strokes, and recapture the beauty of Harvey's batting, and the overwhelming roar of the crowd.

Thus one boy's devotion was sealed. There were visits to Alan Kippax's shop, and Stan McCabe's, and Bert Oldfield's, with its leathery smell and gallery of framed photos – the Hammond cover-drive, 'Tibby' Cotter, and dozens more – and Charles Macartney usually beyond access in the upstairs office. Then came the first steps towards building a cricket library. A matriculation was obtained in spite of the distraction of Test broadcasts from eight at night till three in the morning in the memorable English summer of 1953. A portable radio provided the lifeline to an addict at work at the counter of a bank (one of whose clients, joy of joys, was Arthur Mailey), augmented by not desperately serious sore throats and migraine attacks when England played in Sydney. There were abandonments, later in life, of a bemused family, to trace and talk with old players in both countries – Jack Gregory, Harold Larwood, S.F. Barnes, 'Stork' Hendry, Frank Woolley, Arthur Gilligan, Herbert Strudwick, 'Tiger' Smith, Bill O'Reilly, Wilfred Rhodes, Percy Fender, George Geary, Ian Peebles, Herbert Sutcliffe, Jack Fingleton, Les Ames, Eddie Paynter, Cyril Walters, Andy Sandham, Bob Wyatt, and warriors less venerable – even to discover the unclaimed ashes of C.T.B. Turner in a cardboard box in a Waverley funeral director's office. What disruption these Tests can breed.

And so it went on, with O'Neill, who came from among us, taking the position once held by Harvey at number three in the Australian order, Harvey having tenanted it after such as Bradman, Macartney, Hill, Giffen, and Murdoch. Evans, who wore England's wicketkeeping gloves in succession to Lyttelton, MacGregor, Lilley, Strudwick, Duckworth, and Ames, was to hand them to other representatives, from whom they were passed eventually to his Kent successor Knott. The duels of my slender, pale-faced idol Hutton with my other idol, the fiery, rhythmic Lindwall, gave way to duels between Edrich and McKenzie. Lillee and Thomson regenerate the electrifying breed of blitz bowlers, sired by Spofforth and Richardson and Lockwood and Jones last century. The flow continues.

There must have been something like five thousand hours of England-Australia Test cricket so far. In this book we have a thousand particles of time, arranged so that the reader may choose a time and place and go to it. Visual chroniclers of the next hundred years will have far greater resources upon which to draw. Whether they will know the same sepia charm of antiquity remains to be seen. Whether the deep emotional links between Britain and Australia as nations remain firm also remains to be seen. It says much for cricket that it has continued to render each country important to the other even though adverse politico-economic forces lately have thrown shadows over old relationships.

'We're gonna tan the hide off ya!' big Ernie Jones, the fast bowler turned stevedore, used to bellow as a greeting to MCC teams as they berthed at Fremantle, while Sir Robert Menzies has written* that 'Great Britain and Australia are of the same blood and allegiance and history and instinctive mental processes. We know each other so well that, thank Heaven, we don't have to be too tactful with each other.' So let it be.

*Wisden 1963

Guildford, 1976   DAVID FRITH

1876–77
Melbourne, March 15, 16, 17

FIRST TEST

Australia *245 (C. Bannerman 165 ret.ht) and 104 (A. Shaw 5 for 38, G. Ulyett 4 for 39); England 196 (H. Jupp 63, W.E. Midwinter 5 for 78) and 108 (T. Kendall 7 for 55). Australia won by 45 runs.*

The first of some 800 Test matches during Test cricket's first hundred years was played between sides that were hardly fully representative. The term 'Test' was as yet unknown, and few of the participants or onlookers could have had any idea of the vast importance that England-Australia matches – let alone cricket contests between other countries – would assume in years to follow. It was sunny and warm as, at one o'clock on Thursday, March 15, Charles Bannerman received the first ball from Alfred Shaw. By the end of play, at five o'clock, Australia were 166 for 6, Bannerman 126 not out; he played with great freedom, and punished Armitage's lobs so mercilessly that the bowler began trying to drop the ball on the full over the batsman's head onto the bails before resorting to 'grubbers' along the ground. Bannerman's historic innings was ended when a fast ball from Yorkshireman Ulyett split a finger, causing his retirement. Next-highest score came from Garrett, 18 not out, a run for every year of his age. Southerton, then aged 49, and Shaw were England's best bowlers, taking three wickets each. England replied with 196 – a deficit of 49 – but Australia's second-innings collapse left the touring team with only 154 for victory. The task would have been simpler without the last-wicket stand of 29 by Kendall and Hodges. England's first wicket fell without a run on the board, and a steady procession of batsmen followed as left-arm fast bowler Kendall broke through time and again. The crowd, which had built up to around 3000, gave both teams a hearty reception at the end. For years Australia's cricket had been developing fast. The three earlier English touring sides – Stephenson's in 1861-62, Parr's in 1863-64, and Grace's in 1873-74 – had played only against odds. Now Dave Gregory's side had won a famous victory on even terms over Lillywhite's professionals, and a great sporting tradition had begun.

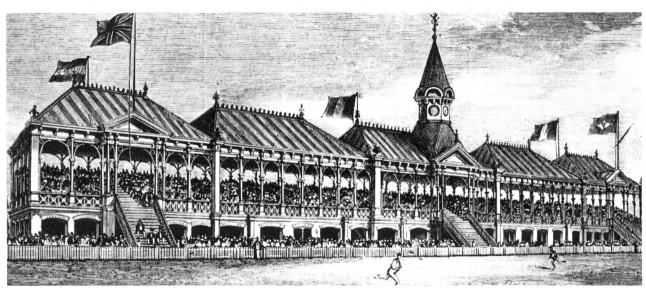

1, above: *The newly-built grandstand at Melbourne, from which the more privileged had a comfortable view of play.* 2, below, left: *Alfred Shaw, who bowled the first ball for England.* 3, right: *Charles Bannerman, who faced it – and many more before being compelled by injury to retire*

4: *The 1876–77 English touring team: back – H. Jupp, T. Emmett, R. Humphrey, A. Hill, T. Armitage; seated – E. Pooley, J. Southerton, James Lillywhite (captain), A. Shaw, G. Ulyett, A. Greenwood; in front – H.R.J. Charlwood, J. Selby*

1876–77
SECOND TEST
Melbourne, March 31, April 2, 3, 4

Australia *122 (A. Hill 4 for 27) and 259 (D.W. Gregory 43, N. Thompson 41, J. Southerton 4 for 46, J. Lillywhite 4 for 70); England 261 (G. Ulyett 52, A. Greenwood 49, A. Hill 49, T. Emmett 48, T. Kendall 4 for 82) and 122 for 6 (G. Ulyett 63).* England won by 4 wickets.

English pride was restored in a return fixture in which they fielded the only eleven players fit and available. Pooley, the first-choice wicketkeeper, did not rejoin the team after being caught up in some off-the-field trouble in New Zealand. For Australia, Spofforth, who refused to play in the earlier match because Murdoch was not to keep wicket, announced himself with some decidedly quick bowling, but Blackham, Australia's craftsman wicketkeeper, stood up at the stumps and even effected a stumping off Spofforth. Australia lost their first four wickets to Hill and finished dismally with 122, with Midwinter (31) top-scorer. Five Yorkshiremen contributed 219 of England's 243 from the bat, but an opening stand of 88 by Gregory and Thompson bit into the arrears, and though wickets fell steadily, Australia eventually led by 120. England began disastrously. Three wickets fell for nine runs, and even at 76 for 5 the match was anyone's. Then Ulyett, top-scorer in the first innings, hammered his side to the brink of victory and Hill did the rest. Lillywhite's team failed to generate high regard in Australia, where in many quarters it was being suggested that only the strongest side available should visit the colony in future.

5, above, left: *Dave Gregory, Australia's captain in the first three Test matches.* 6, above, right: *Harry Jupp, who made England's first half-century in Test cricket. In the second Test Kendall bowled him for 0 and 1.* 7, right: *Allan Hill, the Yorkshire fast bowler, who had fair all-round success in the second Test*

1878–79
Melbourne, January 2, 3, 4

ONLY TEST

England 113 (C.A. Absolom 52, F.R. Spofforth 6 for 48) and 160 (F.R. Spofforth 7 for 62); Australia 256 (A.C. Bannerman 73, T. Emmett 7 for 68) and 19 for 0. Australia won by 10 wickets.

Australia had shown during the 1878 tour of England (when no Tests were played) that they had an enviable array of bowlers. Lord Harris's side, which was all-amateur except for Ulyett and Emmett, was rich in batting. Thus the confrontation between the tourists and a team which with one exception had toured England only months earlier (shocking MCC by bowling them out for 33 and 19 and winning in a day) was anticipated with some fervour. A morning thunderstorm failed to dissuade Lord Harris from batting after winning the toss, and before lunch England were 26 for 7. Spofforth, in dismissing Royle, Mackinnon and Emmett, performed the first Test hat-trick. The captain (33) and Absolom managed to lift the total out of the depths of humiliation, but Australia were 95 for 3 at the close. Alec, small younger brother of Charles Bannerman of first-Test immortality, led Australia to a handsome lead with a slow but chanceless 73. England only just avoided an innings defeat, Lord Harris top-scoring with 36. Spofforth's match figures of 13 for 110 confirmed him as the world's most penetrative bowler. A return match was cancelled after the touring team's match against New South Wales was interrupted by larrikins who invaded the pitch and assaulted some of the players and an umpire.

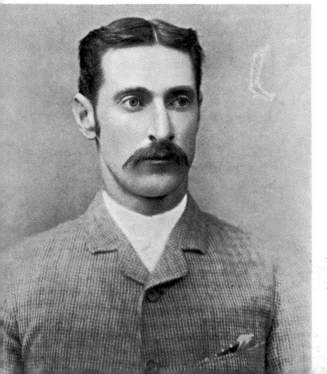

8, above, left: *The amateurs, who formed the bulk of Lord Harris's side: standing – R.D. Walker, F. Penn, Lord Harris, L. Hone, F.A. Mackinnon; centre row – A.P. Lucas, S.S. Schultz, Mrs Hornby, Lady Harris, H.D. Maul, C.A. Absolom; front – A.N. Hornby, Miss Ingram, V.P.F.A. Royle, A.J. Webbe.* 9, right: *Tom Emmett, the bluff Yorkshireman, whose 7 for 68 was not supported by very distinguished England batting.* 10, left: *'Demon' Spofforth, who took the first Test hat-trick among his 13 wickets at Melbourne*

1880
The Oval, September 6, 7, 8

ONLY TEST

England *420 (W.G. Grace 152, A.P. Lucas 55, Lord Harris 52, A.G. Steel 42) and 57 for 5; Australia 149 (F. Morley 5 for 56) and 327 (W.L. Murdoch 153*, P.S. McDonnell 43). England won by 5 wickets.*

The first Test match ever played in England was dominated by Dr W.G. Grace, who made 152 upon his debut, and W.L. Murdoch, who passed the new individual batting record when Australia followed on. Following upon the Sydney riot of 1879, the 1880 Australians had certain difficulties in obtaining fixtures in England, and it was only because of the efforts of the Surrey authorities that the first Test in England was not postponed still further. Apart from Spofforth's absence through injury, both sides were at near-full strength. At the close of the first day England were 410 for 8, Grace having put on 91 for the first wicket with his elder brother EM, and 120 for the second with Lucas. By lunch on the second day Australia were 126 for 9, light rain the previous evening probably having changed the nature of the pitch. All seemed lost when three wickets fell for 14 in the follow-on, but McDonnell and others stayed with the gallant Murdoch, who went in at the fall of the first wicket, and England were eventually set 57 to win. After some frights, the runs were made, though the third Grace brother – GF (Fred) – made his second nought in his only Test appearance, having made one of history's most famous catches off a monster hit by the giant Bonnor – the batsmen were on their third run as the ball was safely caught. G.F. Grace, aged 29, died a fortnight later from a chill and lung congestion.

11: *Lord Harris, England's captain in the first home Test, runs to save a boundary*

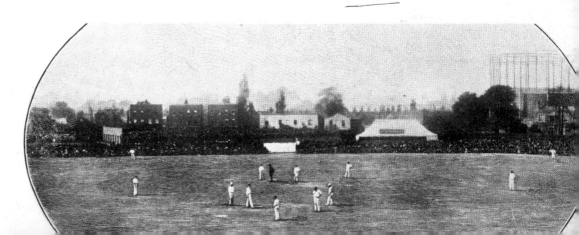

12, above, left: *A commemorative belt buckle.* 13, above, right: *Lord Harris concedes the importance of Spofforth's absence even 50 years later.* 14, right: *General view of the match*

1881–82
Melbourne, December 31, January 2, 3, 4

FIRST TEST

England 294 (G. Ulyett 87, W. Bates 58, J. Selby 55) and 308 (J. Selby 70, W.H. Scotton 50*, W. Bates 47, A. Shaw 40, W.H. Cooper 6 for 120); Australia 320 (T.P. Horan 124) and 127 for 3. Match drawn.

Four Tests were played during the 1881–82 tour, the first of several enterprises embarked upon by the partnership of Shaw, Shrewsbury and Lillywhite, with the first-named as captain, and the team composed entirely of professionals, including W.E. Midwinter, who became the only man ever to play for Australia against England and *vice versa*. England's innings owed most to a second-wicket stand of 137 between the hard-hitting Ulyett and little Selby. Medium-pacer Edwin Evans took 3 for 81 off 71 four-ball overs, of which 35 were maidens. In reply, Australia owed much to Irish-born Horan, whose century was founded on the straight-drive. He added 107 for the fifth wicket with Giffen, who was to become a major all-rounder, and now made 30 on his debut. England soon wiped off the deficit, but Cooper, an ancestor of A.P. Sheahan, who played against England from 1968 to 1972, created some havoc with his leg-breaks, and only an obdurate innings by Scotton, supported by Shaw, saw to it that, on a still blameless pitch, Australia would not have time to bat their way to victory.

15: *Tom Horan, who featured with Giffen in the first century partnership in Tests for Australia*

16: *John Selby, of Notts, who played two staunch innings for England*

17: *William Cooper, whose leg-breaks embarrassed England*

1881–82
Sydney, February 17, 18, 20, 21

SECOND TEST

England 133 (G.E. Palmer 7 for 68) and 232 (G. Ulyett 67, R.G. Barlow 62, T.W. Garrett 4 for 62, G.E. Palmer 4 for 97); Australia 197 (H.H. Massie 49, J.McC. Blackham 40, W. Bates 4 for 52) and 169 for 5 (W.L. Murdoch 49). Australia won by 5 wickets.

Sydney's first Test match fluctuated between Australian ascendancy and an even balance: England were never quite in command after back-pedalling all the first day. Palmer and Evans bowled unchanged for over three hours throughout England's modest first innings, and by the second evening the tourists were in again, facing arrears of 64. Yet Ulyett and Barlow, in their contrasting styles, built an opening of 122, and a sizable task seemed in prospect for Australia. The batting then collapsed before the bowling of Palmer and Garrett, and Murdoch, with care and supported by several determined partners, took Australia to the point of victory. During the match Murdoch and Blackham shared the wicketkeeping duties. Between this and the previous Test, the English party played seven matches in New Zealand.

18: *Hugh Massie, bank officer, strong driver, lethal cutter*

19: *G.E. 'Joey' Palmer, young bowler with a touch of genius*

20: *Edwin Evans, a supreme all-rounder from New South Wales*

1881–82
Sydney, March 3, 4, 6, 7

THIRD TEST

England *188 (A. Shrewsbury 82, G.E. Palmer 5 for 46) and 134 (A. Shrewsbury 47, T.W. Garrett 6 for 78, G.E. Palmer 4 for 44); Australia 260 (P.S. McDonnell 147, A.C. Bannerman 70, E. Peate 5 for 43) and 66 for 4. Australia won by 6 wickets.*

England's first five wickets fell for 56 on a difficult pitch, and only the great skill of Shrewsbury enabled them to approach 200. Australia were allowed to prepare a fresh pitch for their innings, and were themselves 24 for 3 at the end of the first day, a score taken to 146 for 3 when heavy rain cut short the second day. Young McDonnell, London-born, displayed his great hitting powers, once putting Bates over the pavilion. His stand with Bannerman realised 199, but once it was broken, Peate ran through the side. The next-highest scorer after McDonnell and Bannerman was S.P. Jones with seven not out. Shrewsbury again stood almost alone when England batted, and Australia gathered in the necessary runs by the 50th over to go two-up in the series.

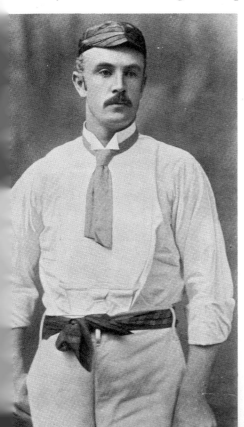

21, left: *Percy McDonnell, another of Australia's mighty hitters.* 22, right: *Tom Garrett, still the youngest player to appear in these Test matches*

1881–82
Melbourne, March 10, 11, 13, 14

FOURTH TEST

England 309 (*G. Ulyett 149, T.W. Garrett 5 for 80*) *and* 234 for 2 (*G. Ulyett 64, R.G. Barlow 56, W. Bates 52*, J. Selby 48**); Australia 300 (*W.L. Murdoch 85, P.S. McDonnell 52, W.E. Midwinter 4 for 81*). Match drawn.

'Happy Jack' Ulyett started his big innings unusually cautiously, but accelerated later. Its value may be assessed against the next-highest score – Emmett's 27. Ulyett was ninth out. In continuing great heat, Australia led off with 110 for the first wicket by A.C. Bannerman (suffering from sunstroke) and Murdoch, but this was easily the highest stand of the innings, and when England progressed to an overall lead of 243 with eight wickets standing they seemed to be headed for a morale-boosting victory at last. Then the weather broke, and the fourth day was washed out. With the Australians due to sail for England, there was no chance of extending the match, which was the last to be drawn in Australia until 1946–47.

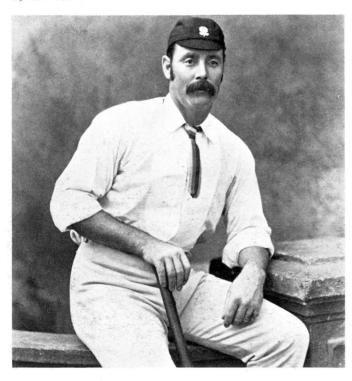

23, left: *George Ulyett, the strong Yorkshire all-rounder.* 24, above: *William Midwinter, the only man to play for Australia against England and vice versa*

1882
The Oval, August 28, 29

ONLY TEST

Australia 63 (*R.G. Barlow 5 for 19, E. Peate 4 for 31*) *and* 122 (*H.H. Massie 55, E. Peate 4 for 40*); England 101 (*F.R. Spofforth 7 for 46*) *and* 77 (*F.R. Spofforth 7 for 44*). Australia won by 7 runs.

One of the most famous of all cricket matches, this extraordinary contest led to the creation of the Ashes. After the 'Colonials', from a dreadful beginning, had fought back to defeat the full might of England in two days, the *Sporting Times* published a mock obituary of English cricket. It concluded: 'The body will be cremated and the ashes taken to Australia.' The man chiefly responsible for the upset was Fred Spofforth, 'The Demon'. Only Bob Massie in 1972 has surpassed his figures of 14 for 90 for Australia in a Test against England. Australia were first bowled out in 2¼ hours by the left-handers Barlow and Peate on a pitch which had absorbed two days' rain. Spofforth bowled Grace for four, and six England wickets fell before a lead was obtained. The 'Demon' bowled with fire and with guile, stirred, it is said, by some derogatory remarks overheard in the pavilion. On the second day, with the ground wet after further downpours, Massie went after the bowling and made 55 in three-quarters of an hour. Missed at 38, he made possible by his strength and audacity a victory that was to be celebrated in prose and verse for decades to come. A.C. Bannerman, his fellow opener, made 13 and Murdoch 29, but no-one else reached double-figures, and Australia's total of 122 left England a mere 85 to win. Grace's running out of Sammy Jones when the youngster left his crease to attend to a divot in the pitch did

nothing to reduce the grim if seemingly farfetched determination of the Australians. At 3.45 pm Grace and Hornby walked out to begin the job. With 15 on the board, England lost Hornby, bowled by Spofforth. Barlow went the same way next ball. Ulyett came in, and the runs began to flow. The fifty came up, and the match seemed over. Then Ulyett was caught at the wicket. Lucas joined Grace, but the Champion himself, having made 32, was caught at mid-off off Boyle. 53 for 4. Lyttelton, the wicket-keeper, joined Lucas, and soon, in almost total silence, the match fell into an eerie stalemate. Twelve successive maiden overs: then a deliberate misfield got Lyttelton opposite Spofforth. Having made 12, the 'keeper was bowled by Australia's master fast bowler. A.G. Steel, the talented amateur all-rounder, came in. Lucas hit a four – loudly cheered by the nervy twenty thousand – then Steel was caught-and-bowled Spofforth. 70 for 6. Maurice Read was then bowled second ball. Barnes hit a two, Blackham allowed three byes, then Lucas played on to Spofforth after a patient five runs. 75 for 8. Barnes was caught off his glove off Boyle's bowling. 75 for 9. Last man Peate joined C.T. Studd, who had oddly been kept back by Hornby to number 10 and had been observed shivering with a blanket around him in the dressing-room. Peate struck a two, then was bowled after heaving at a ball from Boyle. 'Ah couldn't troost Maister Stood,' he said later. Studd had made two centuries already that summer against the Australians. One spectator died of heart failure during the tense closing stages, and another had bitten through his umbrella handle. Henceforth Englishmen knew, if they had not known by now, that Australia offered the sternest of challenges to their national cricket eleven – and their pride.

25, above: *A precious photograph of The Oval during the 'Ashes match'. The players were moving rather too fast for the shutter speed of the camera.* 26, below: *As the artist from* The Illustrated Sporting and Dramatic News *saw play. The batsman is Grace, the bowler Spofforth, and the umpire Bob Thoms*

27, top: *An impression of the famous Oval match from* The Illustrated London News. 28, centre: *The scorecard and the captains' batting lists: Hornby's for England could be said to reflect the tension of the hour.* 29, left: *The urn containing the Ashes, with embroidered velvet bag.* 30, below: *The mock obituary notice in* The Sporting Times *which was to have unforeseen widespread effect*

In Affectionate Remembrance

OF

ENGLISH CRICKET,

WHICH DIED AT THE OVAL

ON

29th AUGUST, 1882,

Deeply lamented by a large circle of sorrowing
friends and acquaintances.

R.I.P.

N.B.—The body will be cremated and the
ashes taken to Australia.

1882–83
Melbourne, December 30, January 1, 2

FIRST TEST

Australia 291 (G.J. Bonnor 85, W.L. Murdoch 48, P.S. McDonnell 43) and 58 for 1; England 177 (G.E. Palmer 7 for 65) and 169 (G. Giffen 4 for 38). Australia won by 9 wickets.

The Hon. Ivo Bligh took a fairly strong side to Australia in a crusade to recover the Ashes, but had to withstand a setback precipitated by the weather in the first Test. Australia's sound 291 owed much to the huge, muscular Bonnor, who lofted a number of balls towards – and over – the boundary. After rain on the Sunday, the pitch was slower. Australia's last three wickets fell for 33 and England's first three for eight. Wicketkeeper Tylecote top-scored with 33, and repeated the feat with 38 in the follow-on, when, despite a more agreeable pitch, England managed only 169. 'Joey' Palmer, a talented young medium-pace spinner (and married to Blackham's sister), took 10 for 126 in the match.

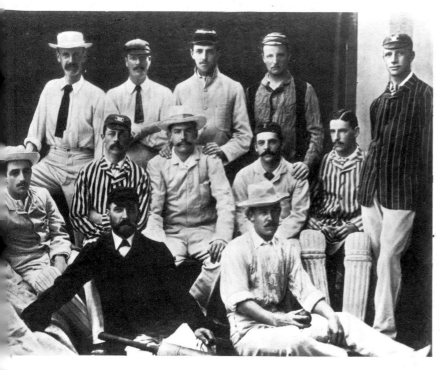

31, above, left: *The team that brought back the Ashes: standing – W. Barnes, F. Morley, C.T. Studd, G.F. Vernon, C.F.H. Leslie; seated – G.B. Studd, E.F.S. Tylecote, Hon. Ivo Bligh (captain), A.G. Steel, W.W. Read; in front – R.G. Barlow, W. Bates.* 32, above, right: *The 1773 George III penny used by Bligh to toss in these Tests.* 33, left: *George Giffen, 'the Australian WG'.* 34, right: *George Bonnor, one of the heftiest hitters of them all*

1882-83
Melbourne, January 19, 20, 22

SECOND TEST

England 294 (*W.W. Read 75, W. Bates 55, C.F.H. Leslie 54, G.E. Palmer 5 for 103, G. Giffen 4 for 89*); Australia 114 (*H.H. Massie 43, W. Bates 7 for 28*) and 153 (*W. Bates 7 for 74*). England won by an innings and 27 runs.

Fred Morley, who was seriously injured during the voyage out when the ship collided with another, was brought into England's team, but his fast, left-arm, roundarm deliveries lost their effect with his disability, and he was to die the following year. This was 'Billy Bates's match'. The Yorkshireman, coming in at the fall of the seventh wicket at 199, dominated a stand of 88 with Read. Then, coming on as England's fifth bowler, he found a spot at the northern end which Giffen had used to perplex some of England's batsmen, and proceeded to decimate Australia. Massie and Bannerman had posted 56 for the first wicket – the former making 43 of them – and this was all but half the final total. The crescendo of Bates's success came as he bowled McDonnell, caught-and-bowled Giffen next ball, then bluffed Bonnor out for the hat-trick. By placing a short mid-on he persuaded the big hitter to poke timidly at his first ball, jabbing it for a catch to Read. Murdoch's unbeaten 19 occupied 2½ hours. In the follow-on only Bonnor showed any real resistance. His 34 contained three hits over the boundary, which then counted as only five runs. Bates's slow-medium roundarm bowling, breaking appreciably from the off, was again too much for the home batsmen. His 14 wickets linked with a half-century is a unique distinction in a Test match against Australia. For his hat-trick, admirers presented him with £31 and a tall hat made of silver.

35, below: *How a cartoonist saw Australia's pathetic batting procession.* 36, bottom, left: *Walter Read, the splendid Surrey amateur.* 37, right: *Billy Bates – a fifty, a hat-trick, and 14 wickets in the match*

1882–83
THIRD TEST
Sydney, January 26, 27, 29, 30

England 247 (W.W. Read 66, E.F.S. Tylecote 66, F.R. Spofforth 4 for 73) and 123 (F.R. Spofforth 7 for 44); Australia 218 (A.C. Bannerman 94, G. Giffen 41, F. Morley 4 for 47) and 83 (R.G. Barlow 7 for 40). England won by 69 runs.

A stand of 116 between Read and Tylecote saved the England innings when it stood at 75 for 5. By the end of the first day, which had attracted over 20,000 spectators, Australia, batting on a fresh pitch, by arrangement, to offset the advantage of the toss, were eight without loss. There was rain about during the night and on the second day, but Bannerman and Giffen raised 76 for the first wicket, and Australia were strongly set at 133 for one on Saturday evening. More rain on Sunday left the pitch treacherous, and but for poor English fielding Australia would not have made as many as 218. Resuming on the pitch they had used in their first innings, England did not expect – and did not make – many runs to add to their early advantage of 29. There was an inevitability about the play as Spofforth used the conditions as he pleased. Australia's target of 153 was distant in the circumstances, and receded from sight altogether as Barlow, the slow-medium left-arm bowler from Lancashire, keeping a full length, confounded the opposition, for whom Blackham top-scored with 26. Following England's triumph, some Melbourne ladies (one of whom became Bligh's bride) burnt a bail, sealed it in an urn, and presented it to the England captain. Lord Darnley (as he became), who died in 1927, bequeathed the Ashes to Lord's, where they now remain as an eternal symbol of England v Australia competition.

38, left: *The ill-fated Fred Morley, an early commuter casualty.* 39, above: *Edmund Fernando Sutton Tylecote, England wicketkeeper and joint saviour of the first innings*

1882–83
FOURTH TEST
Sydney, February 17, 19, 20, 21

England 263 (A.G. Steel 135*, C.T. Studd 48) and 197 (W. Bates 48*); Australia 262 (G.J. Bonnor 87, J.McC. Blackham 57) and 199 for 6 (A.C. Bannerman 63, J.McC. Blackham 58*). Australia won by 4 wickets.

Australia levelled the series in this additional match, though it was accepted that Bligh had already restored England's honour in the decisive third Test. Here, in a match where a fresh pitch was prepared *for each innings,* an evenly-contested game was won at the crucial stage by Bannerman's uncharacteristic flair and Blackham's determination. Steel's innings on the first day was in two distinct parts. Missed by Murdoch before he had scored, the Lancashire amateur moved unimpressively to his fifty, then revealed the polished batsmanship that had made his name. Bonnor's innings was hardly typical: he was unwell. But the runs were invaluable, as were Blackham's – this is a rare instance of two half-centuries in a match by a wicketkeeper.

40, left: *A.G. Steel – a 'curate's egg' of a century at Sydney.* 41, centre: *C.T. Studd – 48 here; a missed opportunity at The Oval six months earlier.* 42, right: *Jack Blackham – two half-centuries for Australia*

1884
Old Trafford, July 10, 11, 12

FIRST TEST

England 95 (*A. Shrewsbury 43, H.F. Boyle 6 for 42, F.R. Spofforth 4 for 42*) and 180 for 9 (*G.E. Palmer 4 for 47*); Australia 182. Match drawn.

Manchester's first scheduled day of Test cricket was washed out, and in muddy conditions batsmen struggled thereafter. Shrewsbury gave a wonderful display of wet-wicket batsmanship against the feared partnership of Spofforth and bearded medium-pace spinner Boyle. Seven Australians made double-figures, with Midwinter, now playing against England once more, heading the innings with 37. On a drier pitch England had to exercise care in regaining the lead, and again the stylish Lucas batted with patience and fine judgment. Grace's 31 was of great value, but it was well into the final day before England were out of danger.

43, left: *Harry Boyle, excellent foil for Spofforth, and pioneer of the silly mid-on position.* 44, right: *A.P. Lucas, correct, elegant batsman, sometime opener, sometime in the middle order*

1884
Lord's, July 21, 22, 23

SECOND TEST

Australia 229 (H.J.H. Scott 75, G. Giffen 63, E. Peate 6 for 85) and 145 (G. Ulyett 7 for 36); England 379 (A.G. Steel 148, G.E. Palmer 6 for 111). England won by an innings and 5 runs.

Steel's century, made out of 261 while he batted, was a splendid innings, surpassing in quality of strokeplay his hundred at Sydney the previous year. When he went in, England were 90 for 3, and a long way from their eventual triumph. Spofforth bowled unluckily, and unwittingly aided England in cutting up the pitch with his spikes. Ulyett brought the ball back sharply off the rough area, and sank Australia in their second innings. His dismissal of Bonnor was notable: he clung to a ferocious straight drive in his followthrough. Australia's first innings owed much to a last-wicket stand of 69 between Scott and Boyle. The former was caught by his own captain, Murdoch, fielding as substitute for Grace, whose finger was injured.

45, left: *Dr H.J.H. 'Tup' Scott, who was to lead Australia in England in 1886.* 46, right: *Ted Peate, one of the long line of clever slow left-arm bowlers from Yorkshire*

1884
The Oval, August 11, 12, 13

THIRD TEST

Australia 551 (W.L. Murdoch 211, P.S. McDonnell 103, H.J.H. Scott 102, A. Lyttelton 4 for 19); England 346 (W.W. Read 117, W.H. Scotton 90, G.E. Palmer 4 for 90) and 85 for 2. Match drawn.

Australia's innings, in hot conditions and with a fast pitch and outfield, was spread over 9½ hours, and Murdoch was in for over eight hours for the first double-century in Test cricket. McDonnell, in contrast, having opened the innings, was out with the total 158, a stand of 143 for the second wicket. Murdoch added 207 for the third with Scott in even time, Australia ending the first day at 363 for 2. By the end of the mammoth innings all eleven England players had bowled, the Hon. Alfred Lyttelton, the wicket-keeper, taking four cheap wickets with underarm lobs. By mid-afternoon on the final day England were 181 for 8, but Read, seething at having to bat at number 10, struck a furious century in just under two hours and added 151 with the somnolent left-hander Scotton, who had opened the innings. This is now the oldest partnership record in England-Australia Tests. Scotton's 90 took 340 minutes and inspired some satirical verse in *Punch.* The follow-on was enforced as a matter of routine. The Ashes remained in England's custody.

47, below, left: *Hon. Alfred Lyttelton, 'keeper-bowler.* 48, centre: *William Scotton, dour left-hander.* 49, right: *Billy Murdoch, first double-centurion*

1884-85
Adelaide, December 12, 13, 15, 16

FIRST TEST

Australia 243 (P.S. McDonnell 124, J. McC. Blackham 66, W. Bates 5 for 31) and 191 (P.S. McDonnell 83, G. Giffen 47, R. Peel 5 for 51); England 369 (W. Barnes 134, W.H. Scotton 82, G. Ulyett 68, G.E. Palmer 5 for 81) and 67 for 2. England won by 8 wickets.

The first five-Test series was closely fought, though Australia, rent by internal disputes, were under full strength. McDonnell's second Test century in succession was made in typically robust manner, and he might have repeated the performance in the second innings but for Giffen's refusal to respond to his call for a single. Australia were 190 for 3 at one point, but fell away before Bates's bowling. England were 232 for 2 at the close of the second day – a day of dust-storms. Barnes's innings lasted five hours, and Scotton's 5¾. Peel's slow-medium left-arm bowling tore the heart out of Australia's second innings – from which Alec Bannerman was missing because of a hand injury sustained in fielding a lusty hit by Ulyett.

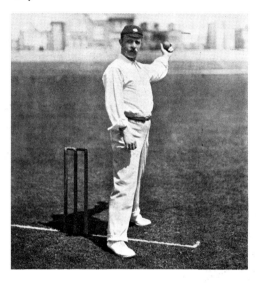

50, left: *Bobby Peel, in the first of his 20 Tests against Australia, took eight wickets. 51, right: Billy Barnes, the Notts all-rounder*

1884-85
Melbourne, January 1, 2, 3, 5

SECOND TEST

England 401 (J. Briggs 121, A. Shrewsbury 72, W. Barnes 58, S.P. Jones 4 for 47) and 7 for 0; Australia 279 (A.H. Jarvis 82, T.P. Horan 63, J.W. Trumble 59) and 126 (W. Bruce 45, W. Barnes 6 for 31). England won by 10 wickets.

Australia, with nine new caps pressed into service, contained England reasonably well – apart from Shrewsbury's virile innings – until the later stages of the innings, when Briggs batted with increasing confidence. His 121 took only 2½ hours and included 15 fours: he was missed twice towards the end. His stand of 98 with wicketkeeper Joe Hunter (39 not out) disheartened the home side. The efforts of Horan, Trumble and Jarvis almost saved the follow-on, but a fine catch at mid-on by Briggs at a crucial time helped end the innings. Bruce, who went in second-last, opened the second innings and was the only Australian to withstand Peel and the fast-medium Barnes for any length of time.

52, left: *Johnny Briggs, the little Lancashire left-hander, who excelled himself with the bat at Melbourne. 53, right: 'Affie' Jarvis, from South Australia: 82 in his first Test innings*

1884–85
Sydney, February 20, 21, 23, 24

THIRD TEST

Australia 181 (T.W. Garrett 51*, W. Flowers 5 for 46, W. Attewell 4 for 53) and 165 (W. Bates 5 for 24); England 133 (T.P. Horan 6 for 40, F.R. Spofforth 4 for 54) and 207 (W. Flowers 56, J.M. Read 56, F.R. Spofforth 6 for 90). Australia won by 6 runs.

A brilliant catch by Edwin Evans at point, to dismiss England's most successful batsman in the match, Wilfred Flowers, off Spofforth, gave Australia a thrilling victory and brought them back into the series. Flowers and Read had taken England to the brink of victory with a seventh-wicket stand of 102, but the last four wickets fell for 13 runs. Australia's opening innings had been saved by a last-wicket stand of 80 by Garrett and Evans after a lunchtime hailstorm had turned the ground into a great white expanse. England, batting on a fresh pitch, found Horan too difficult as he exploited a responsive patch where Spofforth's foot had come down. Smart fielding and catching kept England in contention, but in their quest for the required 214 runs, the turning point came with the glorious ball with which Spofforth bowled Shrewsbury, England's captain.

54, above, left: *William Attewell, steadiest of fast-medium bowlers.* 55, centre: *J.M.(Maurice) Read, all-rounder from Surrey.* 56, right: *Wilfred Flowers – wickets, runs, and in at the death at Sydney*

1884–85
Sydney, March 14, 16, 17

FOURTH TEST

England 269 (W. Bates 64, W. Barnes 50, J.M. Read 47, A. Shrewsbury 40, G. Giffen 7 for 117) and 77 (F.R. Spofforth 5 for 30, G.E. Palmer 4 for 32); Australia 309 (G.J. Bonnor 128, A.C. Bannerman 51, S.P. Jones 40, W. Barnes 4 for 61) and 40 for 2. Australia won by 8 wickets.

Bonnor's innings was magnificent. Starting uncertainly, he then began to employ his peerless power, sometimes trusting to luck, and in just under two hours he made 128 out of 169. When he entered, Australia were 119 for 6 – still 150 behind. He was missed at slip from the stroke that brought him his century – his only one in Tests – but in conditions which favoured the bowlers, his was an extraordinary innings. England batted a second time on the pitch used by Australia, but it broke up, and they were helpless against Palmer and Spofforth, who bowled unchanged. The home side then decided to use England's first-innings pitch, and squared the series.

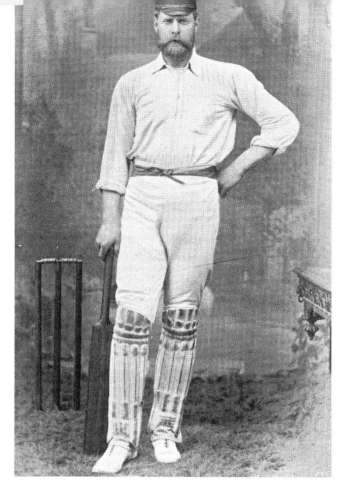

57, left: *Bonnor, the giant, whose only Test century was made in better than even-time.* 58, above: *Sammy Jones, who stayed with him while 154 runs were added*

1884–85
Melbourne, March 21, 23, 24, 25

FIFTH TEST

Australia 163 (F.R. Spofforth 50, G. Ulyett 4 for 52) and 125; England 386 (A. Shrewsbury 105*, W. Barnes 74, W. Bates 61, J. Briggs 43). England won by an innings and 98 runs.

The pitch was still damp from heavy watering, and Peel, Ulyett and Barnes took the first nine Australian wickets for 99. Then last man Spofforth, with some exotic strokes, put on 64 with J.W. Trumble (34 not out). Nevertheless, England were 44 without loss that evening, and progressed steadily to a commanding lead. Shrewsbury's century, the first by an England captain, was scored at the rate of 19 an hour, but contained many sweet pulls to rising off-side balls. Bates's contribution was valuable, though he was dropped several times, and retired unwell at one stage. Again Australia began disastrously, and never recovered, Ulyett, Flowers and Attewell taking three wickets apiece as England went on to retain the Ashes. One of the home players, Garrett, took the place of umpire Hodges when he refused to continue after tea on the third day. Hodges was protesting at the complaints by some of the Englishmen at some of his decisions.

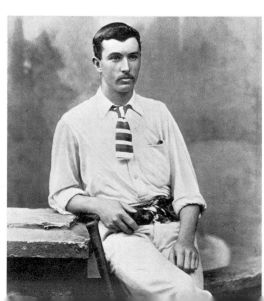

59, left: *Arthur Shrewsbury, the premier professional batsman in England in the 1880s.* 60, right: *Billy Bruce, who top-scored with 35 in Australia's second innings*

1886
FIRST TEST

Old Trafford, July 5, 6, 7

Australia 205 (S.P. Jones 87, A.H. Jarvis 45, G. Ulyett 4 for 46) and 123 (H.J.H. Scott 47, R.G. Barlow 7 for 44); England 223 (W.W. Read 51, F.R. Spofforth 4 for 82) and 107 for 6. England won by 4 wickets.

Australia, again under strength – without Murdoch, Horan, McDonnell, Bannerman and Massie – and unsettled by camp squabbles, had a disastrous series. With Jones and Jarvis at the wicket, the score had reached 134 for 2, but the innings then fell away. England, with Spofforth bowling almost at his fastest, were made to fight for the lead, but Australia went to pieces again in the second innings. They saw a glimmer of hope when Grace, Shrewsbury and Read were dismissed cheaply, but Barlow's dourness made sure that his bowling success was not wasted.

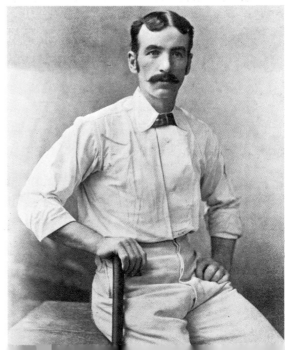

61, above, left: *Dick Barlow, the Lancashire all-rounder, who made 38 not out and 30 and took 7 for 44.* 62, above, right: *A silk scorecard of the match, presented to Barlow.* 63, right: *Dick Pilling, also of Lancashire, who kept wicket for England on his home ground*

1886
Lord's, July 19, 20, 21

SECOND TEST

England 353 (A. Shrewsbury 164, W. Barnes 58, F.R. Spofforth 4 for 73); Australia 121 (J. Briggs 5 for 29) *and 126 (G.E. Palmer 48, J. Briggs 6 for 45).* England won by an innings and 106 runs.

Shrewsbury's was one of the most praiseworthy innings in the history of the game. Rain soon after the start left the pitch ideal for bowling, and Shrewsbury's skill against the skidding ball, the kicking ball, the sharp turner, and the one that stops was put to the ultimate test, and with the aid of three difficult chances he survived for almost seven hours. At the end of the first day he was 91 and England miraculously had made 202 for the loss of Grace, Scotton, W.W. Read and Steel. The Shrewsbury-Barnes stand eventually realised 161. That evening Australia were 12 for one in the follow-on – still 220 behind – after Briggs had demolished them with his slow-medium left-arm bowling. He was even more successful on the last day, bowling from the pavilion end. Palmer, who opened, stayed 2½ hours, shaming some of his team-mates.

64, above: *An interpretation of the match, with Lord's still looking more rural than metropolitan.* 65, left: *Shrewsbury, an exceptionally skilful defensive player.* 66, right: *Briggs – his bowling and Shrewsbury's batting gave England a handsome victory at Lord's*

1886
The Oval, August 12, 13, 14

THIRD TEST

England 434 (*W.G. Grace 170, W.W. Read 94, J. Briggs 53, A. Shrewsbury 44, F.R. Spofforth 4 for 65*); Australia 68 (*G.A. Lohmann 7 for 36*) and 149 (*G. Giffen 47, G.A. Lohmann 5 for 68*). England won by an innings and 217 runs.

The weather dealt cruelly with the disappointed and disappointing Australians. After England's heavy innings, rain fell and assisted England's clever pair, Lohmann and Briggs, who bowled unchanged through Australia's first innings. Giffen, making runs at last after a poor series, saved his side from complete humiliation. Grace's 170 was made out of only 216 scored while he was in. His opening partner Scotton had taken 3¾ hours for 34, and the 19 posted in the first hour's play might have been less unexpected in a modern Test match. The first-wicket stand – 170 – was the highest so far for any England wicket, and Grace's was the best individual score for England to date. It took him 4½ hours and included 22 boundaries, one a huge drive off Spofforth into the crowd.

67, above: *Another of the earliest 'location' photographs – the Oval Test 1886. The batsman appears to be marking his guard.* 68, left: *Dr W.G. Grace, whose 170 added just one more to his numerous records.* 69, right: *George Lohmann, taker of 77 wickets in only 15 Tests against Australia*

1886–87
Sydney, January 28, 29, 31

FIRST TEST

England 45 (*C.T.B. Turner 6 for 15, J.J. Ferris 4 for 27*) and 184 (*J.J. Ferris 5 for 76*); Australia 119 and 97 (*W. Barnes 6 for 28*). England won by 13 runs.

McDonnell put England in and had the pleasure of seeing them humbled by a pair of new bowlers, 'Terror' Turner, right-arm, fast-medium off-break, and Ferris, left-arm fast-medium. Often taking advantage of each others' 'footprints' at the other end, they became a feared and almost incredibly successful partnership. Bowling unchanged, and with the help of some superb catches – two by Spofforth – they reduced the tourists to a score which is still England's lowest in Test cricket. Lohmann (17) alone reached double-figures. Australia were ahead with only two men out, but wickets fell steadily and the lead was confined to 74. This was absorbed before England's second wicket fell, but there was a mid-innings collapse, and England owed much to the last three wickets, which added 81. Well controlled by Shrewsbury, England somehow prevented Australia from reaching their target of 111 (which took on an ominous ring in the 1950s). Barnes bowled 46 four-ball overs, of which 29 were maidens. This match and the next were poorly promoted and attended.

  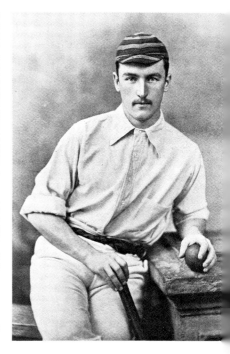

70, left: *The only known action picture of Charlie 'Terror' Turner.* 71, centre: *Turner in Australian cap.* 72, right: *Jack Ferris, his partner in destruction*

1886–87
Sydney, February 25, 26, 28, March 1

SECOND TEST

England 151 (*C.T.B. Turner 5 for 41, J.J. Ferris 5 for 71*) and 154 (*R.G. Barlow 42*, C.T.B. Turner 4 for 52, J.J. Ferris 4 for 69*); Australia 84 (*G.A. Lohmann 8 for 35*) and 150 (*W. Bates 4 for 26*). England won by 71 runs.

Several names were missing, including that of Spofforth, who had thus played his final Test, and Barnes, the Notts all-rounder, who had damaged his hand in throwing a punch at McDonnell; he hit a wall instead. The best stand of England's first innings was 57 by Barlow and Flowers for the eighth wicket, Turner and Ferris again carrying all before them. The genius of Lohmann, of Surrey, overcame Australia, for whom Moses top-scored with 28, and Barlow set about stretching England's lead: coming in at number three, he stayed over three hours. Bates made a robust 30. McDonnell, Allen and Moses (who once hit Lohmann over the fence) all reached the thirties, but it would have been expecting too much for Australia to have attained what would have been by some way the highest score of the match. This was England's sixth victory in as many Tests.

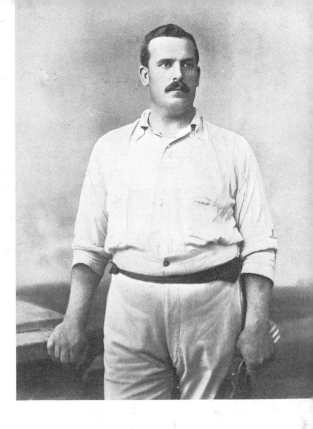

73, above: *Harry Moses, a fine left-hander who favoured the leg glance, top-scored with 28 in the first innings, and only McDonnell exceeded his 33 in the second.* 74, right: *Mordecai Sherwin, the massive wicketkeeper, who made four dismissals in Australia's second innings*

1887–88
Sydney, February 10, 11, 13, 14, 15

ONLY TEST

England *113 (A. Shrewsbury 44, C.T.B. Turner 5 for 44, J.J. Ferris 4 for 60) and 137 (C.T.B. Turner 7 for 43); Australia 42 (G.A. Lohmann 5 for 17, R. Peel 5 for 18) and 82 (R. Peel 5 for 40, G.A. Lohmann 4 for 35).* England won by 126 runs.

Lillywhite, Shaw and Shrewsbury's third touring team joined forces with another English side taken to Australia by Lord Hawke to play what can only be considered in somewhat loose terms as a Test match. At least one other contest during the season was played between respective sides of greater strength. On a rain-ruined wicket only Shrewsbury could cope with Turner and Ferris: the latter often spun the ball across to slip, and Blackham's task behind the stumps often bordered upon the impossible. In an hour before the close of the first day Australia lost eight for 35. Their final 42 remains their second-lowest ever in Tests. J.M. Read enjoyed the greatest luck in England's second innings on a pitch still extremely difficult. Hitting boldly, he made 39 on the fourth day after the second and third were washed out. That evening, Australia, needing 209, were 47 for 5.

75: *In 1887–88 two English teams toured Australia. This is Lillywhite's party: standing – G. Brann, L.C. Docker, James Lillywhite, J.M. Read, A.D. Pougher; seated – G. Ulyett, R. Pilling, C.A. Smith (captain), A. Shrewsbury, G.A. Lohmann; in front – J.M. Preston, J. Briggs, W. Newham*

1888
Lord's, July 16, 17

FIRST TEST

Australia 116 (R. Peel 4 for 36) and 60 (R. Peel 4 for 14, G.A. Lohmann 4 for 33); England 53 (C.T.B. Turner 5 for 27) and 62 (J.J. Ferris 5 for 26, C.T.B. Turner 5 for 36). Australia won by 61 runs.

Of the ten innings in this three-Test series, seven were completed for 100 or less. Australia began with a long-awaited victory, but their satisfaction was short-lived. The pitch at Lord's was muddy, and despite a dropped catch or two England soon had the visitors on their knees. The biggest stand was for the last wicket – 34 by Edwards and Ferris. The pitch grew even worse, and England actually came close to following on (the margin was then only 80 runs), being 26 for 7. Briggs's 17 and Grace's 10 were the highest scores. Australia, with a lead of 63, then collapsed to 18 for 7 before Ferris heaved 20 not out. England's target of 124 was always distant, and ostensibly disappeared with the dismissal of Grace, who made an admirable 24. More licence in the batting might just have brought off an odds-against victory.

77, below, left: *The 1888 Australians: standing – J.J. Ferris, A.H. Jarvis, J. Worrall, C.W. Beal (manager), J.McC. Blackham, H.F. Boyle, J.D. Edwards; seated – G.J. Bonnor, C.T.B. Turner, P.S. McDonnell (captain), G.H.S. Trott, A.C. Bannerman. S.M.J. Woods played instead of Boyle at Lord's and The Oval. 78, right: Blackham, the great wicketkeeper*

79: *Returning batsman's view of the Lord's pavilion assembly. An 1888 impression*

1888
The Oval, August 13, 14

SECOND TEST

Australia *80 (J. Briggs 5 for 25) and 100 (W. Barnes 5 for 32, R. Peel 4 for 49); England 317 (R. Abel 70, W. Barnes 62, G.A. Lohmann 62*, C.T.B. Turner 6 for 112).* England won by an innings and 137 runs.

There was little wrong with the wicket as Australia plunged to 50 for 7 by lunch. Bannerman's 13 lasted 100 minutes, and ended with an amazing full-stretch slip catch by Lohmann, who had already caught McDonnell at the start with a low, left-handed catch. Abel and Barnes arrested an early England slide by adding 112 for the fifth wicket, and Lohmann, at number 10, hit hard and cleanly. McDonnell made 32 of Australia's first 34, and Alec Bannerman dropped anchor this time for 75 minutes for five runs. Australia's performance was a great disappointment since the pitch presented no problems. Five Surrey men represented England.

80, left: *Bobby Abel, England's small, tenacious opener.* 81, right: *His 'opposite number', Alec Bannerman, from Sydney*

1888
Old Trafford, August 30, 31

THIRD TEST

England *172 (C.T.B. Turner 5 for 86); Australia 81 (R. Peel 7 for 31) and 70 (R. Peel 4 for 37).* England won by an innings and 21 runs.

Grace top-scored for England with a freely-struck 38, which included a hit off Turner over the sightscreen and ended with an astonishing catch by Bonnor at long-on: the fieldsman, when seemingly unable to reach the ball, thrust out a hand and the catch stuck. The pitch was dead after recent rains, and was kept so with occasional showers. 32 for 2 overnight, Australia had the misfortune to bat on a pitch now sticky under a hot sun. Lyons top-scored with 22, and seemed certain to save the follow-on, but he became one of Peel's 11 victims in the match, and Australia had to go in again. Their start was appalling: 0 for 1, 0 for 2, 1 for 3, 7 for 4, 7 for 5, 7 for 6. Turner (26) and Lyons (32) then added 48, but Peel, Lohmann and Briggs bowled England to an innings victory shortly before lunch on the second day, making this the shortest Test match of all time.

82, left: *Jack Lyons, the strong and willing South Australian opener.* 83, right: *Sammy Woods, Australian-born, residing in England, was called up by the 1888 touring team*

1890
Lord's, July 21, 22, 23

FIRST TEST

Australia *132 (J.J. Lyons 55, W. Attewell 4 for 42) and 176 (J.E. Barrett 67*);* England *173 (G. Ulyett 74, J.J. Lyons 5 for 30) and 137 for 3 (W.G. Grace 75*).* England won by 7 wickets.

Lyons gave the match a frantic start with 55 in 45 minutes, but Australia failed to capitalise. The last seven wickets fell for 23 runs. England's innings also began sensationally: Grace was caught-and-bowled by Turner second ball for a duck. At 20 for 4, they were saved by J.M. Read and Ulyett, who added 72. Lyons, medium-pace, got them both out, and restricted England to a narrow lead. Australia's second innings was built around Barrett, a left-hander, who carried his bat through the innings in his first Test. Lyons continued to imprint his personality on the match with a swift 33, but Grace steered England to victory in favourable conditions, though dropped at 44. No byes were conceded throughout the match, which marked the return of Murdoch as Australia's leader.

84: *Quick sketches of events during the final day's play. The new Lord's pavilion had recently been opened*

85, left: *Dr John Bar-rett, who carried his bat through the Australian innings.* 86, right: *'WG' – his very presence in the England XI was worth two men*

1890
The Oval, August 11, 12

SECOND TEST

Australia 92 *(F. Martin 6 for 50)* and 102 *(F. Martin 6 for 52);* England 100 *(J.J. Ferris 4 for 25)* and 95 for 8 *(J.J. Ferris 5 for 49).* England won by 2 wickets.

Three players – Stoddart, Peel and Ulyett – chose to play for their counties rather than for England. The other oddity was that 'Nutty' Martin, Kent left-arm fast bowler, was brought in for what was to be his only Test, apart from an appearance in South Africa a year later. His 12 for 102 was a remarkable debut performance. On the opening day 22 wickets fell for 197 runs. Preceding rain was the underlying cause. Harry Trott's 39 was easily Australia's top score, and William Gunn made 32 for England in 1¾ hours. Australia were 54 for 7 after Lyons had made a forceful 21; then Trott and Charlton put on 36, and England were left with the exciting prospect of making 95 for victory on a still-difficult pitch. Grace almost suffered a 'king pair', Trott putting him down at point. Even so, England were soon floundering at 32 for 4. J.M. Read (35) and Cranston (15) then added 51 in even time, but Turner trapped them with successive balls. Lohmann went at 86, Barnes at 93. Sharpe played at Ferris for an entire over without connecting; a single was run; three maidens passed; then Sharpe and MacGregor were stranded in mid-pitch attempting a run, but Barrett threw wide and the winning run was scampered.

A third Test, scheduled at Old Trafford for August 25, 26, 27, was completely washed out.

87, below, left: *Gregor MacGregor, England's Scots-born wicketkeeper, whose gloves offered little by way of protection.* 88, centre: *Frank Martin – 12 for 102 in his only Test against Australia.* 89, right: *Harry Trott, top-scorer in both Australian innings with 39 and 25*

1891–92
Melbourne, January 1, 2, 4, 5, 6

FIRST TEST

Australia 240 (W. Bruce 57, A.C. Bannerman 45, J.W. Sharpe 6 for 84) and 236 (J.J. Lyons 51, A.C. Bannerman 41, W. Bruce 40); England 264 (W.G. Grace 50, G. Bean 50, J. Briggs 41, R.W. McLeod 5 for 55) and 158 (C.T.B. Turner 5 for 51). Australia won by 54 runs.

The English side, which went to Australia under Lord Sheffield's auspices, was led by W.G. Grace, whose only other tour of Australia was 18 years before. Bruce and Bannerman put on an important 87 for Australia's third wicket, but the innings was kept in check by Sharpe and Peel, who bore the brunt of the bowling duties. Grace and Abel began with 84 in reply, but McLeod then got them both and Stoddart in 12 balls. Bean, J.M. Read and Briggs fought England into a narrow lead which Lyons soon wiped away with characteristic power. Grace and Stoddart began with 60, but Australia's varied bowling, following some very determined batting, won a welcome victory.

90, left: *Billy Bruce, Victorian left-hander.* 91, centre: *George Bean, Sussex all-rounder, formerly with Notts.* 92, right: *Bob McLeod, one of a talented Melbourne brotherhood.* 93, below: *Lord Sheffield's team pictured upon their return to England: standing – R. Carpenter (umpire), W. Attewell, G.A. Lohmann, J.M. Read, G. Bean, J.W. Sharpe, R.A. Thoms (umpire); seated – J. Briggs, G. MacGregor, W.G. Grace, R. Peel, A.E. Stoddart, R. Abel*

1891–92

Sydney, January 29, 30, February 1, 2, 3

SECOND TEST

Australia *145 (J.J. Lyons 41, G.A. Lohmann 8 for 58) and 391 (J.J. Lyons 134, A.C. Bannerman 91, W. Bruce 72, G. Giffen 49, J. Briggs 4 for 69); England 307 (R. Abel 132*, G. Giffen 4 for 88) and 157 (A.E. Stoddart 69, G. Giffen 6 for 72, C.T.B. Turner 4 for 46). Australia won by 72 runs.*

By the end of the second day Australia seemed in a hopeless position. They had failed miserably after Lyons's robust opening, and England, in the small figure of Abel, had piled up a lead of 162. That evening Trott was lost, and it was known that Moses' leg injury would prevent him from batting. Grace fell out of favour with the crowd for refusing Moses either a runner in the first innings or a substitute in the field (until late in the match) because Blackham knew of the injury before the start. The match was turned in a stand of 174 by the contrasting Lyons and Bannerman, the former batting for 2¾ hours, the latter for 7½ (12 runs per hour) during which he was at the crease on three separate days and hit a mere three boundaries. Lyons was missed twice at slip by Abel when 49. Briggs finished the innings with a hat-trick, and England needed 230. That night they were 11 for 3. Rain had fallen, but the pitch rolled out well, and Grace was condemned for not sending in nightwatchmen. Stoddart alone batted with assurance, hitting Turner for a second time into the crowd. Australia thus deservedly won the series, and Lohmann's grand effort and Abel's feat of carrying his bat through the innings were to no avail.

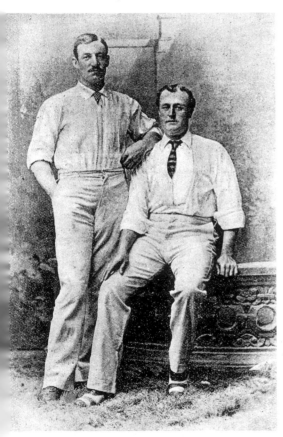

94, left: *George Giffen with G.E. Palmer.* 95, above: *Bobby Abel – carried his bat.* 96, below: *George Lohmann – 8 for 58.* 97, right: *Murdoch, Spofforth, Boyle, and A.C. Bannerman*

1891–92

Adelaide, March 24, 25, 26, 28

THIRD TEST

England *499 (A.E. Stoddart 134, R. Peel 83, W.G. Grace 58, J.M. Read 57, W. Attewell 43*); Australia 100 (J. Briggs 6 for 49) and 169 (J. Briggs 6 for 87). England won by an innings and 230 runs.*

A classic case of victory going with the winning of the toss. England made the most of a good pitch, but rain on the second day turned it into a juicy strip full of good things for bowlers. Briggs often bowled the unplayable ball, and ran through Australia the first time unchanged with Lohmann. Attewell took three wickets in the follow-on. Grace again did little for his popularity by insisting on quarter-hourly inspections of the pitch during the rain interruptions. Stoddart's century was punctuated by several misses, and also some mighty hits. He batted just under four hours.

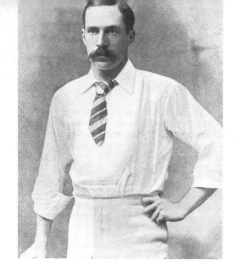

98, left: *A.E. 'Drewy' Stoddart, whose century set up England's victory at Adelaide. 99, right: Bobby Peel, who excelled with the bat this time*

1893
Lord's, July 17, 18, 19

FIRST TEST

England 334 (A. Shrewsbury 106, F.S. Jackson 91, C.T.B. Turner 6 for 67) and 234 for 8 dec (A. Shrewsbury 81, W. Gunn 77, G. Giffen 5 for 43); Australia 269 (H. Graham 107, S.E. Gregory 57, W.H. Lockwood 6 for 101). Match drawn.

Shrewsbury, beginning cautiously on a rain-affected pitch, and Jackson, who batted gloriously on his debut, added 137 for the third wicket, and England's 334 was achieved before close of play. Jackson drove and pulled with masterful ease. Shrewsbury became the first batsman to reach 1000 Test runs. That evening Lockwood bowled Lyons and Giffen, and went on to take the next three wickets the following day before being rested after a stoical spell of almost two hours. Soon he was called up again, and eventually broke the saving partnership of Gregory and Graham, which realised 142 in only 100 minutes. This was 'Tich' Gregory's first substantial innings in a Test career which was to span 22 years. Graham, missed three times, batted for 140 minutes in his maiden Test innings – the first century for Australia at Lord's. Shrewsbury and Gunn scored 152 for England's second wicket, and though wickets tumbled thereafter, the lead was formidable when rain came. In mid-afternoon, Stoddart (captaining England this match in Grace's absence) made the first declaration in Test matches, but the drizzle returned.

100, below, left: *The Hon. F.S. Jackson, immaculate all-rounder for Cambridge, Yorkshire, and England.* 101, centre: *William Gunn, partner to Shrewsbury for county and country.* 102, right: *Harry Graham – century on Test debut*

103: *Lord Sheffield's greeting in fireworks at Sheffield Park to Blackham's 1893 Australians*

1893
The Oval, August 14, 15, 16

SECOND TEST

England 483 (*F.S. Jackson 103, A.E. Stoddart 83, W.G. Grace 68, A. Shrewsbury 66, A. Ward 55, W.W. Read 52, G. Giffen 7 for 128*); Australia 91 (*J. Briggs 5 for 34, W.H. Lockwood 4 for 37*) and 349 (*G.H.S. Trott 92, A.C. Bannerman 55, G. Giffen 53, H. Graham 42, J. Briggs 5 for 114, W.H. Lockwood 4 for 96*). England won by an innings and 43 runs.

England's strong XI took command from the start, though Stoddart had much luck in his opening stand of 151 with Grace. The score at the end of the first, hot day was 378 for 5. Jackson batted on next day with power and poise to be 98 when last man Mold joined him. Run-outs were narrowly avoided, Jackson drove Giffen high onto the pavilion stand to reach his century, and soon his reckless partner did run him out. The tired Australians were without an answer to Lockwood and Briggs, and followed on 392 behind. Bannerman and Bruce began with 54, and Trott and Graham added 106 for the fifth wicket, raising their side's hopes of escape. But with Trott caught at mid-on Australia's tail offered little resistance, though Lyons made a few thunderous hits. England had had to work for the victory which was to regain them the Ashes.

104, below, left: *Bill Lockwood, a top-class all-rounder, whose fast bowling had much to do with England's supremacy in the 1893 series.* 105, right: *The Vauxhall end at The Oval as seen from the Press box during the Test match of 1893*

1893
Old Trafford, August 24, 25, 26

Australia 204 (W. Bruce 68, T. Richardson 5 for 49, J. Briggs 4 for 81) and 236 (A.C. Bannerman 60, T. Richardson 5 for 107); England 243 (W. Gunn 102*, W.G. Grace 40, G. Giffen 4 for 113) and 118 for 4 (W.G. Grace 45, A.E. Stoddart 42). Match drawn.

Jackson and Peel were absent – playing instead for Yorkshire – and Lockwood, with a strained side, was replaced by Surrey team-mate Richardson, who took ten wickets upon debut. Bruce, hitting well to leg, made his 68 in 100 minutes, but the next-highest score was only 35, from Trumble. As Gunn began to run out of partners, he went after the bowling – with some elegance. His century took just over four hours, and his second 50 was twice as fast as the first. Bannerman was, as so often, the anchor-man as Australia fought for a sizable lead. His 60 – his final Test innings – took 205 minutes. Turner and Blackham, in a last-wicket stand of 36, cheated England of a run-a-minute chase, and after Grace and Stoddart had 70 up in 78 minutes, England were content to play out time for their fifth home series victory running.

106, below, left: *Moments and musings during the Manchester Test.* 107, right: *Tom Richardson, the lion-hearted Surrey fast bowler, who took 10 wickets in his first Test.* 108, bottom, right: *Albert Ward, whose modest start in 1893 preceded greater deeds*

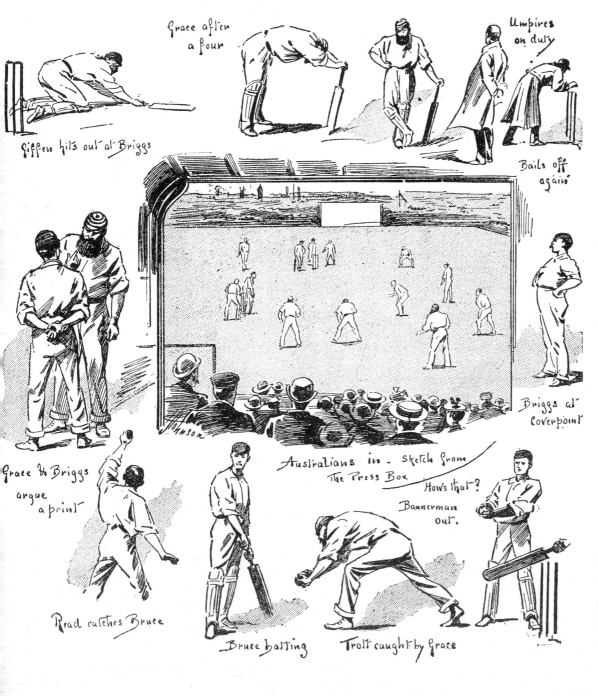

1894–95
Sydney, December 14, 15, 17, 18, 19, 20

FIRST TEST

Australia 586 (*S.E. Gregory 201, G. Giffen 161, F.A. Iredale 81, J.McC. Blackham 74, T. Richardson 5 for 181*) *and 166 (J. Darling 53, G. Giffen 41, R. Peel 6 for 67); England 325 (A. Ward 75, J. Briggs 57, W. Brockwell 49, G. Giffen 4 for 75) and 437 (A. Ward 117, J.T. Brown 53, F.G.J. Ford 48, J. Briggs 42, G. Giffen 4 for 164).* England won by 10 runs.

An enthralling series began with one of the strangest turnabouts of all time. Following on, England made enough a second time to place unanticipated pressure on Australia in the fourth innings after overnight rain had converted the pitch into a quagmire. Australia had started the match badly, three men being bowled by fast bowler Richardson while 21 runs were scored. Giffen added 171 with Iredale and 139 with Gregory, who registered Test cricket's second double-century in only 244 minutes. The run quest reached a peak with Gregory and Blackham together: 154 were added in an hour and a quarter. The stamina of Peel and of Richardson in particular were marvelled at. There were few complete failures in England's innings, and Ward batted stoutheartedly. Batting seemed even a trifle easier in the follow-on, Ward and Brown hitting 102 for the third wicket and Ford and Briggs a crucial 89 for the seventh, when England were just ahead. Only wicketkeeper Gay failed to obtain double-figures, and with several dropped catches, Australia had placed themselves in need of 177 to win. On the fifth evening, with dark clouds banking up, they had made 113 for 2, Darling having hit a brisk 44 in contrast to Giffen's cautious 30. Some English players 'relaxed' that night, thinking the game lost. Peel was one, but Stoddart ordered him under a cold shower, and on a pitch saturated by heavy overnight rain the Yorkshireman proceeded to run through Australia. Briggs (3 for 25) took the other end, and after some nerve-shattering cricket England stole a narrow victory. Blackham, in his final Test, batted with a painful hand injury and was last out.

109, above: *Stoddart's team line the ship's rail as the great journey begins.* 110, below: *The contented Sydney crowd during the Gregory-Blackham partnership. The Hill now rises from this area, and the flimsy scoreboard has long since been replaced*

The Australia Cricket Club v. the England Cricket Club

Match Played at Sydney on 14. 15. 17. 18 December 189_

1st Innings of Australia   Result

BATSMAN.	RUNS SCORED.	HOW OUT.	BOWLER.	TOTAL
1.1 Lyons J		Bowled	Richardson	1
2.2 Trott H		Bowled	Richardson	12
5.3 Giffen G		caught Ford	Brockwell	161
3.4 Darling J		Bowled	Richardson	0
4.5 Iredale F		caught Stoddart	Ford	81
9.6 Gregory S		caught Peel	Stoddart	201
6.7 Reedman J		caught Ford	Peel	17
7.8 McLeod C		Bowled	Richardson	15
8.9 Turner		caught May	Peel	1
10 Blackham J		Bowled	Richardson	74
11 Jones E		Not out		11

UMPIRE		
	Byes 44	8
	Leg Byes	3
	Wide Balls	1
	No Balls	

Runs at the fall of each Wicket: 1 – 10, 2 – 21, 3 – 21, 4 – 192, 5 – 331, 6 – 379, 7 – 400, 8 – 409, 9 – 563, 10 – 586   Total of Innings 586

BOWLING ANALYSIS.

BOWLER.	RUNS FROM EACH OVER.	Overs	Maidens	Wides	No Balls	Runs	Wickets
Richardson		55.3	13	.	.	181	5
Peel		53	14			140	2
Briggs		25	4			96	0
Brockwell		22	7			78	1
Ford		11	2	1		47	1
Stoddart		3	.			31	1

Published by ALFRED SHAW & ARTHUR SHREWSBURY, Football and General Athletic Sports Warehouse, Carrington St. Bridge, Nottingham.

111, above: *The scorebook records some relentless batting and gallant bowling.* 112, left: *Syd Gregory, Australia's little double-century hero.* 113, below: *Stoddart and the Kangaroo – the Ashes war is on again*

I say "Old Man"
"Who's got those Ashes?"

114: *View of play from the Randwick end at Sydney. In 1936 the Noble Stand was built on the far side*

1894–95   SECOND TEST
Melbourne, December 29, 31, January 1, 2, 3

England 75 (*C.T.B. Turner 5 for 32*) *and 475 (A.E. Stoddart 173, R. Peel 53, A. Ward 41, G. Giffen 6 for 155); Australia 123 (T. Richardson 5 for 57) and 333 (G.H.S. Trott 95, F.A. Iredale 68, W. Bruce 54, G. Giffen 43, R. Peel 4 for 77).* England won by 94 runs.

Giffen was elected Australia's new captain just before the start, and he put England in to bat. Two hours later they were all out on a pitch that still presented difficulties to batsmen. Coningham, in his only Test, had removed MacLaren with the first ball of the match. Only Ward (30) prospered for any length of time. Australia were ahead with six wickets in hand, but Richardson held their first-innings advantage to 48, and on the Monday, the pitch having had 15 minutes' rolling, heavy scoring was expected. That evening England were 287 for 4, Stoddart 150 made coolly and authoritatively. He went on to pass Grace's England record of 170, and his 173 (in 320 minutes) was to be the highest by an England captain in Australia for 80 years. Last man Richardson's 11 was the lowest score of the innings, and England's courage and concentration presented Australia with a weighty task. They were 98 for one on the fourth evening: 330 still required. Giffen went at 191, Trott, to a boot-high caught-and-bowled by Brockwell, soon afterwards. Iredale defended with scarce support until Turner shared 65 with him for the last wicket. England, hardly clear-cut superiors, were two-up.

115, left: *Andrew Stoddart, whose 173 led England to a big second innings.* 116, below: *Arthur Coningham – a wicket with his first ball.* 117, right: *Billy Brockwell – three vital wickets in the last innings*

118: *All eyes on the middle as the second Test match runs its enthralling course at Melbourne*

1894–95
Adelaide, January 11, 12, 14, 15

THIRD TEST

Australia *238 (G. Giffen 58, G.H.S. Trott 48, S.T. Callaway 41, T. Richardson 5 for 75) and 411 (F.A. Iredale 140, W. Bruce 80, A.E. Trott 72*, R. Peel 4 for 96); England 124 (S.T. Callaway 5 for 37, G. Giffen 5 for 76) and 143 (A.E. Trott 8 for 43).* Australia won by 382 runs.

England were beaten as much as anything by the intense heat and Albert Trott, who, in his first Test, made 110 runs without losing his wicket, then hounded England to abject defeat with varied fast-medium bowling on a pitch which the tourists never quite trusted. Richardson won universal admiration for his courageous bowling effort, but even he wilted in temperatures which touched 155°F in the open. Australia enjoyed two big last-wicket stands by Trott and Callaway – 81 and 64 – but the damage to England was done in their first innings. Only J.T. Brown, with a stylish 39 not out, maintained any English pride. Iredale's century was polished, and ended only through fatigue, and Bruce batted with charm. As young Trott ran amok, only the majestic MacLaren and Stoddart held fast long enough to pass 30. Albert Trott was a national hero overnight.

119, left: *Albert Trott, fit for canonisation after his startling debut.* 120, right: *'The Cause of Defeat' – a cynical view of the Englishmen's alleged drinking excesses*

121, left: *Frank Iredale – a monumental 140 at Adelaide in stifling heat.* 122, right: *Syd Callaway, who had a good all-round match*

1894–95
Sydney, February 1, 2, 4

FOURTH TEST

Australia 284 (H. Graham 105, A.E. Trott 85*, J. Briggs 4 for 65); England 65 and 72 (G. Giffen 5 for 26, C.T.B. Turner 4 for 33). Australia won by an innings and 147 runs.

With this trouncing, Australia drew level two-all and set up a highly exciting prospect for the decider in Melbourne. Stoddart won his only toss of the series and put Australia in on a dubious pitch. Six wickets fell for 51, but Giffen had rearranged the batting order, and Graham added 68 with Darling (who once hit Briggs into the tennis courts) and 112 with Albert Trott (who now had 195 Test runs without a dismissal). Graham, who batted gamely and enterprisingly against the fierce bounce of Richardson, achieved the unique double of a century in his first Test innings in both England and Australia. England lost MacLaren that evening, and Saturday's play was washed out. More rain Sunday night left the pitch in a dreadful condition when play resumed, and Stoddart expressed doubts that England would last out the day. He was right. Strangely, A.E. Trott, the destroyer at Adelaide, was not called upon to bowl a ball. Charlie 'Terror' Turner was dropped after this match, having taken 101 wickets at 16.53 in 17 Tests – an illustrious career ended in controversy.

123, left: *Harry Graham, 'The Little Dasher', who completed a unique double when he made a century at Sydney.* 124, top, right: *Spectators examine the pitch on which England were all but bowled out twice in a day.* 125, right: *The England players prepare to take the field at Sydney*

1894–95
Melbourne, March 1, 2, 4, 5, 6

FIFTH TEST

Australia 414 (J. Darling 74, S.E. Gregory 70, G. Giffen 57, J.J. Lyons 55, G.H.S. Trott 42, R. Peel 4 for 114) and 267 (G. Giffen 51, J. Darling 50, G.H.S. Trott 42, T. Richardson 6 for 104); England 385 (A.C. MacLaren 120, R. Peel 73, A.E. Stoddart 68, G.H.S. Trott 4 for 71, G. Giffen 4 for 130) and 298 for 4 (J.T. Brown 140, A. Ward 93). England won by 6 wickets.

Thousands converged on Melbourne by all manner of means for 'the match of the century'. It was said that even Queen Victoria took a close interest in reports of the contest. Those in attendance on the final day saw one of the greatest attacking innings as well as one of the finest supporting roles. Australia's 414 after winning the toss seemed an insurance against defeat, even though England came within 29. Gregory and Darling put on 142 for the fifth wicket, and runs came from most of the side. MacLaren's century, the first of his five against Australia, ended when he trod on his stumps in pulling at a short ball from Harry Trott. His important stand with Peel (who had made a 'pair' in each of the previous Tests) amounted to 162. This together with Ward and Stoddart's second-wicket stand of 104 kept England in the fight. Another heroic effort by Richardson, supported by Peel, confined Australia to an overall lead of 296, and though Brockwell was out that evening, the fifth day began with England hopeful. Immediately, however, Stoddart was lbw, and under an overcast sky, Brown of Yorkshire came in. He square-drove his first ball to the boundary and hooked the next for four. In less than half an hour he had his fifty – the fastest ever in Tests – and with rain still threatening, he raced to his century in 95 minutes. The stand reached 210, then the highest in Test cricket, before Brown was caught at slip. Ward, his partner, missed his century, but had taken England to the threshold of a famous victory.

126: *The Englishmen practise before the deciding Test at Melbourne*

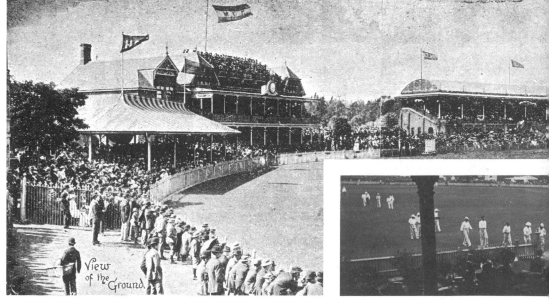

127, above, left: *The Melbourne Argus office displays progress scores for those who cannot get to the ground.* 128, above, right: *The bat with which Brown made his historic 140.* 129, right: *The crowded stands and (inset) players leaving the field.* 130, below, left: *Scoreboard during the vital first-innings MacLaren-Peel partnership.* 131, below, right: *J.T. Brown, pride of Yorkshire and England*

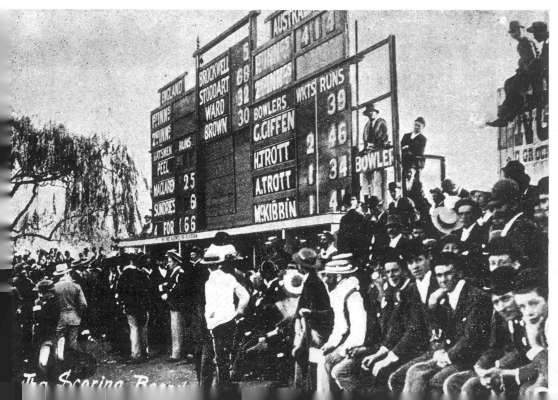

1

Brisbane Street
Launceston March 16th 1895

Dear Father and Mother, Brother and Sister

It gives me pleasure to write you a few lines and let you know how we are going on. As you can imagine we are all very happy now that we have won the final Test match and what a match it was. The greatest match on record. The excitement was intense. We outplayed them at every point. When we had 297 to get to win and Brockwell was out at 6 and then Stoddart at 28 the betting men offered 5 to 1 against us. If I ever felt determined to do well I did when I heard the people say 'It's all over now.' I got 51 in 24 minutes and then the people

2

began to think that 'It was not all over yet' and it was not for Albert Ward and myself took the score to 238 before I was out. Of course you will have read all about the match before you recieve this letter but I am glad to say that everybody gave us great credit for winning. It was a glorious win one that we shall never forget. The gate reciepts were 4003£ so you me guess what a lot of people saw the match. The cricketers out here are very good players indeed and take a lot of beating. We left Melbourne on Thursday night at 6-30 and arrive here that is Launceston in Tasmania at 2 in the afternoon on Friday after a very rough voyage. It was a terrible night the ship rolled awfully and nearly everybody was bad, but I

132, above: *Jack Brown's letter, written four days after the great Melbourne match, tells of his fast fifty and of the tremendous interest and excitement generated by this decider.* 133, below: *It is all over, and the Australians, with MacLaren and Peel, leave the field*

1896
Lord's, June 22, 23, 24

FIRST TEST

Australia *53 (T. Richardson 6 for 39) and 347 (G.H.S. Trott 143, S.E. Gregory 103, J.T. Hearne 5 for 76, T. Richardson 5 for 134); England 292 (R. Abel 94, W.G. Grace 66, F.S. Jackson 44) and 111 for 4.* England won by 6 wickets.

The mighty Richardson, bowling from the pavilion end, bowled six Australians before lunch, by which time England were already setting about their reply. The pitch was fast, and Richardson's success was based on sheer speed. Only Darling (22) stayed for any length of time. That evening England were 233 ahead with two wickets left. About 30,000 had crammed into Lord's that day, and there was much rowdyism in some quarters. Those with an uninterrupted view of play saw Grace notch his 1000th Test run and Abel bat studiously. Australia were 62 for 3 on the second day, and apparently well on the way to defeat, when Trott, the captain, who failed to score in the first innings, was joined by Gregory, and bravely they added 221 – a new all-wicket Test record – in only 160 minutes. Even Richardson was driven to the boundary. Australia fell away after this breathtaking stand, but after rain on the second night England had to fight for victory, and Brown considered his 36 against Jones at his most aggressive and in failing light to have been quite as satisfying as his magnificent century at Melbourne.

134, above: *Photograph of Lord's during England's first innings.* 135, below: *W.B. Wollen's painting of the match, probably set during the Trott-Gregory partnership. Lohmann chases the ball; WG at point*

136, above: *England batting at Lord's, 1896, with the bowler coming in from the Nursery end.* 137, right: *The four South Australians in the tourists' side: Joe Darling, George Giffen, Ernest Jones, and (in front) Clem Hill*

1896
Old Trafford, July 16, 17, 18

SECOND TEST

Australia 412 (F.A. Iredale 108, G. Giffen 80, G.H.S. Trott 53, T. Richardson 7 for 168) and 125 for 7 (T. Richardson 6 for 76); England 231 (A.F.A. Lilley 65*, K.S. Ranjitsinhji 62) and 305 (K.S. Ranjitsinhji 154*, A.E. Stoddart 41). Australia won by 3 wickets.

Richardson and Ranjitsinhji were the heroes who caught the imagination, but the victory was Australia's – though Richardson's relentless attack on the last day almost reversed the match. Lilley's spilling of Kelly, his opposite number, as his arm hit the ground gave the visitors the respite they needed in the closing stages. The first day ended with Australia in command: 366 for 8. Iredale's was a pleasant innings, and with Giffen he added 131. Trott was dismissed by Lilley, England's wicketkeeper, whom Grace gambled upon to break a threatening partnership. Richardson bowled 68 five-ball overs, and was to manage another 42.3 in the second innings. Trott had Grace and Stoddart stumped off his leg-breaks at the start of England's innings, and only 'Ranji' and Lilley saved complete embarrassment. The Indian prince was making his Test debut at last, the Lord's authorities having considered him ineligible. In the follow-on he played an enchanting innings, all ease and fluidity, hooking Jones's thunderbolts, cutting wristily, glancing with sweet precision. He batted for 185 minutes, and made 113 runs before lunch on the third morning. He showed no sign of fallibility, but the others did, and he was left undefeated. Richardson then took over to make Australia's task more difficult than could ever have been foreseen 24 hours earlier.

138, above, left: *Tom Richardson, who bowled his heart out in the second Test.* 139, right: *Ernie Jones bowls at practice on Mitcham Green.* 140, below, left: *'Dick' Lilley, England's wicketkeeper, whose unfortunate error probably cost his side victory.* 141, right: *'Ranji', maker of a brilliant century in his first Test*

1896

The Oval, August 10, 11, 12

THIRD TEST

England *145 (F.S. Jackson 45, H. Trumble 6 for 59) and 84 (H. Trumble 6 for 30); Australia 119 (J. Darling 47, J.T. Hearne 6 for 41) and 44 (R. Peel 6 for 23, J.T. Hearne 4 for 19).* England won by 66 runs.

England retained the Ashes, though when five players threatened strike action over match fees before the start it seemed the home team would be appreciably weakened. Three – Abel, Richardson and Hayward – relented, but Gunn and Lohmann withdrew their services. England made 69 for one in the 95 minutes' play allowed by the weather on the first day, but subsided before the medium-pace of tall Trumble, who got among the wickets in a Test for the first time. He was to finish, in 1904, with a record 141 wickets in England-Australia Tests. Darling and Iredale made 75 in 45 minutes for Australia's first wicket, the latter being run out on a fifth run by a prodigious throw from Ranji. Medium-pacer Hearne forced a collapse, and England made a painful 60 for 5 that evening. Abel top-scored with a fine defensive 21, and Australia, set 111 on a worsening pitch, were devastated. Last man McKibbin made 16 of the total of 44.

142, above, left: *As Punch saw the players' threatened strike: 'Now, gentlemen all, I'll give you a toast that every good cricketer may join in – "Fair Play, Fair Pay, and Friendliness!"'* 143, above, right: *Harry Trott, Jones and Iredale leave the Oval pavilion to do battle.* 144, right: *MacLaren, resplendent in tie, and WG trot off at the end of Australia's first innings*

145, above: *Clem Hill about to be run out by Wynyard for one after turning a ball to leg – part of the Australian first-innings collapse.* 146, left: *The vast crowd stays to cheer England after their Oval victory*

1897–98
Sydney, December 13, 14, 15, 16, 17

FIRST TEST

England 551 (*K.S. Ranjitsinhji 175, A.C. MacLaren 109, T.W. Hayward 72, G.H. Hirst 62, W. Storer 43*) and 96 for 1 (*A.C. MacLaren 50**); Australia 237 (*H. Trumble 70, C.E. McLeod 50*, S.E. Gregory 46, J.T. Hearne 5 for 42*) and 408 (*J. Darling 101, C. Hill 96, J.J. Kelly 46*, J.T. Hearne 4 for 99*). England won by 9 wickets.

Stoddart's second team flattered to deceive in the first Test. The captain himself withdrew, grief-stricken, after news of his mother's death a few days before the start – which was postponed because of rain, allowing Ranji to regain some sort of fitness after a bout of quinsy. George Giffen's grand Test career came to an end when, after speculation and many 'quotes', he announced his retirement to pursue his career in the Post Office. MacLaren, captaining England, made a chanceless century on his favourite ground, adding 136 with Hayward. Ranji, still unwell, took his 39 overnight to 175, also chanceless, and was last man out, having dealt wonderfully well with Jones's fast and often short-pitched attack. Richardson, having helped in a final stand of 74, made his usual wholehearted effort with the ball, but was carrying surplus weight. Trumble surprisingly top-scored for Australia, but in the follow-on Darling displayed his skill and Hill batted with dash and flair. McLeod, who was deaf, left his ground after being bowled, but it was a no-ball; he had not heard the umpire's call, and Storer ran him out.

147, above, left: *The captain goes aboard – Stoddart sets out on his second tour as skipper.* 148, right: *The 'Pro-Test' match: a frustrating situation for everyone involved.* 149, below: *Sydney, first Test, 1897*

150, above, left: *Ranji runs in at the end of his great innings.* 151, above, right: *England take the field, wearing mourning bands out of respect for Stoddart's mother, who died before the match.* 152, left: *Painting by A. Henry Fullwood from the popular side during the first Test.* 153, below: *The scorebook records Ranjitsinhji's 175 and MacLaren's cultured century*

First Test at Sydney

A CRICKET MATCH between Australia and England

FIRST INNINGS OF England   13·14ᵗʰ December 97

	STRIKER.	SCORE.	TOTAL	HOW OUT.	BOWLER.	REMARKS.
1	Mason	24	6	Bowled	Jones	
2	McLaren		109	caught Kelly	McLeod	
3	Hayward		72	caught Trott	Trumble	
4	Storer		43	caught & bowled	Trott	
5	Druce		20	caught Gregory	McLeod	
6	Hirst		62	bowled	Jones	
7	Ranjitsinhji		175	caught Gregory	McKibbin	
8	Wainwright	1441	10	bowled	Jones	
9	Hearne		17	caught & bowled	McLeod	
10	Briggs	1	1	run out		
11	Richardson		24	not out		
	Byes	—				
	Leg Byes	—		11		
	Wide Balls	—		1		
	No Balls	—				
		TOTAL	551			

RUNS AT THE FALL OF EACH WICKET	For 1	For 2	For 3	For 4	For 5	For 6	For 7	For 8	For 9	For 10
	26	162	224	256	258	382	422	471	47	

ANALYSIS OF THE BOWLING OF THE FIRST INNINGS.

	BOWLER.	RUNS FROM EACH OVER.	WIDE BALLS.	NO BALLS.	RUNS.	WICKETS.	MAIDEN OVERS.
1							
2	McKibbin		-	-	113	1	5
3	Jones		-		130	3	8
4	McLeod				80	3	12
5	Trumble		-		135	1	7
6	Trott		1	-	78	1	2
7							

154: *McLeod and Trumble go forth after lunch on the third day*

1897–98
Melbourne, January 1, 3, 4, 5

SECOND TEST

Australia 520 (C.E. McLeod 112, F.A. Iredale 89, G.H.S. Trott 79, S.E. Gregory 71, C. Hill 58); England 315 (K.S. Ranjitsinhji 71, W. Storer 51, J. Briggs 46*, N.F. Druce 44, H. Trumble 4 for 54) and 150 (M.A. Noble 6 for 49, H. Trumble 4 for 53). Australia won by an innings and 55 runs.

In uncomfortable heat Australia piled up 283 for 3 on the first day, with McLeod compiling a careful century. England's bowling inadequacy was completely exposed, and the seven who tried (Wainwright was ignored by MacLaren) were defeated by broad bats and fatigue. Australia's impressive resurgence hiccoughed when Ernie Jones was no-balled for throwing by Anglo-Australian umpire Jim Phillips, but the incident seemed soon forgotten. England passed 200 with only four men out, but Ranji's, the key wicket, was taken by Trumble and only a ninth-wicket stand of 87 by Briggs and Druce saved a total collapse. The pitch by now was cracked all over, and in the follow-on Noble (in his first Test) and Trumble proved insuperable.

We are given to understand that the English cricketers, on seeing the ladies piled up behind those iron railings at the M.C.C. ground, imagined the officials had taken this precaution to prevent the Australian girls from getting at Prince Ranji, and eloping with him in a mass.

155, left: *The England fielders come off for lunch at Melbourne.* 156, centre: *Charlie McLeod, century-maker: sweet revenge for the controversial run-out in the preceding Test.* 157, right: *Ranji, the Indian prince, was a 'pop idol' in Australia*

158, left: *Norman Druce, who made runs at Melbourne.* 159, above: *The cracked pitch after England's second innings – a snapshot by Jim Phillips*

1897–98
Adelaide, January 14, 15, 17, 18, 19

THIRD TEST

Australia 573 (*J. Darling 178, F.A. Iredale 84, C. Hill 81, S.E. Gregory 52, T. Richardson 4 for 164*); England 278 (*G.H. Hirst 85, T.W. Hayward 70, W.P. Howell 4 for 70*) *and 282 (A.C. MacLaren 124, K.S. Ranjitsinhji 77, C.E. McLeod 5 for 65, M.A. Noble 5 for 84*). Australia won by an innings and 13 runs.

Australia batted into the third day to reach 573, a new second-highest total in Test cricket, having ended the first day at 310 for 2. The left-handers, Darling and 20-year-old Hill, struck 148 for the second wicket after McLeod had raised 97 with Darling for the first. The latter reached his century in grand style, hoisting Briggs out of the ground. England's misfortunes continued to pile up: Richardson was unwell, Hirst and Ranji were injured, and catches were spilt. Howell, an off-spinner, Jones and Noble cut swathes through the England batting a first time, and in the follow-on, after a promising second-wicket resistance of 142 by MacLaren and Ranji, McLeod broke through the middle order and Noble, using a wind that earlier created a dust-storm, did the rest. Stoddart, having resumed the England captaincy, batted low down and made only 15 and 24.

160: *Again a pitch is the focus of attention: Hayward, Board, and MacLaren study the Adelaide strip*

161, left: *Joe Darling – three centuries in the series, including one on his home ground, Adelaide.* 162, right: *Archie MacLaren – two centuries in the series for England*

1897–98
Melbourne, January 29, 31, February 1, 2

FOURTH TEST

Australia 323 (C. Hill 188, H. Trumble 46, J.T. Hearne 6 for 98) and 115 for 2 (C.E. McLeod 64*); England 174 (E. Jones 4 for 56) and 263 (K.S. Ranjitsinhji 55, A.C. MacLaren 45). Australia won by 8 wickets.

The 50th England-Australia Test match further established the renascence of the home side, though when, on the first day, Australia were 58 for 6 it seemed England were at last about to come back into the series. Hearne and Richardson made the breakthrough, but without the support of Hirst they wilted in the heat and young Hill mounted his rescue act, chiefly with Trumble. Their 165 remains a record for the seventh wicket in these matches. Hill drove beautifully and treated anything outside leg stump with vicious contempt; he batted for 294 minutes and gave only one chance. With bushfires filling the air with smoke, England gave their feeblest display yet, and did little better in the follow-on. MacLaren claimed a fly in his eye caused his dismissal, and this – with several English players' protests at crowd behaviour – reduced the popularity of the touring team and increased its misery.

163, below: *Clem Hill, only 20, made 188 at Melbourne (wicketkeeper in picture is Jim Kelly).* 164, right: *The coin drops, and Trott (left) beats Stoddart for choice of innings*

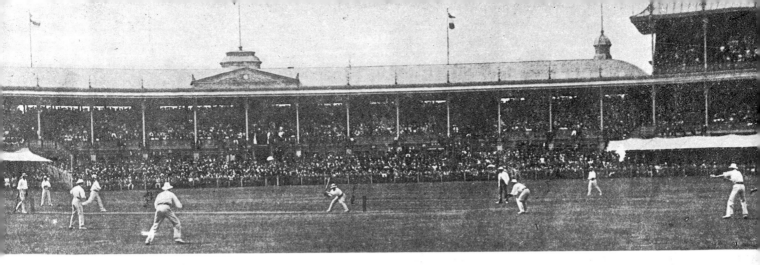

165, opposite: *A satirical account of the fly that got in MacLaren's eye, and some of Ranji's published remarks.*
166, above: *Hill cuts Richardson during his 188 at Melbourne. Trumble non-striker, Storer wicketkeeper*

1897–98
Sydney, February 26, 28, March 1, 2

FIFTH TEST

England 335 (A.C. MacLaren 65, N.F. Druce 64, E. Wainwright 49, T.W. Hayward 47, W. Storer 44, G.H. Hirst 44, E. Jones 6 for 82) and 178 (T.W. Hayward 43, H. Trumble 4 for 37); Australia 239 (C.E. McLeod 64, T. Richardson 8 for 94) and 276 for 4 (J. Darling 160, J. Worrall 62). Australia won by 6 wickets.

A large total seemed probable when England finished the first day at 301 for 5, but Jones wiped out the tail. MacLaren and Wainwright began with a stand of 111, and several previous failures found form rather too late in the series. Richardson, free of rheumatism at last, and playing in what transpired to be his final Test, bowled his fastest and got most of the wickets bowled or caught behind the wicket. Trumble and Jones bowled well enough to keep England's overall lead down to 274, but, setting out on the chase for their fourth straight victory, Australia lost two wickets for 40. Worrall then helped Darling add 193, which effectively decided the match. Darling's superb innings lasted only 175 minutes and contained 30 fours and only 18 singles. He drove Richardson furiously in a concerted attempt to hit him from the firing line, and reached his hundred – his third of the series – in a mere 91 minutes (20 fours) – an Australian speed record against England. It was said that Australia's overwhelming success in the Test matches had done more to promote the idea of Federation than any number of conferences.

ohn Bull's First Question.

167, left: *John Bull: 'Now, Stoddart, what was it?' It was a long story.* 168, below: *The ball with which Richardson took 8 for 94.* 169, right: *Ernie Jones – nine wickets at Sydney*

1899
Trent Bridge, June 1, 2, 3

Australia 252 (C. Hill 52, S.E. Gregory 48, J. Darling 47, M.A. Noble 41, W. Rhodes 4 for 58, J.T. Hearne 4 for 71) and 230 for 8 dec (C. Hill 80, M.A. Noble 45); England 193 (C.B. Fry 50, K.S. Ranjitsinhji 42, E. Jones 5 for 88) and 155 for 7 (K.S. Ranjitsinhji 93*). Match drawn.

The first Test of the first five-match series played in England was the last of W.G. Grace's 22 Test appearances and the first of Wilfred Rhodes's 58. The Test careers of the two spanned 50 years all but a few months. After Australia had fought every inch of the way for their 252, Grace – now almost 51, and often uncomfortable against the pace of Jones – put on 75 with Fry for the first wicket. The only other real stand was 55 by Ranji and Tyldesley. Australia then went after a largish lead while leaving time to bowl England out. The challenge was 290 in four hours, and when four wickets fell for 19, defeat for England loomed large. However, Ranji played with genius and Hayward, dropped once, stayed with him while 58 were added and the crisis was overcome.

170, above, left: *The Australians at breakfast at the Inns of Court Hotel, Holborn – from left: Trumper, Iredale, Worrall, Gregory, Howell.* 171, right: *Hill packs his bag for the match.* 172, left: *Jones, relaxed with pipe, packs his cane-ribbed pads.* 173, below, left: *W.G. Grace c Kelly b Noble 28 – his penultimate Test innings.* 174, right: *WG and Fry open for England at Trent Bridge*

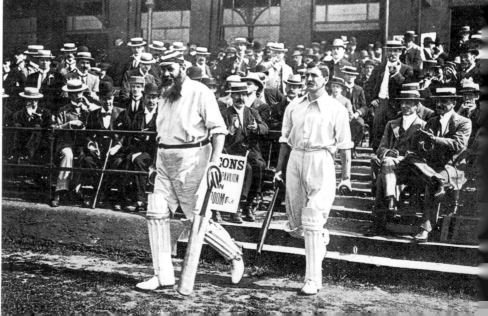

175: *Darling and Iredale open Australia's innings*

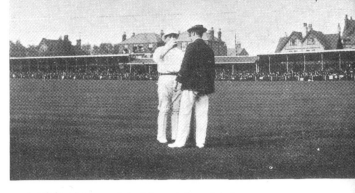

176: *Hill celebrates his fifty with a drink . . .*

177: *and comes in soon afterwards, run out 52*

178: *England come in on the first evening*

179: *WG, Laver, Jackson, and Ranji leave the field at Trent Bridge*

180: *Fry hurries in after making 50*

1899
Lord's, June 15, 16, 17

SECOND TEST

England 206 (F.S. Jackson 73, G.L. Jessop 51, E. Jones 7 for 88) and 240 (A.C. MacLaren 88*, T.W. Hayward 77); Australia 421 (C. Hill 135, V.T. Trumper 135*, M.A. Noble 54) and 28 for 0. Australia won by 10 wickets.

This proved to be the decisive Test of the series, and Jones's fast-bowling onslaught on the first day did much to bring ultimate victory to Australia. He dismissed Fry, MacLaren, Ranji and Tyldesley as England slumped to 66 for 6. Jessop and Jackson hit 95 in little more than an hour, but the total soon faded into insignificance as Hill and Noble added 130 for Australia's fourth wicket and Trumper, a fresh-faced 21-year-old in his second Test, 82 with Hill for the fifth. Fry, Ranji and Townsend again went early, but Jackson stayed with Hayward, who resisted further on the last day with MacLaren. Laver's three good wickets then settled the outcome.

181, 182, 183: *Frank Gillett's views in* The Daily Graphic *of the three days' play at Lord's*

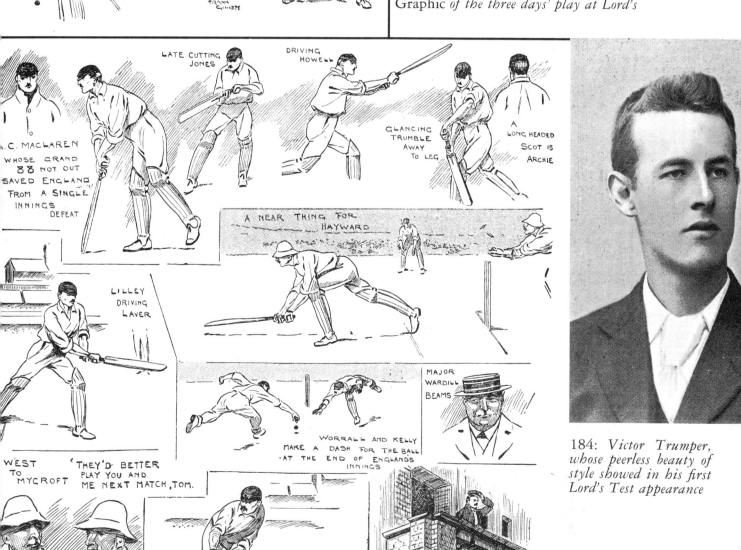

184: *Victor Trumper, whose peerless beauty of style showed in his first Lord's Test appearance*

1899
THIRD TEST
Headingley, June 29, 30, July 1

Australia 172 (J. Worrall 76, H.I. Young 4 for 30) and 224 (H. Trumble 56, F. Laver 45, J.T. Hearne 4 for 50); England 220 (A.F.A. Lilley 55, T.W. Hayward 40*, H. Trumble 5 for 60) and 19 for 0. Match drawn.

Rain before the start of this first-ever Test at Leeds caused widespread conjecture over the state of the pitch. Darling decided to bat, expecting conditions to worsen. His first three men were dismissed without a run between them. Worrall, who opened, made the first 24 runs, and his 76 came out of 95 in 90 minutes before he was run out. 'Sailor' Young, fast left-arm, had Hill and Trumper among his victims. That evening England were already 119 for 4, the tiny W.G. Quaife's 20 taking 1¾ hours. That night real-life tragedy struck when Johnny Briggs had a violent fit while watching a performance at the Empire Theatre. He was to spend most of the few months left to him in Cheadle Asylum. Hayward and Lilley took England into the lead with a stand of 93, and Australia were in grave danger after their first four wickets fell at 34, Hearne doing the hat-trick with the distinguished wickets of Hill, Gregory and Noble (the last two registering 'pairs'). Five runs later Darling was out, but Trumper, Trumble and Laver in turn held on resolutely, and England were set 177. When all was poised for a fascinating final day the rain returned, causing abandonment.

185: *The third Test, at Leeds – an eventful first day*

A Great Crowd of Spectators.
Exceedingly pleasant weather prevailed during the greater part of the afternoon, although there were times when some heavy clouds threatened rain, but a

C. B. Fry's fine one-handed catch which dismissed Kelly.

Johnny Briggs in the team again.

CRICKET FEVER IN THE CITY: TEST MATCH RESULTS IN QUEEN VICTORIA STREET.

slight breeze carried them away, and the first stage of the encounter was concluded in brilliant sunshine. The match proved a huge attraction, and before lunch time there were nearly 20,000 people on the ground, and this number was largely increased as the afternoon advanced. To keep the crowd in order there were over a hundred police present, and though they had no great disorder to deal with, several thousand people forced their way right up to the boundary after lunch, obstructing the view of those who occupied the proper seats, and for the rest of the day the cricket went on to a ceaseless accompaniment of shouting and cries of "Sit down." Except for this nuisance the first stage of the match passed off quite satisfactorily.

Brockwell Unable to Play.
Not until within a few minutes of the start was it definitely settled to play Hayward instead of Brockwell, who had hurt his hand. Brockwell must have been greatly disappointed, for it will be remembered that he was twelfth man both at Nottingham and at Lord's. The Australians left out Iredale—now recovered from his recent illness—McLeod and Johns, the Colonial team being exactly the same as that

(Continued on page 3.)

Worrall takes the first ball.

Noble fools away his wicket.

Lilley plays delightful cricket.

Willie Quaife stands up pluckily to Jones.

An uncomfortable way of watching a cricket match.

Brown does some vigorous boundary cutting. A good catch by Worrall dismisses Ranjitsinhji.

Jones never bowled faster.

186, above (inset): *Jack Hearne, who performed a high-quality hat-trick at Headingley.* 187: *Frank Gillett chose to record other incidents*

1899
Old Trafford, July 17, 18, 19

FOURTH TEST

England 372 (T.W. Hayward 130, A.F.A. Lilley 58, F.S. Jackson 44, H.I. Young 43) and 94 for 3 (K.S. Ranjitsinhji 49*); Australia 196 (M.A. Noble 60*, H. Trumble 44, W.M. Bradley 5 for 67, H.I. Young 4 for 79) and 346 for 7 dec (M.A. Noble 89, V.T. Trumper 63, J. Worrall 53). Match drawn.

A fine innings by Hayward, who went in at 47 for 4 and was 20 at lunch after 1½ hours, put England in command of the match on a pitch which interested bowlers throughout. Lilley added 113 with him for the seventh wicket. Australia reeled before Young and Bradley, and were only 57 when the seventh wicket fell. Trumble then stayed with Noble, who batted altogether for 8½ hours in the match in one of the most remarkable defensive fights ever. MacLaren drained Bradley so that in the follow-on Australia were not so severely tested. There were moments when England glimpsed victory, but Darling and Iredale saw to it that Noble's grim efforts were not wasted. The compulsory follow-on rule was dispensed with as a result of this contest.

188, above, left: *Bill Bradley, Kent fast bowler.* 189, centre: *'Sailor' Young – 12 top wickets in his only two Tests.* 190, right: *Tom Hayward – first century against Australia. Another followed next Test.* 191, below: *The first day's play at Old Trafford depicted in not the most fluid of illustrations.*

Quaife gets considerably knocked about.

Darling leads out his men.

Fry opens England's account with a single.

M. A. Noble.

Darling catches Quaife.

Lilley taking Bradley on the leg side—(no child's play this).

Tom Hayward's favourite stroke—rather high and rather late.

Station end.

Young about to deliver the ball.

Quaife shines at cover point.

192, 193: *Failures and triumphs on the second and final days at Old Trafford*

Montague Noble, the saviour of his side.

Beautiful catch by Ranjitsinhji.

Brockwell catches Worrall.

1899
The Oval, August 14, 15, 16

England 576 (*T.W. Hayward 137, F.S. Jackson 118, C.B. Fry 60, K.S. Ranjitsinhji 54, A.C. MacLaren 49, E. Jones 4 for 164); Australia 352 (S.E. Gregory 117, J. Darling 71, J. Worrall 55, W.H. Lockwood 7 for 71) and 254 for 5 (C.E. McLeod 77, J. Worrall 75, M.A. Noble 69*).* Match drawn.

An orgy of runs – 435 for 4 – on the first day led to the second-highest total in Tests so far, and left England over 10 hours to bowl Australia out twice. On a still-perfect pitch the task proved too much for England's varied array of bowlers. Jackson and Hayward put up a record 185 for the first wicket in better than even-time after making only two runs off the first 10 overs. The score was 316 before the second wicket – Ranji's – fell. A further century stand took place between MacLaren and Fry, who made 110 for the fourth wicket in only 65 minutes. Ernie Jones toiled through 53 five-ball overs. Lockwood was England's hero, Gregory, with Darling, Australia's. Hill was missed, as in the previous Test. It was two hours into the last day when Australia went to the wicket a second time, and after Worrall and McLeod opened with 116 and Lockwood left the field with a strain it was never seriously supposed that Australia would let England in to level the series.

194, above, left: *England's successful first day.* 195, right: *Australia's resistance on the second day.* 196, below: *Ranjitsinhji batting in the fifth Test – just the man to come in after an opening stand of 185*

1901–02
Sydney, December 13, 14, 16

FIRST TEST

England 464 (A.C. MacLaren 116, A.F.A. Lilley 84, T.W. Hayward 69, L.C. Braund 58, C.E. McLeod 4 for 84); Australia 168 (S.E. Gregory 48, C. Hill 46, S.F. Barnes 5 for 65) and 172 (S.E. Gregory 43, L.C. Braund 5 for 61, C. Blythe 4 for 30). England won by an innings and 124 runs.

As happened four years earlier, England blazed away to an opening victory only to finish second-best in the remaining matches. Ranji, Fry, Jackson, Hirst and Rhodes were all unavailable for the tour, but it hardly seemed to matter here at Sydney. MacLaren and Hayward started with a brisk 154, and Lilley and Braund added 124 for the seventh wicket. Australia bowled around 25 six-ball overs an hour throughout. S.F. Barnes, an 'unknown' whose great ability MacLaren had perceived, gave Australia an immediate taste of the bowling skills that were to bring him 106 wickets in 20 Tests. Braund (leg-breaks) and Blythe (slow left-arm) had Australia out a second time in under three hours.

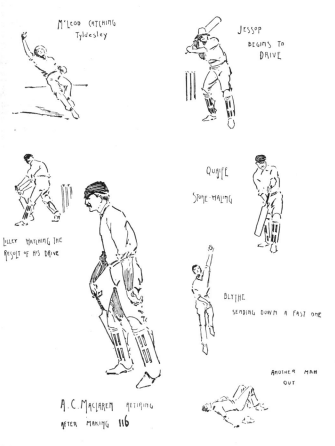

197, left: *Fred Leist's impressions of the first day's play at Sydney.* 198, above: *'Charlie' Blythe – seven wickets with slow left-arm.* 199, right: *Len Braund – seven wickets with leg-breaks.* 200, below: *View towards Randwick end; Jones bowling for Australia*

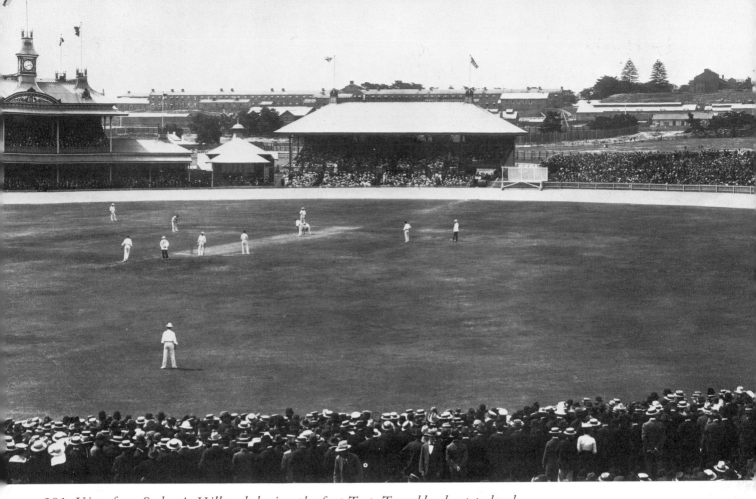

201: *View from Sydney's Hill end during the first Test; Trumble about to bowl*

1901–02
Melbourne, January 1, 2, 3, 4

SECOND TEST

Australia *112 (S.F. Barnes 6 for 42, C. Blythe 4 for 64) and 353 (R.A. Duff 104, C. Hill 99, W.W. Armstrong 45*, S.F. Barnes 7 for 121); England 61 (M.A. Noble 7 for 17) and 175 (J.T. Tyldesley 66, M.A. Noble 6 for 60, H. Trumble 4 for 49). Australia won by 229 runs.*

Barnes took Trumper's wicket with the second ball of the match, and on a rain-affected pitch runs were only ever likely to come from bold batsmanship. Barnes and Blythe bowled unchanged, and Duff, in his initial Test, top-scored with 32. England in turn were bundled out, lasting a mere 68 minutes, with Jessop coming out best with 27 in 20 minutes. Noble and Trumble (3 for 38) also bowled throughout the innings. Darling almost reversed his batting order and at the close of the opening day Australia were 48 for 5. Hill was dropped – a vital miss – on the second day, but Australia took hold of the match in an unusual last-wicket stand of 120, Duff coming in at No. 10 and Armstrong at 11. Barnes bowled 42 overs unchanged and 64 in all. Set 405 for victory on a reformed pitch, England slid to 147 for 5 by the third evening. Heavy rain then rendered the pitch spiteful again, and Trumble cleaned up with a hat-trick: A.O. Jones, John Gunn and Barnes.

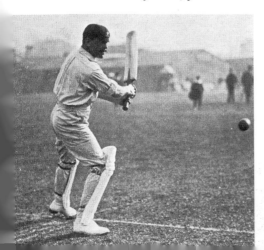

202, left: *Reg Duff – century for Australia on debut – batting No. 10.*
203, right: *Johnny Tyldesley – a brilliant cutter*

204, left: *S.F. Barnes, MacLaren's momentous discovery.* 205, above: *M.A. Noble, master swerve bowler – 13 for 77 at Melbourne*

206: *No room in the grandstand during the second Test*

1901–02
Adelaide, January 17, 18, 20, 21, 22, 23

THIRD TEST

England 388 (*L.C. Braund 103*, T.W. Hayward 90, W.G. Quaife 68, A.C. MacLaren 67*) and 247 (*T.W. Hayward 47, A.C. MacLaren 44, W.G. Quaife 44, H. Trumble 6 for 74*); Australia 321 (*C. Hill 98, V.T. Trumper 65, S.E. Gregory 55, R.A. Duff 43, J. Gunn 5 for 76*) and 315 for 6 (*C. Hill 97, J. Darling 69, H. Trumble 62**). Australia won by 4 wickets.

The loss of Barnes with a twisted knee after only seven overs was critical to the balance of the match – and the series, for he was unable to resume his place at the head of England's attack. MacLaren and Hayward got England off to a strong start: 149; but the innings was slipping away when Quaife and Braund added 108 for the sixth wicket. Led by Hill's 98, Australia responded well until Gunn ran through the second half of the order. England extended their lead, with rain falling on the third evening and a dust-storm cutting play on the fourth. Set 315, Australia were 201 for 4 by the fifth evening, Hill having been bowled by Jessop towards the end to complete a bizarre sequence of 99, 98 and 97. Despite one worn end, the pitch remained fairly sound, and Australia went 2–1 up on the sixth day.

207: *Jessop at cover throws to 'keeper Lilley with Trumble, having crossed with Darling, still well out of his crease. The batsman survived*

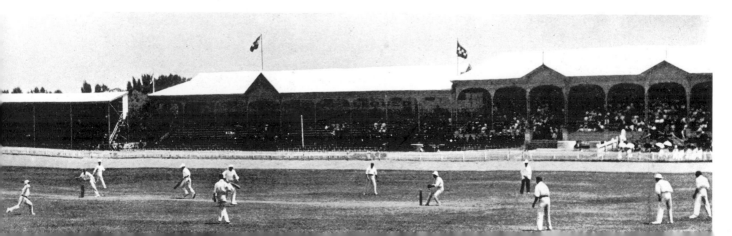

208, above: *Trumble catches A.O. Jones off his own bowling.* 209, left: *John Gunn – eight wickets at Adelaide.* 210, right: *W. G. Quaife – a valuable double of 68 and 44, but in a losing cause*

1901–02
Sydney, February 14, 15, 17, 18

FOURTH TEST

England 317 (A.C. MacLaren 92, J.T. Tyldesley 79, T.W. Hayward 41, A.F.A. Lilley 40, J.V. Saunders 4 for 119) and 99 (J.V. Saunders 5 for 43, M.A. Noble 5 for 54); Australia 299 (M.A. Noble 56, W.W. Armstrong 55, A.J.Y. Hopkins 43, G.L. Jessop 4 for 68, L.C. Braund 4 for 118) and 121 for 3 (R.A. Duff 51*). Australia won by 7 wickets.

England scored 179 before their second wicket fell, but persistent outcricket by Australia under their new captain, Trumble, prevented a mammoth score. Jessop's fast bowling cut down the first four Australian wickets for only 48, but the middle batsmen resisted stoutly, and the first-innings margin was kept to insignificance after all. Then England collapsed unaccountably against Noble and Saunders, who bowled unchanged through the innings, supported by smart fielding and catching. Saunders, fast-medium left-arm, had match figures of 9 for 162 but was omitted from the following Test.

211, left: *Montague Alfred Noble – a superb all-round match: 56 and eight wickets.* 212, right: *Jack Saunders, the Victorian left-hander*

1901–02
Melbourne, February 28, March 1, 3, 4

FIFTH TEST

Australia 144 (*T.W. Hayward 4 for 22, J. Gunn 4 for 38*) *and* 255 (*C. Hill 87, S.E. Gregory 41, L.C. Braund 5 for 95*); England 189 (*A.F.A. Lilley 41, H. Trumble 5 for 62*) *and* 178 (*A.C. MacLaren 49, M.A. Noble 6 for 98*). Australia won by 32 runs.

Australia, winning the toss for the first time in the series, failed on a pitch which several times changed character as showers occurred during the four days. Jessop (35) and MacLaren had 50 up for England in a mere 20 minutes, but Australia restored a balance and set about building up a new lead, and were ahead by 181 with four wickets left on the second evening. Hill was missed twice during his stylish innings. Eventually set 211 to win, England finished the day 87 for 3. Jessop went first ball next morning and against Noble and Trumble on a lifting pitch the going was difficult. Tyldesley, a master in such circumstances, held one end secure, but lost partners steadily and was last out.

213, left: *A.O. Jones leads out some of his men – from left: Tyldesley, Braund, Blythe, Jessop (in sunhat), and McGahey.* 214, below, left: *Hugh Trumble, whose total of 141 wickets in these Tests is still unapproached.* 215, below, right: *Darling and his second side embark for England in Coronation Year*

HERE WE ARE AGAIN!

1902
FIRST TEST
Edgbaston, May 29, 30, 31

England 376 for 9 dec (J.T. Tyldesley 138, F.S. Jackson 53, W.H. Lockwood 52*, G.H. Hirst 48); Australia 36 (W. Rhodes 7 for 17) and 46 for 2. Match drawn.

One of the most fascinating of Test series began with Birmingham's first Test and Australia's lowest-ever score. An England XI perhaps without equal across the hundred years of Test cricket recovered from a shaky start primarily through Tyldesley's artistry, with support from Jackson and Hirst and an unfinished tenth-wicket stand of 81 by Lockwood and Rhodes. Tyldesley played supremely well through the off side, and was missed just twice – when 43. After a delay for rain, MacLaren allowed the innings to continue awhile before declaring. The pitch was now drying but never beastly, and Hirst (who finished with 3 for 15) bowled so well that Rhodes, appearing less lethal to the batsmen, reaped the greater harvest. Trumper's 18 was half the final pathetic total, which was reached in 85 minutes. The two Yorkshiremen bowled through the innings except for one over by Braund to enable them to change ends. Further rain on the second night meant a late start on the last day, and though the crowd burst into the ground with great excitement – several people were injured – the pitch was dead and Australia had no trouble in playing out time. Three days later, in their match with Yorkshire, the Australians were dismissed by Hirst and Jackson for 23.

216: *Glimpses of the first day's play, with hardly a hint of the sensations to follow*

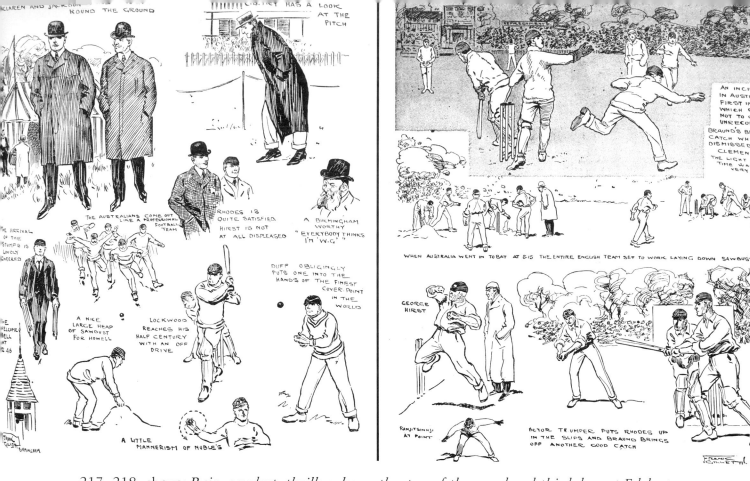

217, 218, above: *Rain, sawdust, thrills galore – the story of the second and third days at Edgbaston*

219, above, left: *The Australians set off from their Birmingham hotel.* 220, above: *Wilfred Rhodes, 7 for 17, was – with Hirst – irresistible on the damp pitch.* 221, left: *How Tom Webster remembered the wonderful England XI*

1902
Lord's, June 12, 13, 14

SECOND TEST

England *102 for 2 (F.S. Jackson 55*, A.C. MacLaren 47*).* Match drawn.

Australia, without Trumble (still injured) and Howell, and with a few other players off-colour, were not too disconsolate at the abandonment of this rain-ruined match, although the opening overs midway through the first day were not without sensation. Hopkins had Fry caught at short leg in his first over and bowled Ranji off his pads in his second to render England 0 for 2. Jackson made a run then gave a sharp chance to slip. That would have made it three down for one run. However, the crisis was overcome, and was soon seen in perspective as rain and more rain washed out the remaining two days.

222: The first day – and Hopkins' moments of glory. There was to be no second or third day

JONES LEADS OFF WITH A MAIDEN OVER

RANJITSINHJI ALL AT SEA WITH ONE OF HOPKINS' BREAK BACKS (2 WICKETS FOR 0)

FRY FALLS INTO AN OBVIOUS TRAP (1 WICKET FOR 0)

ARMSTRONG GIVES JACKSON A LIFE AT SLIP

JACKSON SCORES THE FIRST RUN OF THE MATCH IN THE SIXTH OVER

A WEIRD CHOP OF JACKSON'S BOUNCES OVER KELLY'S HEAD

A.J. HOPKINS WHO DISPOSED OF FRY AND RANJITSINHJI

HIRST AND RHODES CHUCKLE

FRANK GILLETT

1902
Bramall Lane, July 3, 4, 5

THIRD TEST

Australia 194 (M.A. Noble 47, S.F. Barnes 6 for 49) and 289 (C. Hill 119, V.T. Trumper 62, A.J.Y. Hopkins 40*, W. Rhodes 5 for 63); England 145 (J.V. Saunders 5 for 50, M.A. Noble 5 for 51) and 195 (A.C. MacLaren 63, G.L. Jessop 55, M.A. Noble 6 for 52, H. Trumble 4 for 49). Australia won by 143 runs.

Sheffield's only Test match saw a full-strength Australia move into a series lead, though their start was unsteady. MacLaren gave the new ball to Hirst and leg-spinner Braund, and the latter bowled Trumper in his first over. When Barnes came into the attack he took 3 for 3, but from 73 for 5 Australia managed a reasonable total. MacLaren and Abel raised 61 for England's first wicket, but the innings became a procession, some of the batsmen's downfalls doubtless attributable in part to dreadful light due in no small part to the smoke from factory chimneys. Australia grasped the initiative when Trumper began their second innings with 62 out of 80 in only 50 minutes. Darling made a 'pair' (c Braund b Barnes both times), but Hill tore into the bowling, adding 107 with Gregory in 67 minutes, and batting in all for only 145 minutes. England's target of 339 was plainly beyond them in the conditions, yet Jessop opened with 55 at his customary tearaway rate, and MacLaren commanded for a time. Noble cut the ball back briskly and used the wearing pitch cleverly to finish with 11 wickets in the match.

223, left: Australia's grim start at Sheffield as seen by The Daily Graphic. *224, below: England do even less well in their first innings*

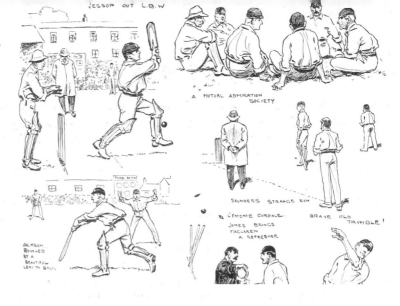

225: *The demise of Jessop and of Jackson in England's second innings*

1902
Old Trafford, July 24, 25, 26

FOURTH TEST

Australia 299 (V.T. Trumper 104, C. Hill 65, R.A. Duff 54, J. Darling 51, W.H. Lockwood 6 for 48, W. Rhodes 4 for 104) and 86 (W.H. Lockwood 5 for 28); England 262 (F.S. Jackson 128, L.C. Braund 65, H. Trumble 4 for 75) and 120 (H. Trumble 6 for 53, J.V. Saunders 4 for 52). Australia won by 3 runs.

One of the most famous cricket matches began with a pyrotechnic innings from Victor Trumper, who reached his century before lunch, when Australia were 173 for one. Trumper and Duff posted 135 for the first wicket – a record for Australia – in 78 minutes. Lockwood got Duff in his first over, much delayed because of slippery footholds, and continued to present the batsmen with problems, especially in his third spell, when he wrapped up the innings with five wickets for eight. Meanwhile, Rhodes had trapped Trumper (who batted only 115 minutes), Noble and Gregory in four overs after lunch, only to be hit right out of the ground twice by Darling. Hill and his captain, apart from the two openers, were the only ones to make more than five runs. England suffered early shocks and were 44 for 5 before Jackson and Braund stayed together in an admirable stand of 141. Jackson was last out, having withstood a high-class attack on a dubious pitch for 4¼ hours. Australia, 37 ahead, lost three for 10, and Fred Tate, on the square-leg boundary, made a fateful miss when he dropped Darling – the eventual top-scorer with 37 – when the total was still only 16. The next wicket did not fall until 64, and after that Australian wickets cascaded. England needed 124, and MacLaren and Palairet saw them to 44 before the first wicket fell. Trumble and Saunders steadily gathered wickets thereafter, and with the last pair at the wicket and eight runs needed, a shower forced a dramatic pause. It was 45 minutes before Rhodes and Tate were able to resume, and the latter then jabbed Saunders for four. Four needed. Saunders bowled a faster ball, Tate played helplessly at it and was bowled. It bears the macabre label 'Tate's match', but the batting of Trumper and Jackson, the bowling of Lockwood, and Hill's diving one-handed boundary catch to dismiss Lilley should never be forgotten.

226, left: *Fred Tate, a fine bowler, who will be remembered for his fielding and batting lapses at Manchester.* 227, below: *A premature memorial card, printed when England were 'certain' of victory.* 228, right: *Trumper's 1902 bat, signed by dozens of Test players*

IN MEMORY OF THE
AUSTRALIANS.

The Australians came like the wolves on the fold
And their faces looked tanned like the Australian gold
To the cricket field they all wended their way,
To see all England at cricket to play.

The Australia men, their players feel
The blighting, withering blast,
For full of hope, they thought to steal
The verdict at last:
'Twas not to be, so let them lie
Deep in the silent grave,
And shed a tear, o'er their bier,
And the match they tried to save.

229, above, left: *Trumper and Duff put on 135 in only 78 minutes before lunch on the first day at Old Trafford.* 230, right: *Braund and Jackson resumed for England on the second day with the score 70 for 5 in reply to Australia's 299. England were 185 before Braund was bowled by Noble.* 231, left: *Chasing 124 for victory, England saw only four batsmen reach double-figures — Palairet 17, Abel 21, MacLaren 35, and Tyldesley 16. Tate was last out, bowled by Saunders four runs from England's target*

1902
The Oval, August 11, 12, 13

FIFTH TEST

Australia 324 (H. Trumble 64, M.A. Noble 52, V.T. Trumper 42, A.J.Y. Hopkins 40, G.H. Hirst 5 for 77) and 121 (W.H. Lockwood 5 for 45); England 183 (G.H. Hirst 43, H. Trumble 8 for 65) and 263 for 9 (G.L. Jessop 104, G.H. Hirst 58*, F.S. Jackson 49, J.V. Saunders 4 for 105, H. Trumble 4 for 108).* England won by one wicket.

'Jessop's match' reached its climax when Rhodes joined Hirst for England's last wicket with 15 needed for victory. The runs were not obtained in singles, as legend has it; not did the two realistic Yorkshiremen plan to get them necessarily in that way. England's chance came only by virtue of Jessop's historic century. He went in when England, needing 263 in the fourth innings, were 48 for 5, and, with lunch intervening, he was 50 in 43 minutes. Jackson continued to bat gracefully as the rugged Jessop charged Trumble and Saunders – especially the latter – on an improving pitch. In only 75 minutes he had his century, and his 104 took 77 minutes and included 17 fours and an all-run five. Three times he drove the ball into the pavilion. He was missed twice. Jackson, who made only 18 of a sixth-wicket stand of 109, was succeeded by Hirst, who added 30 in eight minutes with 'The Croucher'. With Jessop's departure, caught at short leg off Armstrong, much responsibility fell on Hirst. Lockwood made two in a stand of 27 and Lilley 16 in a ninth-wicket stand of 34. Hirst and Rhodes (6 not out) did the rest. The course of this magnificent match was altered by England's success in averting a follow-on on a wet pitch which was worsening under a warm sun, and by Hill's dropping of Lockwood when the follow-on still seemed inevitable. Trumble bowled unchanged throughout both England innings, often spinning sharply from the off, but Saunders was the bowler to wilt most noticeably before the Jessop barrage. Against Trumble Jessop disciplined himself not to sweep hard across the line: he cracked him straight and through the off field. He faced only 80 balls and, after a number of failures, he had shown doubting opponents in that brief time that he was an attacking batsman without equal anywhere.

232, below, left: A memorable innings begins. 233, right: Gilbert Jessop, whose 104 was perhaps the most famous innings in history

ST. DADD

urt by the ball that bowled Palairet.

ssop receiving his first ball.

Jessop hits Trumble on to the Pavilion for the second time in one over.

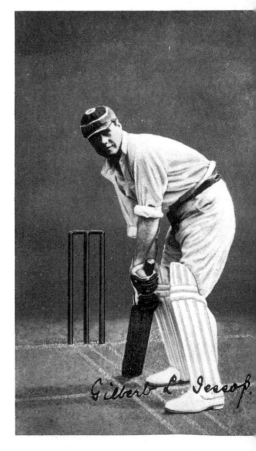

Gilbert Jessop

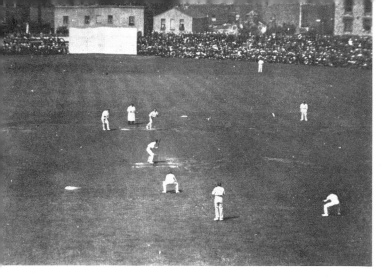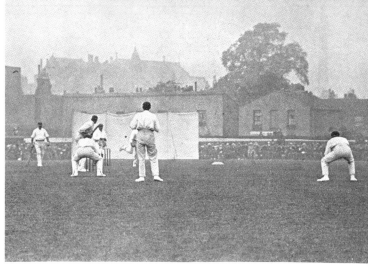

234, above, left: *Lockwood bowls to Trumper in the fifth Test at The Oval.* 235, right: *Australia batting, Lilley keeping wicket, Braund at slip, MacLaren at gully.* 236, below: *Trumper cuts at Lockwood and misses; Lilley takes*

237, above, left: *Jessop pulls Saunders during his matchwinning century.* 238, right: *An extraordinary match ends: Rhodes has hit the winning single, and the players race off to escape the eager clutches of the frenzied spectators*

1903–04
Sydney, December 11, 12, 14, 15, 16, 17

FIRST TEST

Australia 285 (M.A. Noble 133, W.W. Armstrong 48, E.G. Arnold 4 for 76) and 485 (V.T. Trumper 185*, R.A. Duff 84, C. Hill 51, S.E. Gregory 43, W. Rhodes 5 for 94); England 577 (R.E. Foster 287, L.C. Braund 102, J.T. Tyldesley 53, W. Rhodes 40*) and 194 for 5 (T.W. Hayward 91, G.H. Hirst 60*). England won by 5 wickets.

The third truly enthralling Test in succession marked this as a halcyon period. For the first time MCC chose and managed the English touring team, and though Fry, Jackson and MacLaren were unavailable, it was a strong all-round combination. Arnold took Trumper's wicket with his first ball in Test cricket, and Australia were soon 12 for 3. Noble, with his only Test century, saved the innings in a 280-minute devotion on his debut as captain. A thunderstorm made batting anything but easy, and England were 117 for 4 before Braund and a hesitant Foster took the score to 243 that evening. In better conditions on the third day England took control. Foster, much more impressive now, in his first Test innings, reached his hundred and Braund did likewise next over and was then out. Their stand was worth 192 and England were 24 ahead. Three wickets fell, then Relf stayed while 115 were added, Foster off-driving and cutting with ease and charm and forcing through the leg side with powerful wristwork. His footwork, too, was attractive. He was 203 when Relf was out just before tea, but Australia had to wait a further record 130 runs before Foster was caught at mid-off after a seven-hour innings that included 37 fours. He and Rhodes were together only 66 minutes. England's record Test innings was surpassed and Foster's new individual Test record was to stand for 26 years. Australia, 292 behind, retrieved their honour through Trumper, who played probably his greatest innings, treating all the bowlers except Rhodes as if they were schoolboys, and being particularly severe on Braund. His 94-minute hundred is the third-fastest in these Tests, and in all he scored 26 fours. The crowd demonstrated when Hill was given 'run out', and Warner came close to calling his team off the field. Trumper ran out of partners, but England were still left a tallish task on a wearing pitch. Hayward and Hirst made sure of victory with a stand of 99 for the fifth wicket.

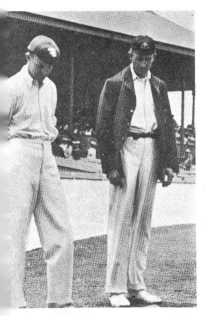

239, left: *Warner (left) and Noble toss at Sydney.* 240, above, right: *The scoreboard proclaims England's 577 and Foster's 287.* 241, below, left: *England enter the field – across the cycle track.* 242, right: *Bosanquet – revolutionary among bowlers*

243, left: *R.E. 'Tip' Foster, whose 287 is still the highest innings by any player in his first Test.* 244, right: *Victor Trumper, whose century at Sydney was probably his finest*

245, above: *Cartoonist's view of the unsavoury crowd behaviour during the first Test.* 246, left: *Ted Arnold – a wicket with his first ball in Tests.* 247, right: *Wilfred Rhodes, 54 years later, holds the emu egg trophy presented to him to mark his 7 for 135 in the match*

1903–04
SECOND TEST
Melbourne, January 1, 2, 4, 5

England 315 (J.T. Tyldesley 97, P.F. Warner 68, T.W. Hayward 58, R.E. Foster 49 ret.ill, W.P. Howell 4 for 43, H. Trumble 4 for 107) and 103 (J.T. Tyldesley 62, H. Trumble 5 for 34); Australia 122 (V.T. Trumper 74, W. Rhodes 7 for 56) and 111 (W. Rhodes 8 for 68). England won by 185 runs.

England progressed slowly, making 221 for 2 on the first day. Warner and Hayward scored 122 for the first wicket. Rain cut the second day short, and the pitch on the third day was very difficult. Yet Trumper stroked 74 in 112 minutes, peerless as ever while bowlers had everything to suit them. Wilfred Rhodes, slow left-arm, exploited the pitch and took more wickets than had ever been taken in an England-Australia Test. Tyldesley saved England's second innings, making his 62 out of 85; Relf, 10 not out, was the next-highest scorer. Three Australians reached double-figures: Trumper 35, Hill 20, and Noble a fine, back-to-the-wall 31 not out. Eighteen Australian wickets fell to catches.

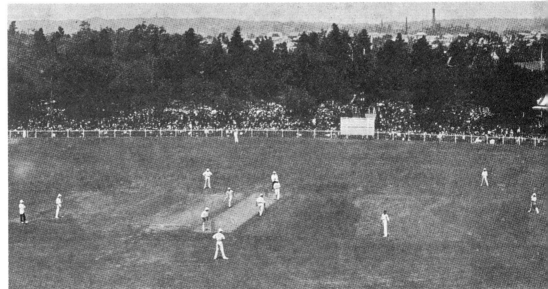

248, above: *Bill Howell, the Penrith beekeeper, who made his off-breaks buzz.* 249, top, right: *Warner and Hayward open for England in the second Test.* 250, centre: *Hayward has cut Howell to the boundary.* 251, right: *Noble forces Hayward to play back*

1903–04
Adelaide, January 15, 16, 18, 19, 20

THIRD TEST

Australia 388 (V.T. Trumper 113, C. Hill 88, R.A. Duff 79, M.A. Noble 59) and 351 (S.E. Gregory 112, M.A. Noble 65, V.T. Trumper 59, B.J.T. Bosanquet 4 for 73); England 245 (G.H. Hirst 58, P.F. Warner 48) and 278 (P.F. Warner 79, T.W. Hayward 67, G.H. Hirst 44, A.J.Y. Hopkins 4 for 81). Australia won by 216 runs.

Australia were 355 for 6 by the first night, Duff having dominated an opening stand of 129 with Trumper, whose century was his third in five Tests. Hill and Trumper took the score to 272 before the second wicket fell. Bosanquet's then-novel googlies were confusing at times, even to his own wicket-keeper, Lilley. England, with only four specialist batsmen, were bowled out comparatively cheaply on a good pitch, and when Australia – for whom Noble and Gregory put on 162 for the fourth wicket – were all out a second time, England needed 495. Warner and Hayward started with 148, but there was no further prolonged resistance.

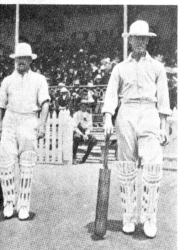

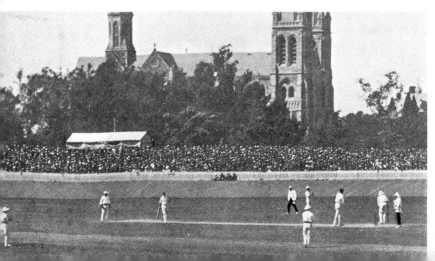

252, top, left: *The toss at Adelaide, and this time Noble wins it.* 253, right: *Duff pulls Fielder for four to start a magnificent opening stand with Trumper.* 254, centre, left: *Duff (left) and Trumper, one of the truly great opening pairs, enter at Adelaide, where the former for once outshone the latter.* 255, right: *Hill pulls Braund with all his considerable strength.* 256, left: *Warner, England's captain, falls to a grand catch by McLeod (out of picture) at mid-on off Trumble for 48*

257, above, left: *George Hirst lofts Trumble to long-off, to be caught by Trumper for 58.* 258, right: *England come off for a welcome respite.* 259, below, left: *Hayward is lbw to Hopkins, and England's opening stand of 148 is ended.* 260, right: *Rhodes is run out, and Australia have won the Adelaide Test by 216 runs*

1903–04   FOURTH TEST
Sydney, February 26, 27, 29, March 1, 2, 3

England *249 (A.E. Knight 70*, M.A. Noble 7 for 100) and 210 (T.W. Hayward 52); Australia 131 (R.A. Duff 47, E.G. Arnold 4 for 28, W. Rhodes 4 for 33) and 171 (M.A. Noble 53*, B.J.T. Bosanquet 6 for 51). England won by 157 runs.*

Knight, batting for 260 minutes, held England's innings together, with main support from Braund, and with occasional delays for rain-showers Australia's reply stuttered before Rhodes and Arnold, with Braund getting the key wicket of Trumper for only seven. Again there were crowd demonstrations, provoked this time by the stoppages. Monday's play was lost, with the pitch aflood, and Australia's last five wickets fell for the addition of 17. Foster and Hayward began well for England, but the best stand was 55 by Warner and Rhodes for the last wicket. On a well-behaved pitch Australia then needed 329, but Bosanquet struck with a 'startling' spell of googlies, taking 5 for 12 at one point. Warner's XI thus regained the Ashes.

261: *Hill has played Braund to leg at Sydney and he and his partner, Trumper, take a run*

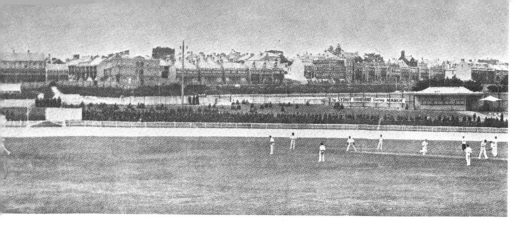
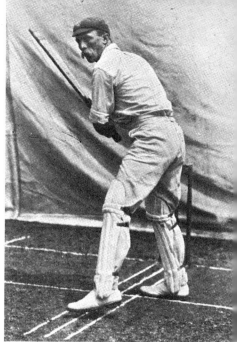

262, above: *Warner hits a four through the off side during his last-wicket stand of 55 with Rhodes in England's second innings.* 263, right: *Albert Knight, whose 70 not out saved England's first innings at Sydney*

1903–04
Melbourne, March 5, 7, 8

FIFTH TEST

Australia 247 (V.T. Trumper 88, L.C. Braund 8 for 81) and 133 (G.H. Hirst 5 for 48); England 61 (A. Cotter 6 for 40, M.A. Noble 4 for 19) and 101 (H. Trumble 7 for 28). Australia won by 218 runs.

Trumper led off with 88 in 110 minutes, but Braund, bowling his leg-breaks slightly faster than usual, proved too much for him and seven others. England lost Hayward and nightwatchman Arnold that evening without a run, and rain delayed the start of the second day's play until 4 pm, when the ball was lifting dangerously. Four were down for five runs before Tyldesley (10) and Foster (18) added 18, the highest stand of the innings. Fast bowler 'Tibby' Cotter, in his second Test, had batsmen retreating. He had the rare ability to keep steady balance even on wet footholds. Hirst was the principal agent in Australia's second-innings destruction; he bowled Trumper for nought. Hayward was absent, stricken with tonsilitis, but England's target was purely academic. Trumble bade farewell to Test cricket with glorious figures, including his second hat-trick: Bosanquet, Warner and Lilley. Foster (30) was caught off him by Trumper, one-handed running back to the long-on boundary.

264, left: *Hill, caught by Braund at slip off Rhodes for 16.* 265, below: *Hopkins hits Braund to square leg*

266, below: *Joy was unbridled at England's success in the 1903–04 series. Medallions were struck by MCC for each player. This is Ted Arnold's.* 267, right: *G. Hillyard Swinstead's drawing from the menu card of the dinner to welcome the team home*

1905
Trent Bridge, May 29, 30, 31

FIRST TEST

England 196 (J.T. Tyldesley 56, F. Laver 7 for 64) and 426 for 5 dec (A.C. MacLaren 140, F.S. Jackson 82*, J.T. Tyldesley 61, T.W. Hayward 47); Australia 221 (C. Hill 54, M.A. Noble 50, A. Cotter 45, F.S. Jackson 5 for 52) and 188 (S.E. Gregory 51, J. Darling 40, B.J.T. Bosanquet 8 for 107). England won by 213 runs.

Cotter, bowling fierily, and Laver, varying his medium-pace, bundled England out on a fair wicket. England then returned the compliment, Jackson cutting the heart of the innings out with the wickets of Noble, Hill and Darling in one over, after Trumper had retired with a back strain sustained earlier while attempting a slip catch. He did not bat in the second innings. MacLaren and Hayward set England off with 145, the former giving delight with his hooking of Cotter. Jackson and Rhodes added 113 unbroken, and Australia, having bowled defensively, now tried to bat out the 4½ hours remaining. Bosanquet, often erratic, was kept on and reaped his reward.

286, left: *Deft penwork shows some of the second-day action at Trent Bridge. A.O. Jones's catching of Gregory was the highlight.* 269, below: *Fast bowler Cotter hurls one down to Hayward*

Price 1d.

NOTTS. COUNTY CRICKET CLUB
Trent Bridge Ground, Monday, May 29, 30, 31, 1905.

ENGLAND v. AUSTRALIA.

Bowler's No.	ENGLAND.	1st Innings		2nd Inn.
1	Mr. A. C. MacLaren (Lc)	c Kelly, b Laver	2	c Duff, b Laver 140
2	T. Hayward (Surrey)	b Cotter	5	c Darling, b Armstrong... 47
3	J. T. Tyldesley (Lanc.)	c Duff, b Laver	56	c and b Duff 6
4	Mr. A. O. Jones (Notts)	b Laver	4	b Duff 30
5	Hon. F. S. Jackson (Cpt)	b Cotter	0	not out 82
6	Mr B. J. Bosanquet (Mx)	b Laver	27	b Cotter 6
7	W. Rhodes (Yorks.)	c Noble, b Laver	29	not out 39
8	A. A. Lilley (Wrk.)	c and b Laver	37	....
9	Mr. G. L. Jessop (Glo')	b Laver	0	....
10	J. Gunn (Notts.)	b Cotter	8	....
11	E. Arnold (Worc.)	not out	2	....
	Byes 21, leg-byes 5, wides 0, no-balls 0...	26	B 11, l-b 9, w 1, n-b 0...	21
	Total	...196	Innings Closed...426	

Wkts fell 1st Inn.	1	2	3	4	5	6	7	8	9	10
	6	24	40	49	98	119	119	139	187	196
2nd Inn.	145	222	276	301	313	...	...	...	...	...

Batsman's No.	AUSTRALIA.	1st Innings		2nd Inn.
1	Mr. J. Darling (Capt.)	c Bosanquet, b Jackson	0	b Bosanquet 40
2	Mr. R. A. Duff	c Hayward, b Gunn	1	c and b Bosanquet 25
3	Mr. C. Hill	b Jackson	54	c and b Bosanquet 8
4	Mr. M. A. Noble	c Lilley, b Jackson	50	st Lilley, b Bosanquet...... 7
5	Mr. W. W. Armstrong	st Lilley, b Rhodes	27	c Jackson, b Bosanquet ... 6
6	Mr. S. E. Gregory	c Jones, b Jackson	2	c Arnold, b Bosanquet ... 51
7	Mr. C. E. McLeod	b Arnold	4	l b w, Bosanquet 13
8	Mr. F. Laver	c Jones, b Jackson	5	st Lilley, b Bosanquet.... 5
9	Mr. J. J. Kelly	not out	1	not out 6
10	Mr. A. Cotter	c and b Jessop	45	b Rhodes 18
11	Mr. V. Trumper	retired hurt	13	absent ...
	Byes 16, leg-byes 2, wides 1, no-balls 0...	19	B 4, l-b 3, w 2, n-b 0...	9
	Total	...221	Total...	..188

Wkts fell 1st Inn.	1	2	3	4	5	6	7	8	9	10
	1	129	130	130	200	204	209	216	216	221
2nd Inn.	62	75	82	93	100	139	144	175	188	...

ANALYSIS

Australia Bowling.	overs	mdns.	runs	wkts.	overs	mdns.	runs	wkts
Cotter	23	2	64	3	17	1	59	1
Laver	31.3	14	64	7	34	7	121	1
Noble	3	0	19	0	7	1	31	0
McLeod	8	2	19	0	28	9	84	0
Armstrong	6	3	4	0	52	24	67	0
Duff	...	...	...	...	15	2	43	2
...	...	...	...	...	...	...	...	...
England Bowling								
Arnold	11	2	39	1	4	2	7	0
Gunn	6	2	27	1	...	...	...	...
Jessop	7	2	18	1	1	0	1	0
Bosanquet	7	0	29	0	32.4	2	107	8
Rhodes	18	6	39	1	30	8	58	1
Jackson	14.5	2	52	5	5	3	6	0
...	...	...	...	...				

Umpires, Jas. Phillips and John Carlin.   Stumps drawn at 6.30

Charles H. Richards, Printer, Lower Parliament Street, Nottingham.

270, above, left: *Gregory and Darling lead the Australians off for lunch on the opening day at Trent Bridge, England 98 for 5, Tyldesley and Bosanquet the not-out batsmen.* 271, right: *The scorecard perpetuates MacLaren's fifth century against Australia and Bosanquet's remarkable analysis.* 272, left: *England build up a winning lead, though Trumper, unable to bat because of injury, was missed when Australia tried to play out time*

1905
Lord's, June 15, 16, 17

SECOND TEST

England *282 (C.B. Fry 73, A.C. MacLaren 56, J.T. Tyldesley 43) and 151 for 5 (A.C. MacLaren 79);* Australia *181 (J. Darling 41, F.S. Jackson 4 for 50).* Match drawn.

Only MacLaren and Tyldesley played with anything approaching freedom after ten days of wet weather had left the pitch helpful to bowlers. Thunderstorms occurred each night of the match, Fry spent 3½ hours over his 73, Darling's field having been placed tightly and Armstrong bowling many overs down the leg side. Trumper and Duff hit a swift 57 before the pitch dried to an awkward state, and a collapse was arrested by Darling and Armstrong, who saved the follow-on. MacLaren attacked on the second afternoon, and Fry held an end (36 not out in 90 minutes), leaving England 252 ahead, but the final day was washed out.

273, above, left: *Charlie McLeod bowls to MacLaren around the wicket with a strong offside field.* 274, right: *Stanley Jackson leads out the amateurs in the England XI at Lord's: MacLaren, Fry, and Jones.* 275, below, left: *Rhodes to Darling – with typically high backlift.* 276, right: *MacLaren majestically places Australian opening bowler McLeod to the legside boundary*

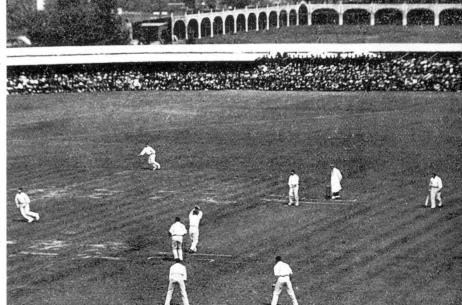

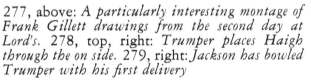

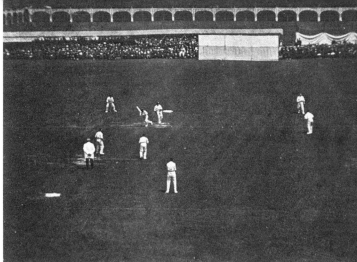

277, above: *A particularly interesting montage of Frank Gillett drawings from the second day at Lord's.* 278, top, right: *Trumper places Haigh through the on side.* 279, right: *Jackson has bowled Trumper with his first delivery*

1905
THIRD TEST
Headingley, July 3, 4, 5

England 301 (F.S. Jackson 144*) and 295 for 5 dec (J.T. Tyldesley 100, T.W. Hayward 60, G.H. Hirst 40*, W.W. Armstrong 5 for 122); Australia 195 (W.W. Armstrong 66, R.A. Duff 48, A. Warren 5 for 57) and 224 for 7 (M.A. Noble 62). Match drawn.

England's captain, going in at 57 for 3, lost Hayward at 64, but found support in Hirst, and went on to make Leeds' first Test century. He batted 268 minutes, hit 18 fours, and was missed just once, at 130. Warren, in his only Test, took Trumper's wicket twice (8 and 0), and bowled with plenty of life. Australia, so far behind, could only play a containing game, and Armstrong bowled 51 overs, mostly down the leg side, with an appropriate field-setting. Tyldesley batted beautifully and sometimes overcame the negative bowling by stepping to leg and hitting through the off side. Many critics felt England should have declared sooner, but Blythe took three early wickets, and only his dropping of a return catch from Noble interfered with England's drive to victory. Noble and Gregory hung on defiantly.

280: *An assortment of straw boaters, panamas, and other hats shelter the heads of the crowd at the Leeds Test match*

ES THE TOSS
TO HILL'S
YANCE

FRY OPENS
ENGLAND'S ACCOUNT
WITH
A CUT (!)

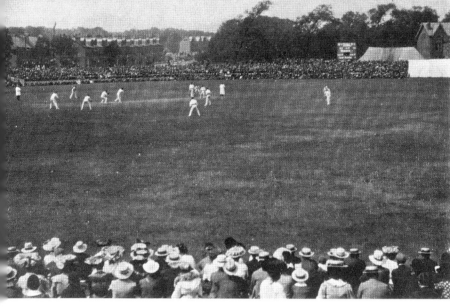

281, top, left: *Darling's third lost toss annoys Hill.* 282, above: *Arnold Warren, the Derbyshire fast bowler, who was highly successful in his only Test.* 283, centre: *Trumper drives.* 284, below, left: *Some of Australia's uncomfortable moments captured . . .* 285, right: *as is some of England's happiness on the final day*

A MISTAKE ONE HARDLY EXPECTED NOBLE TO MAKE
A GENTLE TAP TO TOM HAYWARD AT SLIP

1905
Old Trafford, July 24, 25, 26

FOURTH TEST

England 446 (F.S. Jackson 113, T.W. Hayward 82, R.H. Spooner 52, C.E. McLeod 5 for 125); Australia 197 (J. Darling 73, W. Brearley 4 for 72) and 169 (R.A. Duff 60, W. Brearley 4 for 54). England won by an innings and 80 runs.

On a deadened pitch England went methodically about building a secure score. Hayward was his usual sound self and Spooner batted charmingly. But Jackson, who could do no wrong, was the century-maker, batting 3¾ hours altogether. By lunch on the second day Australia were reduced to 27 for 3, Brearley having bowled with exceptional speed. Throughout the remainder of the innings and in the follow-on the Australians, after the example of their leader, went after the bowling as if victory were imminent. Darling's 73 took only 85 minutes and included five hits clean into the crowd – then worth only four. (One of these blows scattered the inhabitants of the Press box). Following on, Australia were 118 for one that evening, and incredibly wickets were lost with such abandon that the match was all over by lunch on the last day. The pitch was now tricky, but no batsman attempted to 'book in' carefully. When rain began to fall later it was wondered why Australia had not fought harder for a draw, with an eye on the fifth Test.

286, left: *Brearley storms in to bowl to Trumper in the Manchester Test.* 287, below, left: *England stretch their score on the second day.* 288, right: *England press on to victory on the last day*

289, left: *Walter Brearley, the tear-away Lancashire amateur fast bowler.*
290, right: *Reggie Spooner, one of the Golden Age's premier stylists. Both played with credit on their home ground in the 1905 series*

1905
The Oval, August 14, 15, 16

FIFTH TEST

England 430 (*C.B. Fry 144, F.S. Jackson 76, T.W. Hayward 59, E.G. Arnold 40, A. Cotter 7 for 148*) *and 261 for 6 dec (J.T. Tyldesley 112*, R.H. Spooner 79); Australia 363 (R.A. Duff 146, J. Darling 57, J.J. Kelly 42, W. Brearley 5 for 110) and 124 for 4.* Match drawn.

The Hon. F. Stanley Jackson, born the same day as Darling, the opposing captain, won his fifth successive toss, and for the fifth time in the series England took first innings. The draw gave England a 2–0 victory, and Jackson himself topped the batting aggregates and averages and the bowling averages for both sides. Fry at last showed the Australians how he won his great reputation, driving magnificently as he put on 151 for the fourth wicket with Jackson. Cotter bowled heroically on an immaculate pitch, though his field gave him scant support at times. Duff, who began his Test career with a century, ended it with another, attained in barely more than two hours. He was missed three times, once at slip off a high skyer, but his brilliance atoned in some way for the repeated failure of his illustrious partner, Trumper. Darling, also in his last Test match, batted with vigour. England's second innings began shakily but, after a couple of umpiring controversies, Tyldesley and Spooner added 158 in a display of the finest Edwardian batsmanship. The closure, with three England players indisposed, was delayed, and Australia played out time without much trouble.

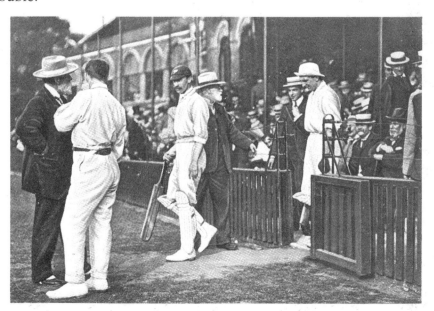

291: *Jackson and Fry return after tea on the first day to extend their fourth-wicket stand to 151. Hill is the fieldsman deep in conversation*

C.B.FRY REACHES HIS HALF CENTURY WITH HIS FAVOURITE STROKE

...AND HIS CENTURY WITH AN OFF DRIVE.

TYLDESLEY STARTS WELL

LUCKY JACKSON!

DUFF SHINES AT COVER POINT

TOM HAYWARD'S BAD LUCK. PULLING A SHORT ONE FROM HOPKINS, HE TREADS DOWN HIS WICKET

HOPKINS ABOUT TO DELIVER THE BALL

DUFF HOOKS A SHORT ONE FROM BREARLEY ACROSS HIS FACE TO THE SQUARE LEG BOUNDARY

HIRST CATCHES DUFF

RHODES HOLDS A SMASHING CUT OF HILLS

PLENTY OF PLUCK DUFF DISCAR ONLY

BREARLEY'S UNMISTAKEABLE SIGNAL TO THE PAVILION

ARNOLD GIVES DUFF A LIFE AT 92

LILLEY HURT

292, above, left: *At The Oval, Fry caught in some stiff attitudes; and Hayward's is positively fatal.* 293, right: *Some of Duff's glorious farewell to Test cricket.* 294, below, left: *The crowd treads the hallowed turf between innings, though rain seems to be threatening.* 295, right: *Tyldesley makes the seventh and last century of the series; Gehrs and Spooner attract attention as substitutes*

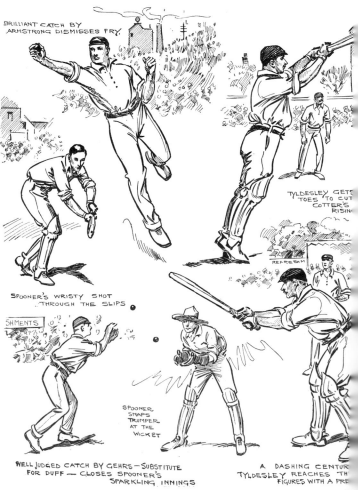

BRILLIANT CATCH BY ARMSTRONG DISMISSES FRY.

TYLDESLEY GETS TO CUT COTTER'S RISING

REFRESH

SPOONER'S WRISTY SHOT THROUGH THE SLIPS

SHMENTS

SPOONER SNAPS TRUMPER AT THE WICKET

WELL JUDGED CATCH BY GEHRS—SUBSTITUTE FOR DUFF—CLOSES SPOONER'S SPARKLING INNINGS

A DASHING CENTUR TYLDESLEY REACHES TH FIGURES WITH A PRE

1907–08   FIRST TEST
Sydney, December 13, 14, 16, 17, 18, 19

England 273 (G. Gunn 119, K.L. Hutchings 42, A. Cotter 6 for 101) and 300 (G. Gunn 74, J. Hardstaff 63, J.V. Saunders 4 for 68); Australia 300 (C. Hill 87, V.T. Trumper 43, A. Fielder 6 for 82) and 275 for 8 (H. Carter 61, W.W. Armstrong 44, P.A. McAlister 41). Australia won by 2 wickets.

A fascinating match had as its first-day highlight a robust century by Gunn, who was in Australia for his health, and called into the side when the captain, A.O. Jones, was unable to play because of a breakdown in his own health. It was Gunn's first Test. He moved from 78 to 102 with boundaries, and added 117 for the fourth wicket with Braund. Gunn put on 113 for the same wicket with Hardstaff in the second innings. The contest embraced some aggressive fast bowling, Cotter, Fielder and Barnes all inflicting hardships on the batsmen. Rain came on occasionally, and indeed the fifth day was washed out. On the last day Australia began at 63 for 3, and soon slipped to 124 for 6, still needing 150. Wicketkeeper Carter, in his first Test, hit about him for 61 in 67 minutes, and Cotter, more cautious than usual, and 19-year-old Hazlitt had a rapid, undefeated ninth-wicket stand of 56 to grasp victory. Young, England's reserve, bespectacled wicketkeeper, had an unfortunate match, and Fane, the stand-in captain, under-bowled Crawford and Rhodes.

296, left: *Albert 'Tibby' Cotter, a wholehearted fast bowler with a slinging action.* 297; right: *George Gunn – in Australia for his health – a lively century in his first Test innings*

1907–08   SECOND TEST
Melbourne, January 1, 2, 3, 4, 6, 7

Australia 266 (M.A. Noble 61, V.T. Trumper 49, J.N. Crawford 5 for 79) and 397 (W.W. Armstrong 77, M.A. Noble 64, V.T. Trumper 63, C.G. Macartney 54, H. Carter 53, S.F. Barnes 5 for 72); England 382 (K.L. Hutchings 126, J.B. Hobbs 83, L.C. Braund 49, A. Cotter 5 for 142) and 282 for 9 (F.L. Fane 50). England won by one wicket.

Jack Hobbs's first Test match was a thriller. Australia were kept down to a modest first-innings total which England passed with only three men out. Hobbs batted for 195 minutes, and added 99 with Hutchings, who went on to his century in 125 minutes and put on 108 with Braund. Cotter and Saunders then had some success, and the deficit was only 116 when Australia went in again. Trumper

and Noble wiped this off before being separated, and Armstrong and Macartney made 106 for the fifth wicket. The tail provided runs too, and England began the task of making 282 early on the fifth afternoon. Hobbs and Gunn fell at 54, and the classical Hutchings was restrained this time. The score reached 159 for 4 that evening. It slumped to 209 for 8, whereupon Humphries, the wicketkeeper, and Barnes managed 34 together. Armstrong had Humphries lbw, and Fielder took his place with 39 still needed. By correct and nerveless batting, against keen fielding and threatening bowling changes, the batsmen brought the scores level. Armstrong, with seven men on the leg side, bowled at Barnes's pads: he drew back and pushed the ball to cover: he ran, but saw his partner motionless: he shouted to Fielder, who started off: Hazlitt gathered the ball and had only to toss it to Carter to make the match a tie: instead, he hurled it at the stumps, missed, and Fielder was home.

298, above, left: *Kenneth Hutchings – 'the English Trumper' – 126 at Melbourne.* 299, above, right: *Frederick Fane, Irish-born, who led England in the first three Tests when illness forced Jones out.* 300, left: *Joe Hardstaff, third in the England batting averages for the series. His son played for England a generation later.* 301, right: *'Rip's' tribute to Barnes and Fielder, the last-wicket heroes*

1907–08
Adelaide, January 10, 11, 13, 14, 15, 16

THIRD TEST

Australia 285 (C.G. Macartney 75, R.J. Hartigan 48, V.S. Ransford 44, A. Fielder 4 for 80) and 506 (C. Hill 160, R.J. Hartigan 116, M.A. Noble 65); England 363 (G. Gunn 65, J.N. Crawford 62, J. Hardstaff 61, F.L. Fane 48) and 183 (J. Hardstaff 72, L.C. Braund 47, J.A. O'Connor 5 for 40, J.V. Saunders 5 for 65). Australia won by 245 runs.

Roger Hartigan made a conspicuous debut, batting at No. 8 in each innings. In the second, when Australia were 180 for 7 (only 102 runs on), he was joined by Hill, who came in late after an attack of influenza, and in tremendous heat they made a century apiece by stumps, when the Englishmen contemplated an Australian score of 397 for 7. Hill was exhausted, but the next day, after losing Hartigan after an all-wicket Test record partnership of 243 in even-time, he continued again in heat touching 106°F, until he had batted for 319 minutes, with only one chance. Hartigan was missed several times, once from a simple catch to Barnes at mid-off. England thus faced an unexpected and improbable score of 429 for victory, and apart from a stand by Hardstaff and Braund, which took the total from 15 for 3 to 128 for 4, the side faded out, with Hobbs retiring with a side strain. Medium-pacer O'Connor, like Hartigan, entered Test cricket with a fanfare: eight wickets for 150.

302, above, left: *Jack Crawford, who took 30 wickets in the series with medium-pace spin bowling.* 303, above, right: *Roger Hartigan, the fourth Australian to make a century in his first Test against England.* 304, right: *'The Invalid: Do I look very seedy, boys?' A jibe at Clem Hill, whose indisposition did not prevent him from batting over five hours at Adelaide*

1907–08
FOURTH TEST
Melbourne, February 7, 8, 10, 11

Australia 214 (V.S. Ransford 51, M.A. Noble 48, J.N. Crawford 5 for 48, A. Fielder 4 for 54) and 385 (W.W. Armstrong 133*, H. Carter 66, V.S. Ransford 54, A. Fielder 4 for 91); England 105 (J.B. Hobbs 57, J.V. Saunders 5 for 28) and 186 (G. Gunn 43, J.V. Saunders 4 for 76). Australia won by 308 runs.

For the third time running (and they were to do it again in the final Test) Australia returned a formidable second-innings total. Their first innings owed much to Ransford, a hard-cutting left-hander, and Armstrong, who put on 91 for the sixth wicket. Hobbs hit out for England before the pitch livened after rain, scoring ten boundaries in his 57, but the last eight wickets fell for 15 runs. Trumper failed to score in either innings, but from 77 for 5 the innings was rescued by Armstrong, first with Ransford then with Macartney, and Carter, with whom he added 112. The powerful Armstrong took over four hours for his hundred, but then struck Braund for two sixes. England, demoralised, were faced with another astronomical target, and fell dismally short, relinquishing the Ashes to Noble's confident XI.

305, above, left: *Arthur Fielder, the Kent fast bowler, who took 25 wickets in four Tests in the 1907–08 series.* 306, right: *Warwick Armstrong, immovable, ever-growing, uncompromising opponent.* 307, left: *Vernon Ransford, the Victorian left-hander, who contributed fifties in both innings at Melbourne*

1907-08
Sydney, February 21, 22, 24, 25, 26, 27

FIFTH TEST

Australia 137 (S.E. Gregory 44, S.F. Barnes 7 for 60) and 422 (V.T. Trumper 166, S.E. Gregory 56, C. Hill 44, J.N. Crawford 5 for 141, W. Rhodes 4 for 102); England 281 (G. Gunn 122*, J.B. Hobbs 72) and 229 (W. Rhodes 69, F.L. Fane 46, J.V. Saunders 5 for 82). Australia won by 49 runs.

A.O. Jones put Australia in to bat, and when England finished the first day at 116 for one the move could be said to have been successful. Barnes ran through the Australians, rendering the change in batting order of no account. Hobbs and Gunn put on 134 for England's second wicket, but rain interruptions on the second and third days lent frustration to the batting. Gunn batted for 4¾ hours, hitting a six and only seven fours. Australia went into the lead during a third-wicket stand of 114 between Trumper and Gregory, but Rhodes's dropping of Trumper off a ball from Barnes that kicked had a profound effect on the match; the batsman was only one at the time. He proceeded to bat in his most delightful manner, making 117 of his runs on the on side, batting four hours in all, and ending his sequence of failures in the most positive way. England needed 279, but more rain damaged the pitch, and the first six men went for 87.

308, left: *Victor Trumper, who, with luck, ended a depressing run of failures.* 309, above: *The Sydney scoreboard tells a tense tale*

310, below: *Jones and Noble, the captains, bid each other farewell.* 311, right: *Jack Hobbs (with veteran Tom Hayward) – a successful first series*

1909
Edgbaston, May 27, 28, 29

Australia 74 (*C. Blythe 6 for 44, G.H. Hirst 4 for 28*) and 151 (*S.E. Gregory 43, V.S. Ransford 43, G.H. Hirst 5 for 58, C. Blythe 5 for 58*); England 121 (*W.W. Armstrong 5 for 27*) and 105 for 0 (*J.B. Hobbs 62**). England won by 10 wickets.

As the scores reflect, rain beforehand dictated the course of the match. Australia found the swerve of Hirst and the spin of Blythe, also left-arm, too much. They bowled unchanged through the innings. The fourth-wicket 48 by Tyldesley and A.O. Jones was the major stand of England's innings, though Jessop slammed 22 in 20 minutes. The pitch was far from 'impossible' when Australia batted again, and Gregory and Ransford added 81 for the third wicket; but the two left-arm bowlers had their way again, helped this time by some brilliant catching: Jones caught a hard hit by Noble left-handed at short leg, and Tyldesley, back against the pavilion rails, held a drive by Cotter. Hobbs and Fry, both dismissed first ball by Macartney, opened the final innings and gained for England a surprisingly resounding victory. Hobbs showed extraordinary class.

312, *left: George Hirst: he and Blythe took all 20 Australian wickets.* 313, *left, below: Hobbs and captain MacLaren open England's innings. Macartney dismissed them and Fry for five runs between them.* 314, *below: Hirst bowls to Armstrong; Bardsley is non-striker.* 315, *bottom, right: The Birmingham crowd relish England's victory*

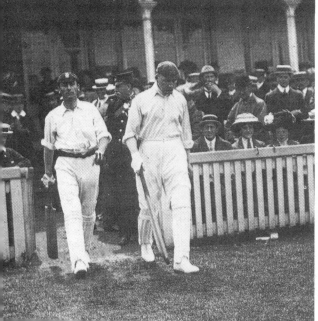

1909
Lord's, June 14, 15, 16

SECOND TEST

England 269 (*J.H. King 60, A.F.A. Lilley 47, J.T. Tyldesley 46, A. Cotter 4 for 80*) and 121 (*W.W. Armstrong 6 for 35*); Australia 350 (*V.S. Ransford 143*, W. Bardsley 46, A.E. Relf 5 for 85*) and 41 for 1. Australia won by 9 wickets.

Noble put England – a much-altered side – in to bat, and the move would have been even more efficacious but for the unanticipated success of King, a 38-year-old left-hander playing in his only Test. England had no really fast bowler, and on a quicker pitch Australia took a useful lead on the second day. Ransford's century, his only one in Tests, lasted four hours, and he was missed three times, twice off King, who finished with one for 99. Relf bowled 45 overs. Armstrong took six good wickets, operating from the Nursery end, with the slope helping his leg-breaks. This victory marked the end of the touring team's poor performances. They lost only once again – at Scarborough towards the end of the season.

316, left: *Armstrong, whose 6 for 35 was the best return of his Test career.* 317, right: *John King – top-scorer for England in his only Test.* 318, below, left: *Albert Relf – Sussex all-rounder who carried the main burden of England's bowling at Lord's.* 319, below, right: *Fashion parade during an interval. The old Tavern is quiet*

1909
Headingley, July 1, 2, 3

Australia 188 (S.E. Gregory 46, V.S. Ransford 45, W. Rhodes 4 for 38) and 207 (W.W. Armstrong 45, S.F. Barnes 6 for 63); England 182 (J. Sharp 61, J.T. Tyldesley 55, C.G. Macartney 7 for 58) and 87 (A. Cotter 5 for 38, C.G. Macartney 4 for 27). Australia won by 126 runs.

Gregory (46 in 130 minutes) and Ransford made 80 for Australia's second wicket, and Tyldesley and Sharp 106 for England's third. Otherwise, the bowlers had things much as they wished. Macartney, slow left-arm, spun the ball and used the 'arm ball' to good effect. The major setback for England, however, came on the first day, when Jessop strained his back. He was unable to bat in the match. Resolute batting by Australia, especially from Armstrong (45 in 2½ hours) and Macartney (18 out of 80 scored for the last three wickets) meant England needed 214, a task seemingly manageable at 60 for 2. But Macartney, this time with Cotter's speed from the other end, overthrew all batting endeavour. Hobbs top-scored with 30.

320, above, left: *MacLaren and Noble toss at Leeds. Australia won all five tosses in the series.* 321, right: *England take the field: Brearley, Fry, Jessop (probably), and MacLaren, followed by Hirst and Lilley.* 322, below: *Barnes bowls to McAlister*

323, above, left: *Peter McAlister and Syd Gregory, Australia's openers.* 324, top, right: *Lilley and MacLaren appeal against Gregory for lbw.* 325, above, right: *Tyldesley and Sharp, England's not-out pair on the first evening.* 326, below, left: *Tyldesley drives Armstrong for four.* 327, below, right: *Sharp st Carter b Macartney 61*

328: *Rhodes caught behind by Carter off Laver for 12*

1909
Old Trafford, July 26, 27, 28

Australia 147 (S.F. Barnes 5 for 56, C. Blythe 5 for 63) and 279 for 9 dec (V.S. Ransford 54*, C.G. Macartney 51, V.T. Trumper 48, W. Rhodes 5 for 83); England 119 (F. Laver 8 for 31) and 108 for 3 (R.H. Spooner 58). Match drawn.

Armstrong (32 not out), going in at 48 for 4, saw Australia clear of humiliation on a damp pitch on which Barnes operated throughout the innings. Cotter once hit Blythe straight out of the ground, and was eventually caught trying to do it again. England were routed by Laver, who used the breeze from leg and sometimes brought the ball back off the pitch. His flight was often puzzling. Rain cut the second day with Australia 77 for 2, and on an easy third-day pitch Noble allowed the innings to continue until England were left with only 2½ hours.

329, above: *Noble plays Blythe to leg.* 330, left: *Frank Laver, whose skilful work on the ball brought him 8 for 31 at Old Trafford.* 331, right: *Opponents Armstrong and Hutchings come in from net practice.* 332, below: *Trumper, now batting in the middle order, is beaten down the leg side*

333, top: *MacLaren turns an eye to the weather as he leads England out; Warner, Tyldesley, Hutchings, and Sharp follow.* 334, above, left: *Blythe bowls, left-arm round-the-wicket.* 335, right: *Bardsley tries to sweep him*

336, left: *Sydney Barnes photographed at Old Trafford, where he took 5 for 56.* 337, top: *Gregory plays back to Barnes.* 338, above: *Bardsley defends with an upright bat. Lilley is England's wicketkeeper*

1909
The Oval, August 9, 10, 11

FIFTH TEST

Australia 325 (W. Bardsley 136, V.T. Trumper 73, C.G. Macartney 50, D.W. Carr 5 for 146) and 339 for 5 dec (W. Bardsley 130, S.E. Gregory 74, M.A. Noble 55); England 352 (J. Sharp 105, W. Rhodes 66, C.B. Fry 62, K.L. Hutchings 59, A. Cotter 6 for 95) and 104 for 3 (W. Rhodes 54). Match drawn.

Carr, 37 years old and in his first season of county cricket, was given the new ball by MacLaren after Noble had won his fifth toss of the series, and in his first seven overs, from the Vauxhall end, he obtained the wickets of Gregory, Noble and Armstrong with his googlies. Ransford fell to Barnes at 58, but Trumper, who batted in the middle order throughout the series with little success, regained the initiative with Bardsley, who went on to become the first batsman ever to make two centuries in a Test match. These two, with Macartney, hit Carr hard and often, and – grossly overbowled – he finished the match with 7 for 280 off 69 overs. Fry and Rhodes put on 104 for England's third wicket, Sharp and Hutchings 142 for the seventh, taking their side ahead. Sharp, missed by Carter off the speedy Cotter at 93, batted for 170 minutes. On a final day lacking in urgency, Australia batted until hardly more than two hours' play remained, Bardsley and Gregory posting 180 for the first wicket – a record for Australia against England until 1964. Left-hander Bardsley batted for 3¾ hours in each innings.

339, opposite: *Warren Bardsley reaches his first century at The Oval with a single off Rhodes. Macartney is his partner.* 340, above: *C.B. Fry is run out after being sent back by Rhodes, who played the ball to cover. Gregory threw to Noble at the stumps.* 341, below, left: *The end of Woolley's first Test innings: b Cotter 8.* 342, right: *Trumper faces the bowling during his stand of 118 with Bardsley for the fifth wicket*

343, left: *Fry hits out at Noble.* 344, below: *The twelfth man, in straw boater, brings welcome drinks.* 345, right: *Sharp cover-drives during his century*

1911–12
Sydney, December 15, 16, 18, 19, 20, 21

FIRST TEST

Australia 447 (V.T. Trumper 113, R.B. Minnett 90, W.W. Armstrong 60, C. Hill 46) and 308 (C. Kelleway 70, C. Hill 65, F.R. Foster 5 for 92, J.W.H.T. Douglas 4 for 50); England 318 (J.W. Hearne 76, J.B. Hobbs 63, F.R. Foster 56, W. Rhodes 41, H.V. Hordern 5 for 85) and 291 (G. Gunn 62, J.W. Hearne 43, H.V. Hordern 7 for 90). Australia won by 146 runs.

There was barely a clue here that England were to run away with the series. Australia made 317 for 5 on the first day, Trumper 95 not out. He and Minnett (in his first Test) added 109 for the sixth wicket. Dr Hordern, in his first Test against England, beset the batsmen with a flow of problems with his googly bowling, only 20-year-old Hearne – himself a leg-break/googly bowler and also on debut – playing him with confidence. Barnes and the left-arm swing bowler Foster foreshadowed their great successes by keeping Australia in check, Kelleway and Hill making the only lengthy stand of the innings. The first-innings advantage, however, gave Australia a long lead, and though several England players applied themselves, the home side had a matchwinner in Hordern, who bowled with uncanny accuracy for one of his kind: Trumper fielded close at short leg for him, and his dipping flight and tantalising pace induced constant doubt. P.F. Warner, who took this MCC side to Australia, fell ill after the opening match, and Johnny Douglas led England in all five Tests.

346, above, left: *Australia's captain Hill run out by Strudwick after smart fielding by Rhodes at backward square leg. Armstrong is non-striker.* 347, right: *Dr H.V. 'Ranji' Hordern, who had conspicuous success on his debut against England.* 348, below, left: *Frank Foster, the young Warwickshire left-arm fast-medium bowler, who took 32 wickets in the series.* 349, right: *Roy Minnett – unlucky to miss a century in his first Test innings*

1911–12
Melbourne, December 30, January 1, 2, 3

SECOND TEST

Australia 184 (*H.V. Hordern 49*, V.S. Ransford 43, S.F. Barnes 5 for 44*) and 299 (*W.W. Armstrong 90, A. Cotter 41, F.R. Foster 6 for 91*); England 265 (*J.W. Hearne 114, W. Rhodes 61, H.V. Hordern 4 for 66, A. Cotter 4 for 73*) and 219 for 2 (*J.B. Hobbs 126*, G. Gunn 43*). England won by 8 wickets.

A famous opening spell by the 38-year-old Barnes gave England a grip on the match which they never relinquished. Unwell before the match and forced to rest after nine overs, Barnes used the new ball with Foster, Douglas conceding that it was not in the side's best interests to take it himself as he did in the first Test. Barnes bowled Bardsley off his heel with his opening delivery; had Kelleway lbw; beat Hill three times before bowling him; had Armstrong caught behind. He now had 4 for one, and at lunch, after a brief rain stoppage, his figures were 9-6-3-4 after 70 minutes' bowling. When Foster bowled Trumper Australia were 33 for 5, and Barnes's dismissal of Minnett made it 38 for 6 – his figures now 11-7-6-5. There was a recovery, during which Barnes was booed for taking time in placing his field, and for a time he refused to bowl. Young Hearne again was the only batsman to play Hordern with assurance. His 114 lasted 3¾ hours, and his second-wicket stand with Rhodes realised 127. Armstrong drove forcefully and saved Australia's innings with a stand of 97 with Ransford, but Hobbs, making the first of his 12 centuries against Australia, spent 3¾ hours seeing his side home. He and Gunn put on 112 for the second wicket.

350, above, left: *Rhodes off-drives during his long stand with Hearne.* 351, right: *Hobbs stands up to play Australian express bowler Cotter.* 352, below, left: *The scoreboard at the end, showing the century by Hobbs (who took the photograph).* 353, right: *Hordern, who rescued Australia's first innings, hits Douglas into the covers*

1911-12
Adelaide, January 12, 13, 15, 16, 17

THIRD TEST

Australia *133 (F.R. Foster 5 for 36) and 476 (C. Hill 98, H. Carter 72, W. Bardsley 63, T.J. Matthews 53, S.F. Barnes 5 for 105); England 501 (J.B. Hobbs 187, F.R. Foster 71, W. Rhodes 59, C.P. Mead 46, A. Cotter 4 for 125) and 112 for 3 (W. Rhodes 57*, G. Gunn 45).* England won by 7 wickets.

England were ahead on first innings before losing a wicket. Foster and Barnes (3 for 71) had bowled Australia out on a fast pitch, Armstrong (33) heading the individual scores. Hobbs batted 334 minutes – flawlessly until he was 116, after which he was missed five times. It was the highest of his centuries against Australia and included many stirring drives, especially off Hordern. Carter went in as night-watchman for Australia on the third evening, and put on 157 with Hill on another very hot day. Further resistance left England with runs to make, but their task might have been more demanding if Trumper had not been reduced to coming in at No. 11 after taking a fierce drive by Woolley on a vein in the leg.

354, above, left: *Kelleway about to bowl to Mead. Hobbs is non-striker.* 355, right: *Another Hobbs century shows on the board.* 356, below: *The Australian Board of Control, for whom serious problems were developing, sits at Sydney, February 1912. Clockwise around table, from C.A. Sinclair (NSW) (in bow tie, extreme left): H.R. Rush (Vic), E.E. Bean (Vic), unidentified, Sydney Smith jnr (secretary), W.P. McElhone (chairman, NSW), unidentified, Col. J.F.G. Foxton (Qld), unidentified, C. Hill (SA) (a central figure in the Board/players dispute), Dr Ramsey Mailer (Vic), and H. Blinman (SA)*

1911–12
Melbourne, February 9, 10, 12, 13

FOURTH TEST

Australia *191 (R.B. Minnett 56, S.F. Barnes 5 for 74, F.R. Foster 4 for 77) and 173 (J.W.H.T. Douglas 5 for 46);* England *589 (W. Rhodes 179, J.B. Hobbs 178, G. Gunn 75, F.E. Woolley 56, F.R. Foster 50).* England won by an innings and 225 runs.

Douglas put Australia in, and the Foster-Barnes combination had done its work by late afternoon. England were 54 without loss that night. Hobbs and Rhodes carried their partnership to 323 in 268 minutes, when Hobbs was caught behind off Hordern. The stand – not chanceless – remains an England-Australia first-wicket record, and was followed immediately by 102 by Rhodes and Gunn. Rhodes, who batted No. 11 in his first series 12 years earlier, batted just short of seven hours – while 425 runs were scored – for his only century against Australia. Rain during the third night freshened the wicket, and Douglas rammed home his decision to field first by taking half the wickets, the final one bringing the Ashes back to England.

357, left: *Trumper, in sunhat, cuts Foster for four at Melbourne.* 358, above: *Hill plays Foster through the off*

359, above: *Umpires Young and Crockett.*
360, above, right: *Armstrong walks away, having been bowled for seven by a ball from Barnes which started on the line of leg stump and hit the off.* 361, right: *Hill (22) is caught by Hearne at long-on off Barnes*

362, top left: *Minnett cuts Barnes to the boundary.* 363, right: *Hobbs and Rhodes, complete with neckerchiefs, resume their record stand at Melbourne. Hobbs's century was his third in successive Tests.* 364, left, centre: *Rhodes plays Minnett, the sixth bowler used, to short leg.* 365, left, below: *Hobbs, on 101 and with the opening stand worth 166, gives a difficult stumping chance to Carter off Jimmy Matthews. The partnership was almost doubled before Carter caught Hobbs off Hordern*

1911–12
Sydney, February 23, 24, 26, 27, 28, 29, March 1

FIFTH TEST

England 324 (F.E. Woolley 133*, G. Gunn 52, H.V. Hordern 5 for 95) and 214 (G. Gunn 61, J.B. Hobbs 45, H.V. Hordern 5 for 66); Australia 176 and 292 (R.B. Minnett 61, V.T. Trumper 50, S.E. Gregory 40, F.R. Foster 4 for 43, S.F. Barnes 4 for 106). England won by 70 runs.

After a blank third and sixth days because of rain, Australia came commendably close to their victory target of 363, for the seventh-day pitch, with the sun upon it, was anything but docile. Woolley's catch – one of his six in the match – to dismiss Minnett was a brilliant diving effort, and Hobbs's running out of Hordern was his 15th of the tour. Trumper ended his Test career (though this was not realised at the time) with 50 in his 40th consecutive appearance against England. Woolley, from No. 7 in the order, saved England's first innings, adding a seventh-wicket record 143 with Vine. His century was the first by an England left-hander against Australia. Barnes finished the series with 34 wickets, Foster with 32.

366, above: *Trumper, in his final Test, has been caught at slip by Woolley. England's wicketkeeper is 'Tiger' Smith.*
367, right: *Frank Woolley, a considerable left-arm slow bowler, excellent slip fieldsman, and scorer at Sydney of the first century by an England left-hander against Australia*

1912
Lord's, June 24, 25, 26

FIRST TEST

England 310 for 7 dec (J.B. Hobbs 107, W. Rhodes 59, C.B. Fry 42); Australia 282 for 7 (C.G. Macartney 99, C. Kelleway 61). Match drawn.

The Triangular Tournament of 1912 was a failure chiefly because of the ineffectiveness of the South African team and the wet summer. Australia, too, brought a side well below full strength after Hill, Armstrong, Trumper, Carter, Ransford and Cotter had withdrawn following disagreements with the Australian Board of Control, founded in 1905. The pitch at Lord's was saturated, and was becoming difficult as Hobbs entered the later stages of his century. He put on 112 with Rhodes for the first wicket. Only 20 minutes' play was possible on the second day, and when England declared on the Wednesday with 345 minutes remaining, Kelleway's obduracy (275 minutes) and Macartney's brilliance ensured that Australia were never in jeopardy. Macartney, who once pulled Barnes for six, batted only 140 minutes, and fell, caught by wicketkeeper Smith, to one of many leg-side deliveries from Foster.

368, above, left: *Charlie Kelleway, unsurpassed in Australian ranks for patience at the crease. His 61 at Lord's took 4½ hours.* 369, right: *The mercurial Charlie Macartney, a dashing contrast: his 99 took only 140 minutes*

1912
Old Trafford, July 29, 30, 31

SECOND TEST

England *203 (W. Rhodes 92, W.J. Whitty 4 for 43, G.R. Hazlitt 4 for 77); Australia 14 for 0.* Match drawn.

After a delayed start, England finished the first day 185 for 6, Rhodes having given a fine display, 'digging his runs out of the slush', dealing selectively with the bad balls. He was 92 not out at the close, but played on second ball next day, when play began at 5 pm. The third day was washed out.

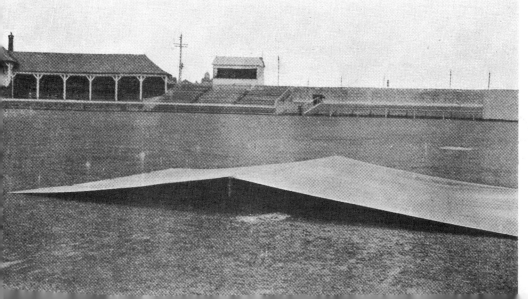

370: *The saddest sight of all. Old Trafford awash – a fairly symbolic picture of the summer of 1912*

1912
The Oval, August 19, 20, 21, 22

England 245 (J.B. Hobbs 66, F.E. Woolley 62, W. Rhodes 49, R.B. Minnett 4 for 34, W.J. Whitty 4 for 69) and 175 (C.B. Fry 79, G.R. Hazlitt 7 for 25); Australia 111 (C. Kelleway 43, F.E. Woolley 5 for 29, S.F. Barnes 5 for 30) and 65 (F.E. Woolley 5 for 20, H. Dean 4 for 19). England won by 244 runs.

England, in this play-to-a-finish Test, ended the opening day 223 for 8 after Hobbs and Rhodes had begun with 107, the former continually finding runs on a soft, slow pitch, the latter content to hold his end. Yet more rain curtailed the second day, which saw Australia 51 for 2, and on the third day, as the pitch dried, Woolley from the pavilion end and Barnes overthrew the last eight wickets for 21 runs. Rain pacified the pitch for England for a time, and Fry played some exquisite strokes – though once he appeared to have trodden on his stumps. Gervys Hazlitt, with medium-pace bowling, had a field day as the pitch dried again, mopping up the last five wickets for one run. Woolley and Dean, both left-arm, then used the conditions well to dispose of Australia. Woolley returning 10 for 49 in the match after his powerful innings of 62 (11 fours). This was Australian captain Syd Gregory's last Test appearance – his 52nd, an England-Australia record still.

371, above, left: *A large crowd gathers at the Vauxhall end to watch the players at pre-match practice.* 372, right: *Bill Whitty, who took seven wickets with fast left-arm bowling*

373, left: *'Gerry' Hazlitt, who disrupted England with mesmeric medium-pace from an action some thought suspicious. Victim of heart trouble, he died three years later, aged 27.* 374, right: *Harry Dean, Lancashire left-armer, who helped Woolley finish off Australia*

375, left: *Charles Fry, England's captain in the Triangular Tournament. He was undefeated, with one victory over Australia and three over South Africa.* 376, above: *Hearne is caught at short leg by Matthews off Hazlitt. Australia's wicketkeeper is Carkeek; Jennings is at slip.* 377, below, left: *Fry plays and misses during his innings of 79*

1920–21
Sydney, December 17, 18, 20, 21, 22

FIRST TEST

Australia 267 (H.L. Collins 70) and 581 (W.W. Armstrong 158, H.L. Collins 104, C. Kelleway 78, C.G. Macartney 69, W. Bardsley 57, J.M. Taylor 51); England 190 (F.E. Woolley 52, J.B. Hobbs 49) and 281 (J.B. Hobbs 59, J.W. Hearne 57, E.H. Hendren 56, W. Rhodes 45). Australia won by 377 runs.

Australia, led by the huge Victorian, Warwick Armstrong, recorded eight successive victories over England upon resumption of Test cricket after the First World War, with a unique (in England-Australia matches) 5–0 ascendancy in the 1920–21 series. Their first six wickets fell for 176, and there were three run-outs in the innings, but 'Jack' Russell played on to the first ball of England's innings and despite a fourth-wicket stand of 74 by Woolley and Hendren England conceded a lead. Australia built massively on this, Collins – a century in his first Test – and Bardsley starting with 123, Collins and Macartney making 111 for the second wicket, and Armstrong making two-thirds of a sixth-wicket stand of 187 with Kelleway to ram the advantage home. Catches were dropped, but Armstrong's 3½-hour assault was chanceless. England, set 659 for victory, were never in a position to feel optimistic. Jack Gregory and Arthur Mailey both took six wickets in their first Test.

378, above: *A passing threat to the resumption of Test cricket after the First War – the MCC side are in quarantine because of an infection aboard ship. Johnny Douglas, the team's captain, has his temperature read.* 379, right: *Hobbs b Gregory 49 – a straight ball, round his legs.* 380, below: *Bardsley c Strudwick b Hearne 22*

Johnny Douglas tore his glove off in anger when Armstrong 'fluked' him off my bowling

381, above: *Rhodes survives a chance to Gregory, who rarely missed slip catches.* 382, left: *Mailey's view of Douglas's demise*

383, top: *A view of the Sydney Cricket Ground on the first day of the first Test of the 1920–21 series. Collins and Kelleway are batting, and a ball from Woolley has just been taken by England wicketkeeper Strudwick.* 384, above: *The Australian XI at Sydney: standing – Bert Oldfield, Edgar Mayne (12th man), Charles Kelleway, Jack Gregory, Jack Ryder, Arthur Mailey, Johnny Taylor; seated – Herbie Collins, Warren Bardsley, Warwick Armstrong (captain), Charles Macartney, Clarrie 'Nip' Pellew*

1920–21
Melbourne, December 31, January 1, 3, 4

SECOND TEST

Australia 499 (C.E. Pellew 116, J.M. Gregory 100, J.M. Taylor 68, H.L. Collins 64, W. Bardsley 51); England 251 (J.B. Hobbs 122, E.H. Hendren 67, J.M. Gregory 7 for 69) and 157 (F.E. Woolley 50, W.W. Armstrong 4 for 26). Australia won by an innings and 91 runs.

A seemingly modest Australian score was inflated by an eighth-wicket stand of 173 on the second day by Pellew, batting No. 7, and Gregory, No. 9. Left-hander Gregory's innings lasted only 137 minutes. Roy Park, batting first-wicket-down, was beaten by the speed of Howell and bowled by the only ball he faced in Test cricket, after Bardsley and Collins had led off with 116; but England's catching let them down, Howell being a key sufferer. After heavy rain on the Sunday, the sun turned the pitch into a gluepot. Hugh Trumble said he would not have backed Australia to make 100 on it. Yet Hobbs (3½ hours) and Hendren stretched their third-wicket stand to 142 before the collapse took place. Hearne was ill and unable to bat in either innings, and in the follow-on had Australia held all their catches England's defeat would have been much more pronounced. Jack Gregory's success with bat and ball has few parallels.

385, above: *Taylor falls forward as he plays at Douglas.* 386, right: *Makepeace is lbw to Armstrong, and England are 32 for 2*

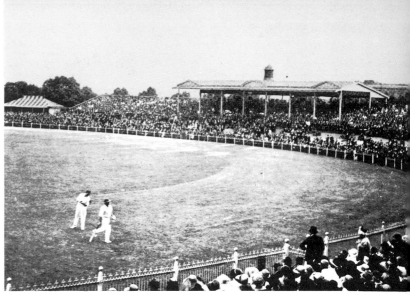

387, left: *Pellew (left) and Gregory, Australia's two centurions, resume their large eighth-wicket stand on New Year's Day 1921.* 388, above: *Hobbs, in trilby hat, comes in to a glad reception after his Melbourne century*

1920–21
Adelaide, January 14, 15, 17, 18, 19, 20

THIRD TEST

Australia 354 (H.L. Collins 162, W.A.S. Oldfield 50, J. Ryder 44, C.H. Parkin 5 for 60) and 582 (C. Kelleway 147, W.W. Armstrong 121, C.E. Pellew 104, J.M. Gregory 78*, H. Howell 4 for 115); England 447 (A.C. Russell 135*, F.E. Woolley 79, J.W.H. Makepeace 60, J.W.H.T. Douglas 60, A.A. Mailey 5 for 160) and 370 (J.B. Hobbs 123, A.C. Russell 59, E.H. Hendren 51, P.G.H. Fender 42, A.A. Mailey 5 for 142). Australia won by 119 runs.

A classic batsman's match, and England were well in it for three days. Howell again bowled with wretched luck; one of several chances off him – Collins to Rhodes at square leg – would have reduced Australia to 96 for 5, but they climbed to 313 for 7 by the first night, Collins's innings lasting 258 minutes. Woolley and Russell steadied England on the second evening, and Douglas added 124 with Russell next day, taking England into the lead. By the close, Australia were 71 for 3 and England felt they were back in the series. Armstrong (whose century was the 100th in these Tests) and the limpet-like Kelleway, however, were not separated until after tea on the third day, having put on 194. Kelleway, dropped before scoring, scored 24 between lunch and tea, and 96 in the day's play of 4¾ hours. When dismissed next day he had batted a shade under seven hours, and Pellew, with whom he added 126, made 84 of their stand. 'Nip' Pellew raced to his century with 16 off an over from Howell, and Gregory's aggression took Australia 489 ahead, a margin clearly beyond England once Hobbs's 2½-hour innings had ended and the middle order was cut away by Gregory, McDonald and Mailey.

389: *Two of the most popular Australian cricketers of the 1920s – Bert Oldfield (in hat) and Arthur Mailey. A tireless and adventurous spin bowler, Mailey was kept on long enough to concede 100 runs or thereabouts in eight innings during the series*

390, left: *A.C. 'Jack' Russell, of Essex – England century-maker at Adelaide.* 391, above: *Time for sandwiches: the crowded grandstand during the third Test.* 392, below: *A crucial miss: Fender at slip drops Kelleway before he had scored. He stayed nearly seven hours to make 147*

1920–21
Melbourne, February 11, 12, 14, 15, 16

FOURTH TEST

England 284 (*J.W.H. Makepeace 117, J.W.H.T. Douglas 50, A.A. Mailey 4 for 115*) and 315 (*W. Rhodes 73, J.W.H.T. Douglas 60, P.G.H. Fender 59, J.W.H. Makepeace 54, A.A. Mailey 9 for 121*); Australia 389 (*W.W. Armstrong 123*, J.M. Gregory 77, H.L. Collins 59, W. Bardsley 56, P.G.H. Fender 5 for 122*) and 211 for 2 (*J.M. Gregory 76*, J. Ryder 52**). Australia won by 8 wickets.

The diminutive Makepeace, in his 39th year, spent 260 minutes over his innings-saving century, adding 106 for the fifth wicket with Douglas, who had won his first toss of the series. There was life in the pitch before lunch, and the batsmen had to withstand some hostile bowling from McDonald and Gregory. Makepeace hit only four boundaries. Australia were in trouble after Collins and Bardsley had started with 117, but Armstrong, though suffering from malaria, put on 145 with Gregory for the sixth wicket. The captain, who went on to his third century of the series, was given a grand reception for having won the Ashes in the previous Test. After Hobbs was lbw to Mailey, Rhodes and Makepeace cleared the arrears of 105, and Douglas again postponed his seemingly inevitable overthrow by Mailey. Fender batted aggressively, and England were 305 for 5 at one point; but the tail was confounded by Mailey. The wry and prodigal little wrist-spinner is still the only Australian to take nine wickets in a Test innings.

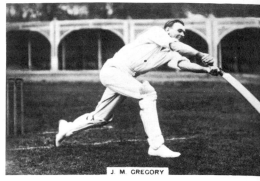

J. M. GREGORY

393, left: *A famous catch – Hobbs caught by wicketkeeper Carter off McDonald at Melbourne. Gregory at slip takes an anticipatory tumble.* 394, above: *Jack Gregory, Australia's beau ideal of an all-round cricketer*

WILLS'S CIGARETTES.

H. MAKEPEACE.

395, above: *Harry Makepeace, a veteran when he scored 117.* 396, right: *Mailey almost catches Fender.* 397, inset: *Douglas somehow avoids being stumped*

1920–21
Sydney, February 25, 26, 28, March 1

FIFTH TEST

England 204 (F.E. Woolley 53, J.B. Hobbs 40, C. Kelleway 4 for 27) and 280 (J.W.H.T. Douglas 68, P.G.H. Fender 40, A.A. Mailey 5 for 119); Australia 392 (C.G. Macartney 170, J.M. Gregory 93, P.G.H. Fender 5 for 90) and 93 for 1 (W. Bardsley 50*). Australia won by 9 wickets.

England, hampered by injuries (Hobbs played despite a strained thigh), again disappointed after a solid start, though Woolley's 53 came in almost even time. Australia were 22 for 3 and 89 for 3, but then Macartney, who missed the preceding three Tests through illness, put on 198 in only 133 minutes with Gregory (who averaged 73.66 in the series, took 23 wickets and held 15 catches). Macartney, the squat, pugnacious 'Governor General', batted only 244 minutes, struck 20 fours, and offered no chances. His footwork was universally admired. Hobbs, obviously lame in the field, was barracked by some of the crowd, who were criticised by Fender and E.R. Wilson in British newspapers. They in turn were shouted at on the third day. England were reduced to 91 for 6 at their second attempt before 'Johnny Won't Hit Today' Douglas resisted for 68 runs as his ship sank for the fifth time. Mailey finished with an Australian record of 36 wickets in the series.

398, above, left: *Percy Fender – 'PGH' – at times for him a troublesome tour, but in spite of restricted opportunities he finished at the head of England's bowling with 12 wickets at 34.* 399, right: *Before a sparsely-populated Hill, Gregory bowls to Hobbs at the start of the fifth Test – a photograph taken by Fender*

400, above: *Makepeace nicely taken by Gregory at slip.* 401, below: *The same fielder holds a more straightforward catch from Russell. Wicketkeeper is 'Sammy' Carter*

1921
Trent Bridge, May 28, 30

FIRST TEST

England *112 (J.M. Gregory 6 for 58) and 147 (E.A. McDonald 5 for 32); Australia 232 (W. Bardsley 66) and 30 for 0. Australia won by 10 wickets.*

England's traumas persisted. Indispositions kept Hobbs from the entire series except the third Test, where acute appendicitis prevented him from batting, and in the five contests England called upon as many as 30 players. The teams, who travelled to England together aboard *Osterley,* faced each other at Nottingham in the 100th England-Australia Test, a match settled in two days after a shocking start by England against the silken speed of McDonald and the violence of Gregory. Percy Holmes, in his only Test against Australia, top-scored with 30. Australia's 232 was almost enough for an innings win, their fast bowlers following up with another vigorous display – to which the crowd sometimes took exception. Ernest Tyldesley was hit in the face by a Gregory bouncer, the ball then falling on his stumps.

H.L. HENDRY (WHO BRILLIANTLY CAUGHT F. WOOLLEY) WAS PLAYING IN HIS FIRST TEST

A. COUPLE OF ENGLISH SELECTORS

TYLDESLEY AND HOLMES WHO ALSO MADE THEIR DEBUT IN TEST CRICKET

J.W.H.T.D WHO MADE A FINE EFFORT TO STOP THE ROT

RICHMOND WHO (BEING A GOOGLEYITE) HAS MY DEEPEST SYMPATHY.

PATSY HENDREN WHO WAS SKITTLED BY THE BEST BALL OF THE MATCH

THE AUST XI WHO ARE NOW COMPELLED TO FIND THEIR WAY TO BED BY CANDLE LIGHT.

ARTHUR MAILEY.

402, left: *Arthur Mailey, who was omitted from the first Test was able to apply himself to his sketches from the pavilion.* 403, above: *The captains, Armstrong and Douglas, go to inspect the Nottingham pitch.* 404, below: *Ted McDonald, whose speed brought him eight England wickets*

405: *Bardsley swings to leg in the first Test. Woolley at slip, Strudwick keeping wicket*

1921
Lord's, June 11, 13, 14

SECOND TEST

England 187 (F.E. Woolley 95, A.A. Mailey 4 for 55, E.A. McDonald 4 for 58) and 283 (F.E. Woolley 93, L.H. Tennyson 74*, A.E. Dipper 40, J.M. Gregory 4 for 76, E.A. McDonald 4 for 89); Australia 342 (W. Bardsley 88, J.M. Gregory 52, H. Carter 46, C.E. Pellew 43, F.J. Durston 4 for 102) and 131 for 2 (W. Bardsley 63*, T.J.E. Andrews 49). Australia won by 8 wickets.

Mailey came in for Collins, whose thumb was broken in the first Test, but England made six changes. C.B. Fry, at 49, was also invited to play, but declined. Woolley's two innings shone with fine drives and cuts, his courage in a losing cause being most conspicuous. He had support only from Douglas (34) in the first innings and Dipper (a stand of 94) in the second before Tennyson, at No. 7, came in and let loose a stream of hearty drives off the fast bowlers. Australia's 342 was made in only 84.1 overs, England having no bowler to match the containing Armstrong, whose 18 overs in England's first innings included 12 maidens. Bardsley topped both Australian innings, cutting soundly and hitting strongly to leg.

406: *Frank Woolley, the favourite of Kent, who scored two memorable nineties at Lord's off the fearsome Australian attack*

407: *Lord's almost full again as Australia forge ahead to their seventh straight victory over England since the post-war resumption*

THE HON L H TENNYSON WAS CHOSEN AT THE LAST MINUTE, RUSHED OUT TO LORD'S, THEN RUSHED OUT TO A "WRONG" UN

408, left: *Curiosity at England's new fast bowler, Durston.* 409, centre: *Armstrong and his men meet King George V.* 410, right: *Lionel Tennyson's late selection and swift dismissal.* 411, below: *Mailey busy with sketchpad again*

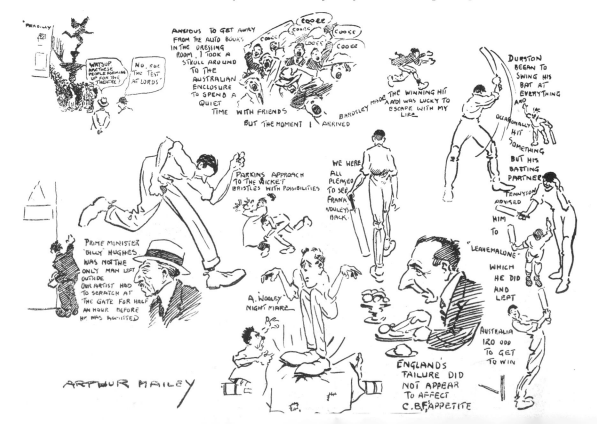

1921
THIRD TEST
Headingley, July 2, 4, 5

Australia 407 (*C.G. Macartney 115, W.W. Armstrong 77, C.E. Pellew 52, J.M. Taylor 50, C.H. Parkin 4 for 106) and 273 for 7 dec (T.J.E. Andrews 92, H. Carter 47);* England 259 (*J.W.H.T. Douglas 75, L.H. Tennyson 63, G. Brown 57, E.A. McDonald 4 for 105) and 202 (G. Brown 46).* Australia won by 219 runs.

England this time made seven changes, as well as transferring the captaincy to the Hon.Lionel Tennyson. Macartney, having just made 345 against Notts, batted 186 minutes for – oddly – Australia's only century of the series. He was not as his best, but dominant nevertheless. One of his drives split Tennyson's hand, and Douglas resumed the leadership for a time. Hobbs then went down with appendicitis, and another backs-to-the-wall situation for England developed. Armstrong hammered home Australia's ascendancy yet again – their 407 took only 296 minutes – and on a cloudy Monday England collapsed to 67 for 5. Here, left-hander Brown, brought in as wicketkeeper in preference to Strudwick to strengthen the batting, helped Douglas add 97, and Tennyson, his lacerated hand protected, but batting virtually one-handed, put on 88 with his deputy in an heroic display that saved the follow-on. Andrews and Carter – one a monumental mason, the other an undertaker – led the way as Australia built a lead, and England were eventually left 4½ hours. It was ample time for the tourists to go three-up.

412: First wicket at Leeds – Bardsley caught by Woolley at slip off Douglas; but England had a great depth of Australian batting still to overthrow

413, above: *Tennyson, England's new captain, gallantly drives Mailey with his one good hand; Gregory and Carter watch.* 414, right: *Headingley, well attended, as usual*

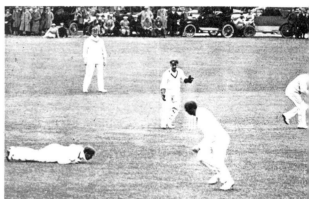

415, left: *Woolley plays on to Mailey for 37, second innings.* 416, above: *Mailey at slip fields a shot from Douglas.* 417, below: *Gregory bowled by Parkin for one in Australia's first innings*

1921
Old Trafford, July 23, 25, 26

131

<h1>FOURTH TEST</h1>

England 362 for 4 dec (A.C. Russell 101, E. Tyldesley 78*, C.P. Mead 47, P.G.H. Fender 44*, F.E. Woolley 41) and 44 for 1; Australia 175 (H.L. Collins 40, C.H. Parkin 5 for 38). Match drawn.

The succession of England defeats was finally stemmed in a match remembered for Tennyson's illegal declaration, which was nullified after Carter, Armstrong's wicketkeeper, pointed out that after loss of the first day it was a two-day match; no declaration could be made in such circumstances within 100 minutes of the end of play. Some of the crowd became unruly, and Tennyson and the umpires had to explain matters to them – by which time 25 minutes were lost. Armstrong then proceeded to bowl the first over, having bowled the last before the break. Russell, batting four hours for his hundred, made 81 of his runs on the leg side, and was missed twice off Gregory at slip. Tyldesley and Fender had added 102 in only 39 minutes before the overnight declaration, but England's overall progress on an easy pitch had never been rapid enough. Even so, Collins dropped anchor for 289 minutes for his 40, ensuring that Australia, though outplayed at last, would not seriously be threatened. At 78 for 5 there were tremors, but Collins continued to kill ball after ball from Parkin, Fender, Parker and Woolley. The innings time of 318 minutes was in stark contrast to some of Australia's performances of the past seven months.

418, left: *Once more to the toss: Tennyson and Armstrong, two pipe-smoking civilians.*
419, below, left: *Cecil Parkin (left), a rebellious player and inventive bowler, who shattered Australia on his home ground, shakes hands with Golden Age champion J.T. Tyldesley. Ted McDonald, who joined Lancashire, looks on.* 420, right: *The easy style of Ernest Tyldesley, JT's younger brother. He was floored at Trent Bridge, rehabilitated at Old Trafford*

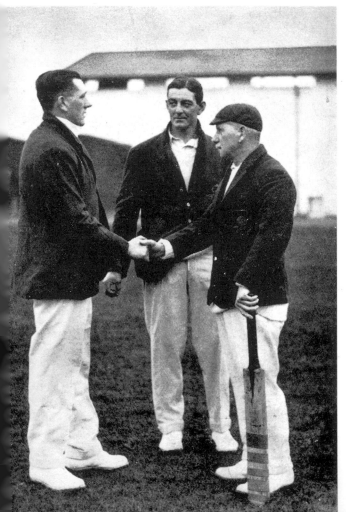

1921
The Oval, August 13, 15, 16

England *403 for 8 dec (C.P. Mead 182*, L.H. Tennyson 51, E.A. McDonald 5 for 143) and 244 for 2 (A.C. Russell 102*, G. Brown 84, J.W. Hitch 51*); Australia 389 (T.J.E. Andrews 94, J.M. Taylor 75, C.G. Macartney 61). Match drawn.*

England's prospects were dim at the end of a rain-interrupted first day (129 for 4), but Phil Mead, having made 19 in 70 minutes, scored 109 in 2½ hours before lunch on the Monday. Missed twice, he batted altogether for 309 minutes, and added 121 with Tennyson. His score was the highest for England against Australia in England, and gave him the freak average for the series of 229. Australia used only four bowlers, McDonald sending down 47 overs and Gregory 38. Hitch removed Collins and Bardsley early and had catches dropped, but Macartney and Andrews consolidated without resorting to undue defence. When England batted again there was no prospect of a result, and Armstrong drifted out to the boundary and left his bowlers and fielders to organise themselves, once picking up a stray newspaper 'to see who we're playing'. It was the 'Big Ship's' way of protesting at Tests limited to three days. Russell and Brown's first-wicket partnership of 158 should therefore be seen in perspective. Hitch's half-century was reached in 35 minutes, second in speed only to J.T. Brown's in these Tests.

421, left: *Armstrong at The Oval, making the bowling seem like 'weak tea' again, his bat 'a teaspoon'.* 422, above, centre: *George Brown, of Hampshire, a rugged all-round player.* 423, above, right: *The skippers toss for the last time: Armstrong soon had to get his flannels on.* 424, below: *The England team in the fifth Test: standing – Andrew Sandham, Phil Mead, Charlie Hallows (12th man), Ernest Tyldesley, George Brown, Jack Russell, Cecil Parkin; seated – Bill Hitch, Johnny Douglas, Hon. Lionel Tennyson (captain), Percy Fender, Frank Woolley*

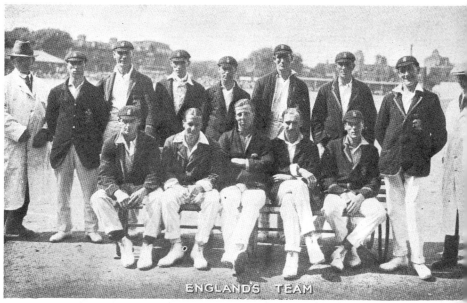

ENGLAND'S TEAM

1924–25
Sydney, December 19, 20, 22, 23, 24, 26, 27

FIRST TEST

Australia 450 (H.L. Collins 114, W.H. Ponsford 110, J.M. Taylor 43, V.Y. Richardson 42, M.W. Tate 6 for 130) and 452 (J.M. Taylor 108, A.J. Richardson 98, H.L. Collins 60, A.A. Mailey 46*, M.W. Tate 5 for 98); England 298 (J.B. Hobbs 115, E.H. Hendren 74*, H. Sutcliffe 59, J.M. Gregory 5 for 111, A.A. Mailey 4 for 129) and 411 (F.E. Woolley 123, H. Sutcliffe 115, J.B. Hobbs 57, A.P. Freeman 50*, A.P.F. Chapman 44). Australia won by 193 runs.

Australia's 4–1 victory in this series was not a faithful reflection of the balance between the sides, though the home side's batting was on the whole more reliable. The series was the first to be played with eight-ball overs, and auspicious debuts were made by Ponsford (who was shielded by Collins from the menace of Tate in the early part of his innings), Arthur Richardson, Sutcliffe (whose opening stands with Hobbs were worth 157 and 110), and Maurice Tate, who took a record 38 wickets in the series. Collins and Ponsford put on 190 for Australia's second wicket, and but for a spell of 4 for 9 on the second day by fast-medium bowler Tate, Australia might have made a mammoth total. As it was, England trailed by a long way after their fine beginning, only Hendren of the remaining batsmen exceeding 13. Australia extended their lead by solid batting all down the order, and England's agony was added to by a last-wicket stand of 127 between Taylor (batting No. 8 because of a boil behind the knee) and Mailey, a record for Australia which still stands. Taylor's second 50 came in a mere 32 minutes. Mailey and Oldfield had added 62 for the tenth wicket in the first innings. Set 605, England began well, but Gregory, Kelleway, Mailey and Hendry whittled away at the order, and it was something of a surprise when Freeman stayed with Woolley while the tall left-hander went past his second century against Australia – the first having been made 13 years previously, also at Sydney.

425, left: *Australia's opening pair, Collins (left) and Bardsley, prepare to do battle at Sydney.* 426, above: *Kelleway and wicketkeeper Strudwick anxiously watch a catch go to slip, where Woolley held it.* 427, below: *Collins reaches his century; Tate at square leg, Woolley, Hearne and Freeman in slips*

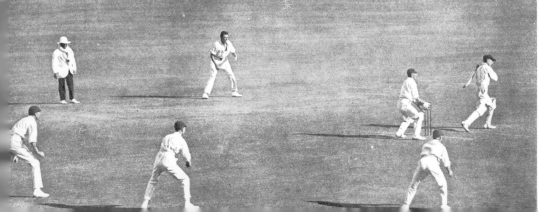

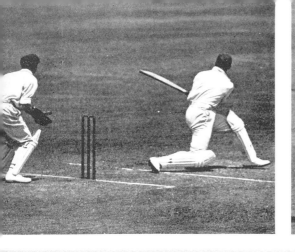

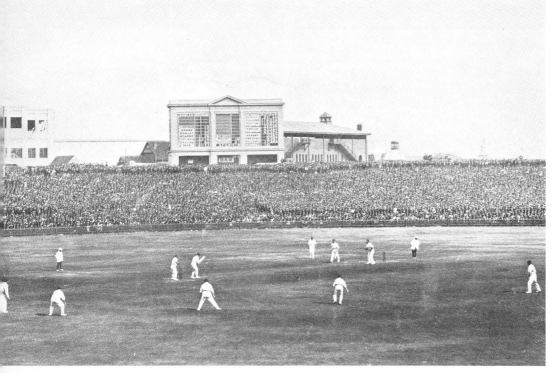

428, top, left: *Herbert Sutcliffe, in his first innings against Australia, sweeps Mailey at Sydney.* 429, right: *A gloveless Collins, when 37, missed by Woolley off Hearne.* 430, above: *Tate bowls, trying to break the last-wicket stand of Oldfield and Mailey which stretched Australia's first innings by 62.* 431, left: *Taylor runs a ball through gully during his 108.* 432, below: *Mailey releases a googly, which Sandham tried to cut. He was bowled by it for seven*

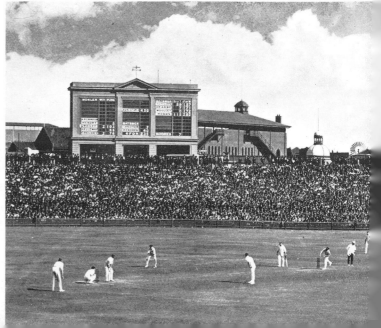

1924–25
SECOND TEST
Melbourne, January 1, 2, 3, 5, 6, 7, 8

Australia 600 (V.Y. Richardson 138, W.H. Ponsford 128, A.E.V. Hartkopf 80, J.M. Taylor 72, J.M. Gregory 44) and 250 (J.M. Taylor 90, M.W. Tate 6 for 99, J.W. Hearne 4 for 84); England 479 (H. Sutcliffe 176, J.B. Hobbs 154) and 290 (H. Sutcliffe 127, F.E. Woolley 50, A.A. Mailey 5 for 92, J.M. Gregory 4 for 87). Australia won by 81 runs.

Collins again beat Gilligan at the toss, and after a quivering start (47 for 3) Australia settled down for two whole days. Ponsford and Taylor added 161, Richardson and Kelleway 123 (of which the latter contributed only 20), and Hartkopf (on debut) and Oldfield 100 for the ninth wicket during which the Test innings record was passed. Richardson moved from 109 to 130 with 4 4 4 2 3 off an over by Douglas. Ponsford's century followed his 110 on debut, but Herbert Sutcliffe went one better with two centuries in this match, giving him three in his first two Tests against Australia. Hobbs and Sutcliffe batted throughout the third day of 288 minutes for an opening stand of 283, without giving a chance, the senior man 154, Sutcliffe 123. It was batting of the highest class, unruffled and perfect in judgment. The stand ended next morning when Mailey began with a full-toss to Hobbs and then another, which hit the stumps almost on the full. Woolley and Hearne quickly followed, and England made not 200 more. Tate struck three times early in Australia's second innings, but Taylor with a pleasant innings and Gregory and Oldfield with vital late resistance saw to it that England's target was a big one. Sutcliffe for the second time in the match batted through a day's play, but apart from Woolley's 50, which started enterprisingly but lost its impetus when he replaced his broken bat at 40 just before the tea interval, the Yorkshireman lacked support.

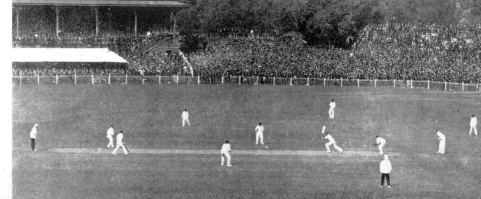

433, above, left: *A gracious gesture: Sutcliffe (left) and Hobbs receive a silver tea and coffee service from the people of Melbourne in recognition of their splendid batting there.* 434, above, right: *Vic Richardson and Bill Ponsford, centurions both, resume their partnership.* 435, right: *Sutcliffe drives spinner Hartkopf during England's first-wicket stand of 283*

436, top, left: *Strudwick, sent in as night-watchman on the sixth evening at Melbourne, parries a short ball from Gregory.* 437, above: *Turning point on the final day – Hendren b Gregory 18.* 438, left: *Sutcliffe out at last, c Gregory b Mailey 127.* 439, below, left: *Gilligan c & b Mailey first ball.* 440, below: *Tate bowled by Gregory, and the Test is over; Chapman the non-striker*

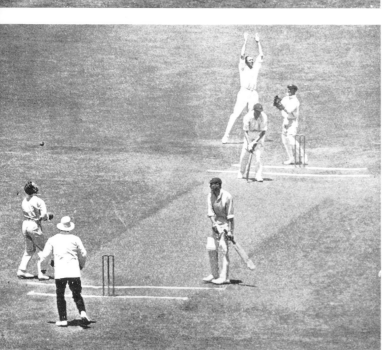

1924–25
Adelaide, January 16, 17, 19, 20, 21, 22, 23

THIRD TEST

Australia 489 (*J. Ryder 201*, T.J.E. Andrews 72, A.J. Richardson 69, W.A.S. Oldfield 47, R. Kilner 4 for 127) and 250 (J. Ryder 88, W.H. Ponsford 43, R. Kilner 4 for 51, F.E. Woolley 4 for 77); England 365 (J.B. Hobbs 119, E.H. Hendren 92) and 363 (W.W. Whysall 75, H. Sutcliffe 59, A.P.F. Chapman 58).* Australia won by 11 runs.

The third successive match to enter a seventh day ended thrillingly when Freeman (24) was caught by 'keeper Oldfield off Mailey, but the margin of runs had yet again diminished, and England, unlucky enough with their third loss of toss, were cruelly reduced by injury during Australia's first innings. They had the home side 119 for 6, but with Tate forced out of action with a raw big toe, Gilligan with a groin strain, and Freeman with a damaged wrist from a fierce Ryder drive, the bulk of the bowling fell to Woolley and Kilner. Australia's last four wickets put on 370 runs, Ryder batting 395 minutes and adding 134 with Andrews and 108 with Oldfield. He hit a six, a five and 12 fours. Gilligan rearranged his batting order, and Hobbs and Sutcliffe were united at 69 for 4, adding 90. Hendren then stayed with Hobbs while 117 were put on. By the end of the fourth day Australia were 211 for 3 – 335 ahead, Ryder 86 – but rain on the fifth morning made the wicket tricky, and the left-arm bowlers Kilner and Woolley soon wrapped up the innings. Hobbs and Sutcliffe gave England a start of 63, but at 133 for 3 that evening, they were still 242 from victory. Whysall, aged 37, in his first Test, batted judiciously, but when rain cut the sixth day short England still needed 27 with two wickets left. With the gates open, 25,000 came to see the last overs, and Mailey, who had been up all night, resumed the bowling with Gregory to Freeman and Gilligan, who had also had a sleepless night. Gregory caught-and-bowled the England captain (31) with an accidental slower ball, and six runs later Mailey induced a fatal snick from Freeman.

441, above, left: *Collins tosses, Gilligan calls, and Australia bat again.* 442, above, right: *Jack Ryder – 201 not out and 88, with some terrific driving.* 443, right: *One Ryder drive struck Freeman a paralysing blow on the left wrist. He is escorted off by Hendren*

444, top: *Another Hobbs century comes to an end. Gregory tosses the ball up after taking a low slip catch off Mailey's bowling in the Adelaide Test.* 445, centre: *The ball is a blur as Andrews prepares to catch Woolley (16) at cover in England's first innings.* 446, left: *A dozen runs from victory, England's last wicket falls: Freeman is caught behind by Oldfield off Mailey, and Australia keep the Ashes*

1924-25
Melbourne, February 13, 14, 16, 17, 18

FOURTH TEST

England 548 (H. Sutcliffe 143, W.W. Whysall 76, R. Kilner 74, J.B. Hobbs 66, E.H. Hendren 65, J.W. Hearne 44, F.E. Woolley 40, A.A. Mailey 4 for 186); Australia 269 (J.M. Taylor 86) and 250 (J.M. Taylor 68, J.M. Gregory 45, C. Kelleway 42, M.W. Tate 5 for 75). England won by an innings and 29 runs.

England at last secured a victory – their first over Australia since 1912. The weather played a part, but the general view was that this popular team deserved its luck. For two days England occupied the crease. Hobbs and Sutcliffe put up another century opening stand, their fourth, and Sutcliffe batted through a day for the third time in the series for his fourth century. Other big stands were 106 by Sutcliffe and Hearne, and 133 by Whysall and Kilner. Several light showers thereafter put some life in the pitch, and Tate was back at his best. Taylor batted twice commandingly and stylishly, but the strong rearguard which the public (and England bowlers) had come to expect did not eventuate in either innings.

447, above: *Hobbs on 19 edges Gregory over gully, Kelleway, who gets his fingertips to the ball. Hobbs and Sutcliffe went on to score 126 for the first wicket.*
448, right: *The stand was broken when Oldfield stumped Hobbs down the leg side off Ryder, a medium-pacer. The wicket-keeper, who made four stumpings in the innings, regarded this one as the best of his career*

449, above, left: *Woolley, toe on line, is stumped by Oldfield off Mailey for 40. 450, right: Yet another Oldfield stumping – Chapman in disarray after stepping out to Mailey. 451, below: Whysall, in the course of another valuable seventy, misses a Mailey googly. Gregory at slip has evidently seen the 'wrong 'un' from the bowler's hand. 452, bottom: Kilner, with a helpful pitch at his disposal, bowls to Kelleway. Taylor is the non-striker, Hendren at silly point*

1924–25
Sydney, February 27, 28, March 2, 3, 4

FIFTH TEST

Australia 295 (W.H. Ponsford 80, A.F. Kippax 42, M.W. Tate 4 for 92, R. Kilner 4 for 97) and 325 (T.J.E. Andrews 80, C. Kelleway 73, W.A.S. Oldfield 65*, M.W. Tate 5 for 115); England 167 (F.E. Woolley 47, C.V. Grimmett 5 for 45) and 146 (C.V. Grimmett 6 for 37). Australia won by 307 runs.

England were confounded in both innings by 33-year-old New Zealand-born leg-spinner Clarrie Grimmett, who swept through the side after Woolley and Hearne had taken the score to 96 for 4. In the final innings he had Hobbs stumped and went on to decimate England, Gregory taking the vital wicket of Sutcliffe – said to be looking stale after his 734 runs in the series – by bowling him for a duck with a sharp breakback. Hobbs had failed to score in the first innings, memorably caught by Oldfield down the leg side off Gregory. Within minutes Sandham was run out, Gregory dislocating a finger as he dived for the stumps. Australia's first innings had slumped to 103 for 5, but the elegant newcomer Kippax then added 105 with Ponsford. Andrews stroked cleanly and placed the ball well in his 80, but the crucial second-innings stand for Australia was that between Kelleway and Collins, who had injured his hand in practice. They saw Australia through the third evening, and Oldfield next day put on an invaluable 116 with Kelleway – the highest stand of the match. Grimmett's accuracy and variation then put a seal on the game.

453, above: *Taylor about to be caught by Whysall off Tate for 15.* 454, centre: *Alan Kippax, in the second innings, chops Woolley wide of Tate at slip.* 455, right: *Hobbs makes a famous 'duck', glancing Gregory, with Oldfield, having sensed the stroke, moving across for the catch. A second later the Hill was in tumult*

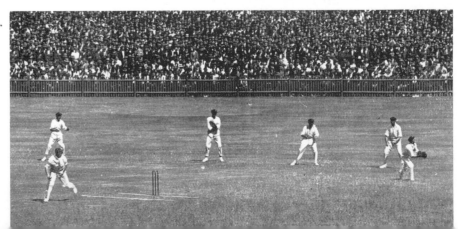

456, top, left: *Mailey takes a competent two-handed catch off Kelleway's bowling to dismiss Sutcliffe for 22, his lowest score in eight innings so far.* 457, above: *Grimmett takes his first Test wicket, bowling Woolley.* 458, above, left: *Kilner, who played Grimmett with least discomfort, swings him for four. He was stumped off Grimmett for 24.* 459, left: *Tate thrashes at Ryder, with fatal results.* 460, below: *Hobbs st Oldfield b Grimmett 13 – a hotly-debated decision at Sydney*

1926
Trent Bridge, June 12, 14, 15

England *32 for 0*. Match drawn.

Herbie 'Lucky' Collins's side arrived in England with no fast attack to compare with that of Armstrong's 1921 side. Gregory, carrying a knee injury, was not quite the same force, and McDonald had settled in Lancashire. This lack of penetration was to show during the series. The opening contest, however, was blighted by the weather, only 50 minutes' batting by Hobbs and Sutcliffe on the first day being possible.

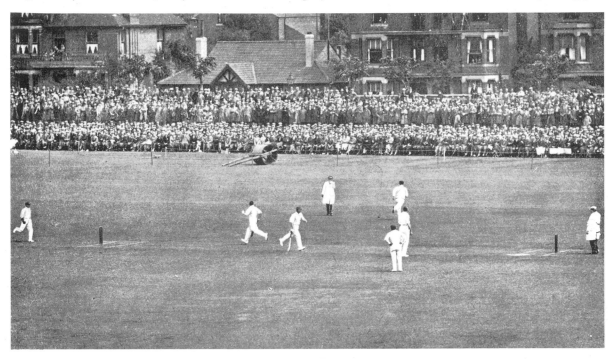

461, top: *Hobbs plays Gregory to leg and takes the first run in the truncated Trent Bridge Test.* 462, left: *The umpires, R.D. Burrows and Frank Chester.* 463, above: *The waterlogged ground – Jupiter Pluvius wins at Nottingham*

1926
Lord's, June 26, 28, 29

SECOND TEST

Australia 383 (W. Bardsley 193*, R. Kilner 4 for 70) and 194 for 5 (C.G. Macartney 133*); England 475 for 3 dec (E.H. Hendren 127*, J.B. Hobbs 119, F.E. Woolley 87, H. Sutcliffe 82, A.P.F. Chapman 50*). Match drawn.

A striking illustration of the difference between timeless Australian and three-day-limit English Tests, this match began with Root, an inswing, leg-trap bowler, removing one of Collins's stumps, and ended with the same batsman existing almost 2½ hours for 24, with Macartney, two days after his 40th birthday, hitting a magical century with deft and sometimes brutal strokeplay. In between, Bardsley, aged 42, had carried his bat through Australia's first innings, which lasted 398 minutes. He hit 14 fours, mostly with nudges off his pads and with cuts, and he was missed three times – all after he had passed 100. Larwood took his first Test wicket when he had Macartney caught. Hobbs and Sutcliffe yet again saw England into three figures: 182; and Woolley and Hendren hit a swift 140 for the third wicket before Chapman joined the latter and put on an unbeaten 116. This was Hendren's first century against Australia, and he was the youngest of the four centurions in the match at 37.

464, above: *England, led by Arthur Carr, take the field.* 465, right: *Collins (1) loses his leg stump to a Root inswinger.* 466, below, left: *Carr at short leg nimbly cuts off a shot from Bardsley. The umpire is Len Braund.* 467, right: *Hendren hits out at Macartney on the second day; Arthur Richardson is at backward point*

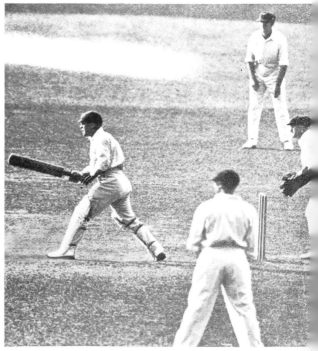

468, right: *Macartney clips a ball from Root, and it is stopped by short leg.* 469, below: *Sutcliffe drives. The sawdust absorbs water from a mains tap inadvertently left running overnight*

470, above, left: *Hobbs, after taking an hour for his last 12 runs, reaches his century.* 471, above, right: *Woolley deals powerfully with a ball from Macartney.* 472, right: *Macartney on-drives Kilner to reach his century*

1926
Headingley, July 10, 12, 13

THIRD TEST

Australia 494 (C.G. Macartney 151, W.M. Woodfull 141, A.J. Richardson 100, J. Ryder 42, M.W. Tate 4 for 99); England 294 (G.G. Macaulay 76, J.B. Hobbs 49, C.V. Grimmett 5 for 88) and 254 for 3 (H. Sutcliffe 94, J.B. Hobbs 88, A.P.F. Chapman 42*). Match drawn.

A.W. Carr asked Australia to take first innings: a fateful decision. Tate's first ball found the edge of Bardsley's bat and Sutcliffe took a neat catch at slip. Macartney came in, cut for two, played the next two with ease, then edged to Carr himself at third slip. The England captain got both hands to the ball but dropped it. Australia's second wicket did not fall until 235 was on the board. Macartney struck boldly in all directions to reach his century (out of 131) in 103 minutes, and to be 112 at lunch – the highest on the first morning of an England-Australia match. When he was caught at mid-on he had hit 21 fours and batted only 172 minutes. There had seemed no likely way of curbing his onslaught, much less dismissing him. Woodfull plodded on for almost five hours, Richardson (aged almost 38) dominating a fourth-wicket stand of 129 and going on to the third century of the innings before Macaulay, the bowler, ran him out as he followed through after driving. England's innings was saved from rout by Geary (35 not out) and Macaulay (No. 10), who added 108 for the ninth wicket. Hobbs and Sutcliffe put on 156 for the first wicket in the follow-on, seeing England to safety while Bardsley, deputising for Collins, who had neuritis, tried seven bowlers.

473, above: *One of the most famous of dropped catches – Carr fails to hold an edge from Macartney (2). Geary (in cap) watches in dismay.* 474, below: *Macartney, on nimble feet, drives during his glorious innings of 151, which started with a century before lunch*

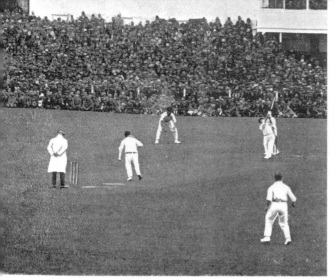

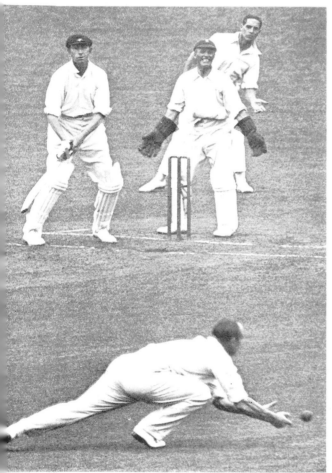

475, above, left: *Macartney lofts Macaulay (bowling round the wicket), to be caught by Hendren (out of picture).* 476, right: *A great innings behind him, Charlie Macartney doffs his cap.* 477, below: *George Macaulay, England's first-innings top-scorer, is let off by Gregory after wicketkeeper Oldfield had touched the catch on its way*

478, above: *Ryder dropped by Carr off Kilner. Strudwick and Sutcliffe show anguish.* 479, right: *Yet another error at Leeds – Geary about to miss Richardson off Macaulay. The batsman was then only 23*

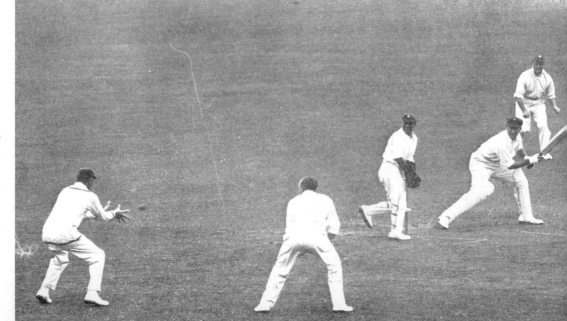

1926
Old Trafford, July 24, 26, 27

Australia *335 (W.M. Woodfull 117, C.G. Macartney 109, C.F. Root 4 for 84); England 305 for 5 (E. Tyldesley 81, J.B. Hobbs 74, F.E. Woolley 58).* Match drawn.

Only ten balls were possible on the first day owing to rain, and on the Monday, as Carr was down with tonsilitis, Hobbs took over the captaincy – the first professional to lead England since the 1880s. Bardsley again led Australia in Collins's absence. Once more Macartney (making his third consecutive Test century) and Woodfull (his second) made a large second-wicket stand: 192. Macartney was almost as brilliant as at Leeds, but Woodfull this time was more forceful than during his maiden century. Wickets fell steadily thereafter to Root's leg-theory (52 overs) and G.T.S. Stevens's leg-spin. England went in at 11.45 am on the last day, and Hobbs batted splendidly. Tyldesley's was a chancy but attractive innings, and Woolley drove beautifully, putting Grimmett over the sightscreen and also hitting Mailey for six. Gregory had still to take a wicket in the series after five England innings.

480, above: *Jack Hobbs becomes England's first professional captain this century after Carr is taken ill. Immediately following Hobbs are (from left) Root, Chapman (12th man), Stevens, and Tate. 481, below: Woodfull drives Root through mid-on, once more depriving the short legs of a touch of the ball*

482, above, left: *Strudwick and Woolley admire a pull by Macartney at Old Trafford – a stroke based on clean footwork, keen eye, and confidence.* 483, above, right: *Macartney b Root 109.* 484, right: *Hobbs deals effortlessly with a full-toss from Mailey*

1926
The Oval, August 14, 16, 17, 18

FIFTH TEST

England 280 (H. Sutcliffe 76, A.P.F. Chapman 49, A.A. Mailey 6 for 138) and 436 (H. Sutcliffe 161, J.B. Hobbs 100); Australia 302 (J.M. Gregory 73, H.L. Collins 61) and 125 (W. Rhodes 4 for 44). England won by 289 runs.

England won back the Ashes five years after losing them, and won a series against Australia for the first time since 1912. This match was to be played to a finish, and England recalled Wilfred Rhodes – then in his 49th year and leading the national bowling averages – and replaced Root with the 21-year-old Notts fast bowler Harold Larwood. Collins returned to the Australian captaincy, Ryder being left out. England were all out on the first day, Mailey, on a pitch that offered a small something to the bowlers, getting rid of six of the first seven batsmen, Hobbs to a full-toss. Australia were 60 for 4 that evening, and not until Collins and Gregory made 107 for the seventh wicket did an Australian lead seem likely. Hobbs and Sutcliffe then made 49 without loss on the second evening, a stand which was to grow to 172, most of it in awkward conditions after heavy overnight rain and morning sun. Arthur Richardson bowled off-breaks round the wicket from the Vauxhall end, and it was felt by many that his figures of 41-21-81-2 ought to have been much better. This was to overlook the great skill shown by England's opening pair, who may just have encouraged – with a high degree of subtlety – the retention of Richardson. Hobbs was bowled by Gregory and Sutcliffe by Mailey (in the day's last over); of the rest, the highest score came from Tate (33 not out). A shower on the fourth morning enlivened the pitch, though it was still far from bad, having a worn patch only at the Vauxhall end. Australia, set 415, lost Woodfull for nought to Larwood – whose six wickets in the match were all top batsmen – and Macartney (16) fell to the same bowler, also caught well by Geary at slip. Rhodes spun the ball off the worn area, and midst noisy jubilation the innings fell apart. Geary bowled last-man Mailey at five past six, and of England's several heroes none was more popular than the drought-breaking, 25-year-old, new skipper, A.P.F. 'Percy' Chapman.

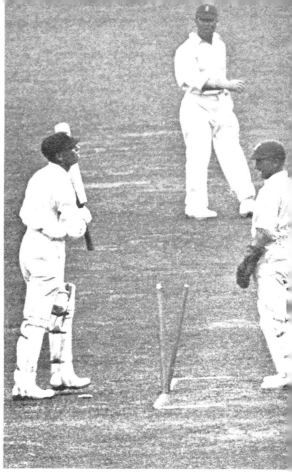

485, above, left: *England's new captain, Chapman, beats Collins at the toss at The Oval.* 486, right: *Woodfull bowled for 35 by the old fox, Rhodes*

487, above, left: *Macartney is bowled by leg-spinner Stevens for 25 in Australia's first innings.* 488, centre: *The action absorbs the Prince of Wales (leaning forward).* 489, above: *Grimmett bowls, Sutcliffe places the ball to extra cover with just the right touch, and without hesitation he and Hobbs steal another single during their classic stand in England's second innings.* 490, left: *Sutcliffe is hit in the mouth during the century partnership with Hobbs – their seventh against Australia*

491, above: *Oldfield removes the dead ball from the flap of Woolley's pad.* 492, top, right: *The Oval, lunchtime, third day: Hobbs and Sutcliffe come in with England 161 for 0.* 493, centre: *Bardsley top-edges Rhodes, and Woolley, running from slip, is about to make the catch*

494, above: *Ponsford neatly caught by Larwood off Rhodes for 12.* 495, left: *The human floodtide washes over the ground as England's victory becomes an exciting reality*

1928–29
Brisbane (Exhibition Ground), November 30, December 1, 3, 4, 5

FIRST TEST

England 521 (E.H. Hendren 169, H. Larwood 70, A.P.F. Chapman 50, J.B. Hobbs 49, W.R. Hammond 44) and 342 for 8 dec (C.P. Mead 73, D.R. Jardine 65*, E.H. Hendren 45, C.V. Grimmett 6 for 131); Australia 122 (H. Larwood 6 for 32) and 66 (J.C. White 4 for 7). England won by 675 runs.

England's strong all-round side began a successful series with an overwhelming victory, made so by the advisability of not enforcing a follow-on in a 'timeless' Test. In such a large total there was but one century partnership, the record 124 of Hendren and Larwood for the eighth wicket. Hobbs was run out by Bradman (playing his first Test, and scoring 18 and one), and Hammond and Jardine, also in their first Test, had a stand of 53. Australia's woes, begun when Jack Gregory's knee finally gave way – forcing his retirement from cricket – and Kelleway later went down with food poisoning, continued with Woodfull's dismissal without scoring as Chapman took a magnificent left-hand catch at gully. Larwood's figures, won on a blameless wicket, were the best of his entire Test career. With a lead of 399, Chapman batted again against a four-man attack, Ironmonger and Grimmett sharing 94 overs, until on the fourth afternoon he made the first declaration in a Test in Australia. Australia were 17 for one when bad light stopped play, and after rain that night Tate, Larwood and White (slow left-arm) had things all their own way, many of the batsmen, by their desperate hitting, acknowledging this. Woodfull carried his bat, though Gregory and Kelleway were absent.

496, above: *The palm-fringed Exhibition Ground, during Brisbane's first Test match. This vista was photographed on the second day of play.* 497, below: *Hobbs is run out for 49, attempting a third run for Mead and failing to beat Bradman's throw and Oldfield's dive. Gregory leaps in delight*

498, above, left: *Hammond, in his first Test innings against Australia, is stranded against Grimmett, but the ball is lodged in Oldfield's pad-flap, and the stumping chance is missed.* 499, above, right: *Mead (back in Australia 17 years after his first tour) is lbw to Grimmett*

500, right: *Hendren cover-drives during his 169 – his second century against Australia.* 501, below, left: *Chapman is caught off Grimmett, Oldfield taking the bails off for good measure.* 502, below, right: *Gregory just fails to achieve a caught-and-bowled against Larwood. (The ball broke a shoulder of the bat.) The Australian's career ended with a knee injury aggravated by this fall. Kelleway (foreground), Oldfield, and Ironmonger watch anxiously*

503, above, left: *Ryder, having tried to hook a short, fast ball from Larwood, has skyed a simple catch for Jardine in Australia's first innings.* 504, right: *Australia's batting misfortunes began with this amazing catch by Chapman to dismiss Woodfull (0)*

1928–29
Sydney, December 14, 15, 17, 18, 19, 20

SECOND TEST

Australia *253 (W.M. Woodfull 68, W.A.S. Oldfield 41*, G. Geary 5 for 35) and 397 (H.S.T.L. Hendry 112, W.M. Woodfull 111, J. Ryder 79, O.E. Nothling 44, M.W. Tate 4 for 99); England 636 (W.R. Hammond 251, E.H. Hendren 74, G. Geary 66, H. Larwood 43, J.B. Hobbs 40, D.D. Blackie 4 for 148) and 16 for 2. England won by 8 wickets.*

Walter Hammond began an extraordinary run of scores with the second double-century ever made for England against Australia, an admirable innings lasting 461 minutes, with 30 boundaries – many from exquisite drives through the off – and with only one difficult chance. He put on 145 with Hendren. Australia's slow bowlers, Grimmett, Ironmonger and 46-year-old debutant off-spinner Blackie, sent down 191 six-ball overs for 481 runs and eight wickets. Geary, the Leicestershire medium-pacer, moved the ball cleverly and was chiefly responsible for Australia's disappointing first innings, but Tate took four good wickets in the second, during which Woodfull and Hendry put on 215 for the second wicket in a most adverse situation. Ponsford's left hand was broken by a flyer from Larwood on the first day, forcing him out of the match. His substitute in the field was Bradman, who had been dropped for the only time in what was to be a 20-year Test career. On the second afternoon, the eve of Jack Hobbs's 46th birthday, 'The Master' was presented out in the middle by M.A. Noble with a shilling-fund collection, the result of a newspaper appeal. He was then escorted around the outfield to the acclaim of a record crowd of 58,456.

505: *'The Kippax Incident': trying to sweep Geary, Kippax was apparently bowled off his pads, but the umpires had to confer before the batsman (left) was confirmed as 'out'*

506, above: *A strange sight for England: Don Bradman as twelfth man, at Sydney.* 507, top, right: *Hendry (37) perplexed and bowled by a ball from Geary.* 508, centre: *Herbert Fishwick's beautiful photo of Hammond, taken during his double-century.* 509, below: *Hammond drives Blackie and goes past 150*

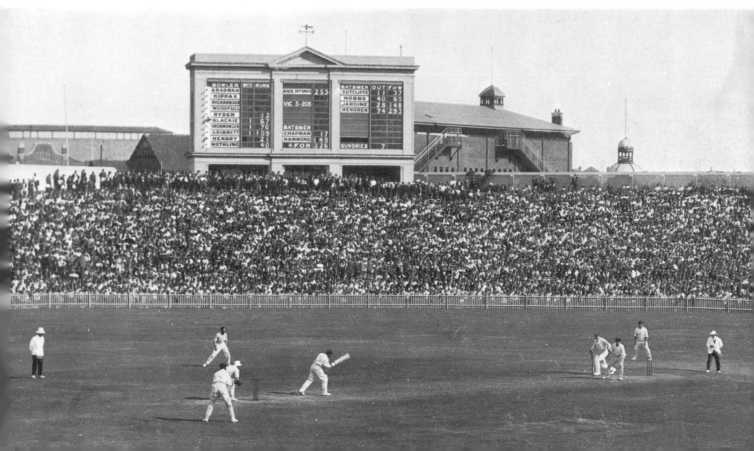

510, above, left: *Jack Hobbs is presented by M.A. Noble (representing a newspaper) with a boomerang and a wallet of notes to mark his 46th birthday.* 511, right: *A confident England take the field on the fifth day: from left – Hobbs, Chapman, Tate, White, Duckworth, Jardine, Larwood, Hammond.* 512, left: *Jack White makes the winning hit in the second Test, and England go two-up*

1928–29   THIRD TEST
Melbourne, December 29, 31, January 1, 2, 3, 4, 5

Australia 397 (J. Ryder 112, A.F. Kippax 100, D.G. Bradman 79, E.L.a'Beckett 41) and 351 (D.G. Bradman 112, W.M. Woodfull 107, A.F. Kippax 41, J.C. White 5 for 107); England 417 (W.R. Hammond 200, D.R. Jardine 62, H. Sutcliffe 58, D.D. Blackie 6 for 94) and 332 for 7 (H. Sutcliffe 135, J.B. Hobbs 49, E.H. Hendren 45). England won by 3 wickets.

England's victories, like Australia's in 1924–25, were by ever-decreasing margins. Success here depended heavily on how Hobbs and Sutcliffe negotiated the sticky wicket on the sixth day. They posted 105 for the first wicket. Jardine (on Hobbs's suggestion) then came in, and the day was seen through. On the final day Sutcliffe steered England to the verge of their target. Australia were 57 for 3 on the opening day before Kippax, hooking well, and Ryder, making a multitude of singles, put on 161. The 20-year-old Bradman took 3¼ hours over his 79. Hammond made history with his second double-century running – batting 398 minutes, giving no chance, hitting only 17 boundaries, and drawing rich applause for his powerful drives, especially off the back foot. He had long stands with Sutcliffe and Jardine. Woodfull's innings lasted 4½ hours, and Bradman's – the first of his 19 centuries against England and 29 in all Tests – took just over four hours. Troubled early on by the accurate floaters of White, he later used swift footwork to advantage, and actually reached his hundred with an all-run four off the back foot through mid-on.

513, above, left: Hammond has driven Blackie and reaches his 200. His partner, in multi-coloured cap, is Jardine. 514, right: In the second innings Hammond advances to Grimmett, jams down on the ball, and is stumped by Oldfield as it curls behind him. 515, left: Bradman goes down the pitch and drives White. 516, below, left: Disastrous start to Australia's second innings: Vic Richardson b Larwood 5. 517, right: Woodfull c Duckworth b Tate 107. Chapman at gully, Hendren short leg

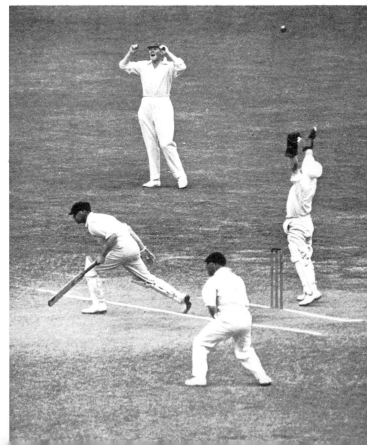

518: *Telegrams of congratulations from the Prince of Wales and Prime Minister Baldwin to Chapman and the team upon their Ashes triumph at Melbourne. Four years later cables of a less cordial nature were being sent back and forth by the administrators*

1928–29
Adelaide, February 1, 2, 4, 5, 6, 7, 8

FOURTH TEST

England 334 (*W.R. Hammond 119*, J.B. Hobbs 74, H. Sutcliffe 64, C.V. Grimmett 5 for 102*) and 383 (*W.R. Hammond 177, D.R. Jardine 98, M.W. Tate 47, R.K. Oxenham 4 for 67*); Australia 369 (*A.A. Jackson 164, J. Ryder 63, D.G. Bradman 40, J.C. White 5 for 130, M.W. Tate 4 for 77*) and 336 (*J. Ryder 87, D.G. Bradman 58, A.F. Kippax 51, J.C. White 8 for 126*). England won by 12 runs.

The seventh day dawned with Australia, 260 for 6, needing 89 for victory, and 48 runs were made before Chapman dived to catch Oxenham. The crucial wicket then followed, Bradman being tragically run out after Oldfield had played a ball to Hobbs at cover. The match was still poised at lunch, but White (124.5 overs in the match) took his seventh and eighth wickets, and England went four-up. Hammond and Jackson were the major figures, the former making 72 of the last 88 runs in England's first innings and batting masterfully in the second until exhaustion defeated him. He was on the field for over 26½ hours, and took his aggregate to 602 in four successive innings. His stand of 262 with Jardine is a third-wicket record for England against Australia. Archie Jackson, opening Australia's innings, saw three wickets fall for 19, but with sweet strokeplay the slightly-built 19-year-old reached his hundred in 250 minutes, adding 60 in a further hour. The Scottish-born Sydneysider, who died four years later of tuberculosis, became the youngest centurion in England-Australia matches in this his first Test.

519: *Wally Hammond, maker of two centuries at Adelaide, comes close to being stumped off Grimmett*

520, top: *Young Archie Jackson's poised and stirring debut innings ends as he is adjudged lbw to White for 164. Duckworth, Hammond, and Jardine are also shown.* 521, above, left: *Jackson reaches the boundary by timing rather than force with an off-drive off White.* 522, above, right: *Duckworth dives but fails to hold a ball from White popped up by Oxenham.* 523, right: *Kippax (51) about to be caught by Hendren (in cap), who took the rebound from second slip Geary*

524, above: *Left-handed Blackie, Australia's last man, has hit White to square leg, where Larwood makes a safe catch – and England have won by 12 runs at Adelaide.* 525, left: *Archie Jackson is congratulated on his maiden-Test success by the scorer of Australia's first century – 52 years earlier – Charles Bannerman, now 77*

1928–29   FIFTH TEST
Melbourne, March 8, 9, 11, 12, 13, 14, 15, 16

England 519 (J.B. Hobbs 142, M. Leyland 137, E.H. Hendren 95) and 257 (J.B. Hobbs 65, M.W. Tate 54, M. Leyland 53*, T.W. Wall 5 for 66); Australia 491 (D.G. Bradman 123, W.M. Woodfull 102, A.G. Fairfax 65, G. Geary 5 for 105) and 287 for 5 (J. Ryder 57*, W.A.S. Oldfield 48, A.A. Jackson 46). Australia won by 5 wickets.

Jack Ryder's side, altered to let in more young players (Wall, Fairfax and Hornibrook), triumphed at last – and worthily, though England lacked Sutcliffe and Chapman. Hobbs's century was the last of his 12 against Australia, and left-hander Leyland's was in his first innings against them. He reached 100 with the last man in, and added 141 with Hendren, whose 95 included an eight (four run and four overthrows). The core of Australia's determined reply was a stand of 183 for the fifth wicket between Bradman and Fairfax. The total of 491 was made at less than two runs an over, Geary bowling 81 overs (36 maidens), captain White 75.3 (22), and Tate 62 (26). Grimmett and Hornibrook managed 59 for the tenth wicket, and the latter, after England's second-innings decline, did a stout job in putting on 51 as nightwatchman opener with Oldfield, who himself stayed 2½ hours. The running-out of Kippax poised the match on the eighth morning, but Ryder and Bradman then saw their side home. Hammond's 54 runs in the match gave him a record series aggregate of 905.

The scoreboard shows:

BATSMEN OUT	FALL OF WKTS	BATSMEN	RUNS	BOWLERS	WKTS	RUNS
JARDINE C1 19	1 FOR 64	HOBBS	99	2 BOWLING		
HAMMOND C1 38	2 „ 146	TYLDESLEY	19	1 WALL	2	45
3 „		EXTRAS	5	2 HORNIBROOK		54
4 „	2 OUT FOR 180			3 OXENHAM		26
5 „		AUSTRALIA		4 GRIMMETT		18
6 „		1ST INNINGS		5 FAIRFAX		29
7 „		2ND INNINGS		6 RYDER		3
8 „		ENGLAND		7		
9 „		1ST INNINGS		8		
10 „		2ND INNINGS				

526: *Jack Hobbs sets off on his 100th run. It was 'The Master's' final century against Australia*

527, above: *Hammond well caught by Fairfax off Wall for 38, England first innings.* 528, right: *Hendren bowled by Grimmett for one, and England's second innings at Melbourne falls away still further*

529, above: *Oldfield's valuable 2½-hour innings of 48 ends as Hammond bowls him.* 530, below: *England, beaten at last, leave the Melbourne ground with their souvenirs*

531: *Some of the former Australian Test players who gathered at the match: from left – V.S. Ransford, C. Hill, M.A. Noble, H. Trumble, J.M. Gregory, J. Darling, J. Worrall, W.W. Armstrong, P.A. McAlister*

1930
Trent Bridge, June 13, 14, 16, 17

FIRST TEST

England 270 (*J.B. Hobbs 78, A.P.F. Chapman 52, R.W.V. Robins 50*, C.V. Grimmett 5 for 107) and 302 (J.B. Hobbs 74, E.H. Hendren 72, H. Sutcliffe 58 ret.ht, C.V. Grimmett 5 for 94); Australia 144 (A.F. Kippax 64*, R.W.V. Robins 4 for 51) and 335 (D.G. Bradman 131, S.J. McCabe 49).* England won by 93 runs.

A grand diving catch at mid-on by a comparatively unknown substitute fieldsman, Syd Copley of the Notts groundstaff, broke a threatening stand between Bradman and McCabe on the last day and opened the way for victory to a mature – perhaps over-mature – England side. The new, young Australian team owed much to their 38-year-old leg-spinner Grimmett, who took ten wickets in the match. Hobbs on the opening day batted over 3½ hours, and Chapman alone – with typical nonchalance – set about the bowling with any success. The tourists unluckily had to bat on a rain-affected pitch: their hero was Kippax, who showed great skill on a drying surface. Tate's opening burst of 3 for 7 reduced Australia to 16 for 3. Hobbs and Sutcliffe put on 125 for England's first wicket in the second innings – their tenth century stand against Australia. The former, at the age of 47, played gloriously. Sutcliffe retired after a blow on the right thumb, and it was left to 41-year-old Hendren, with nimble footwork, to sustain England's command. Set 429, Australia were 229 for 3 when Copley, fielding as 'thirteenth man' for Larwood (stomach upset) with Duleepsinhji already substituting for Sutcliffe, made his fateful catch down near his toes. The target was now 200 in 195 minutes, but when Robins deceived Bradman with a googly all real hope was lost. Some further fine catches were taken, and Chapman had now led England to nine consecutive victories, six against Australia. Bradman's century, in his first Test in England, was the first of 11 in that country.

532, above: *Don Bradman plays to leg during his first Test century in England. Chapman is at gully, Hendren slip, Duckworth wicketkeeper.* 533, below: *Alan Fairfax about to be caught by Hobbs at cover off Robins for 14*

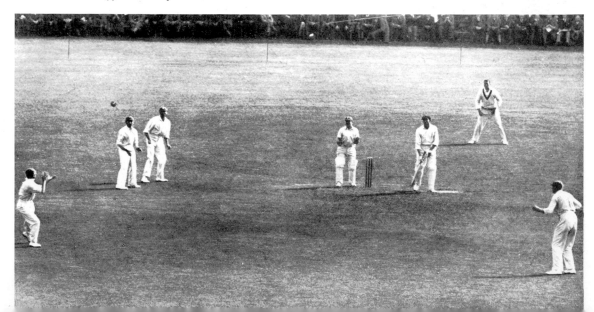

534, above, left: *Sutcliffe sustains a split thumb in trying to hook Wall. Hammond is non-striker.* 535, right: *S. H. Copley, who usually features in England-Australia Test history as plain 'sub'. His catch swung the Trent Bridge match.* 536, left: *Bradman b Robins 131*

1930
Lord's, June 27, 28, 30, July 1

SECOND TEST

England 425 (*K.S. Duleepsinhji 173, M.W. Tate 54, E.H. Hendren 48, F.E. Woolley 41, A.G. Fairfax 4 for 101*) *and* 375 (*A.P.F. Chapman 121, G.O.B. Allen 57, K.S. Duleepsinhji 48, C.V. Grimmett 6 for 167*); Australia 729 for 6 dec (*D.G. Bradman 254, W.M. Woodfull 155, A.F. Kippax 83, W.H. Ponsford 81, S.J. McCabe 44, W.A.S. Oldfield 43**) *and* 72 for 3. Australia won by 7 wickets.

This spectator's Test match began with a brilliant rescuing innings by Duleepsinhji, who emulated his illustrious uncle, Ranji, in scoring a century in his first Test. He drove and cut with great charm, adding 104 with Hendren for the fourth wicket, 98 with Tate for the seventh, and scoring 21 fours before holing out at long-off after 292 minutes. Woodfull (scoring his sixth and final hundred against England) and Ponsford made 162 for Australia's first wicket, and when Bradman joined his captain he was obviously seeing the ball well from the start. They put on 231 in only 154 minutes, and Bradman was 155 at the end of the second day, with Australia already 404 for 2. He passed Murdoch's Australian record of 211 while adding 192 with Kippax, and 585 was on the board before Bradman's, the third wicket, fell. He was in for 339 minutes (25 fours) with only one stroke that could have been considered imperfect before he hit White within the reach of Chapman, who made a thrilling right-hand catch at extra cover. Australia have only once exceeded 729 for 6: against West Indies in 1955, 758 for 8 at Kingston. England, 304 behind, were 93 for 2 at the start of the final day, and Grimmett took his fourth wicket before lunch. Chapman, hitting very hard, then put on 125 with Allen for the sixth wicket. The England captain, who hit three sixes off Grimmett into the Mound Stand and 12 fours, saw the innings defeat staved off before his dismissal. Australia, 22 for 3, still had time and little trouble in making the runs.

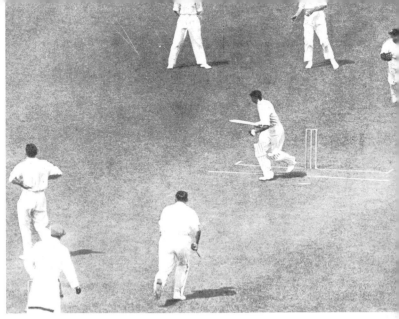

537, left: *Duleepsinhji – with a favourite bat, judged from its binding – pulls Grimmett.* 538, above: *'Duleep', dropped at 98, now cuts Wall to bring up his century, the first by an amateur for England against Australia since 1908 (Hutchings, Melbourne)*

539, above: *On the second day Bradman cuts Tate past Chapman at point. Allen is at short leg, Duckworth wicketkeeper.* 540, right: *Chapman blazes away, salvaging some late honour for England*

166

541, left: *The King greets the Australians at Lord's. Woodfull stands with the monarch, who is shaking hands with McCabe.* 542, above: *Hobbs b Grimmett 19. Woolley is non-striker*

543, above, left: *Bradman (1), in the second innings, back-cuts Tate into the prehensile hands of Chapman.* 544, right, centre: *Hammond dives in an unsuccessful attempt to catch Kippax after a ball from Robins had brushed his glove.* 545, above, right: *An eerie presence – the ill-fated R101 airship makes an appearance during the Lord's Test*

1930
Headingley, July 11, 12, 14, 15

Australia 566 (D.G. Bradman 334, A.F. Kippax 77, W.M. Woodfull 50, M.W. Tate 5 for 124); England 391 (W.R. Hammond 113, A.P.F. Chapman 45, M. Leyland 44, C.V. Grimmett 5 for 135) and 95 for 3. Match drawn.

Bradman, the phenomenon, reached yet new heights with the highest score yet made in Test cricket. A few weeks from his 22nd birthday, he went in when Jackson was out in the second over, and against some testing new-ball bowling from Larwood and Tate he moved to 50 in 49 minutes and his century in only 99 minutes (out of 127 scored). He was 105 at lunch, 220 at tea, and 309 at the end of the day, having passed 1000 Test runs in only his seventh match. In all he batted 383 minutes and hit 46 fours, adding 192 with Woodfull and 229 with Kippax for the third wicket. His only chance was a difficult one to Duckworth (who eventually caught him off Tate) behind the stumps. Bradman's strokeplay, footwork and placement were marvelled at, and if overall his innings fell a trifle short of the perfection of his Lord's double-century, his skills were now comprehensively appreciated by players, Press and public. The pitch began to wear, and England were in difficulties, Hammond staying at the wicket for almost 5½ hours and reaching his 1000 Test runs in this his eighth Test. Rain and bad light came to England's salvation despite the follow-on, and though the series remained alive the prospects depended much upon whether Bradman could be held in check.

546, above, left: *Bradman has passed Foster's England-Australia record 287, and responds to the warm Yorkshire acclaim.* 547, above, right: *The great innings ends: Bradman c Duckworth b Tate 334.* 548, right: *He returns to the pavilion, the luckier spectators getting a touch as he passes*

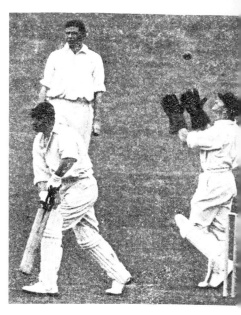

549, left: *McCabe bowled leg stump by Larwood for 30 at Leeds.* 550, above: *England's champion, Hammond, is caught by Oldfield for 113*

1930
Old Trafford, July 25, 26, 28, 29

FOURTH TEST

Australia *345 (W.H. Ponsford 83, W.M. Woodfull 54, A.F. Kippax 51, C.V. Grimmett 50, A.G. Fairfax 49); England 251 for 8 (H. Sutcliffe 74, K.S. Duleepsinhji 54, S.J. McCabe 4 for 41).* Match drawn.

On a slow pitch, after rain, Australia made heavy work of it, and crumpled after Woodfull and Ponsford's tedious 106 opening. Fairfax and Grimmett took them to a respectable total, but England's reorganised attack had had its say. Ian Peebles, bowling more googlies than leg-breaks, took 3 for 150, including Bradman (14), caught at slip. Sutcliffe dominated a first-wicket stand of 108 with Hobbs – their last of three-figures against Australia – before being caught breathtakingly by Bradman at long leg, and after Duleep's fine innings, during which he ran out to Grimmett, Leyland batted cautiously. During the brief period of play at 5.30 on the Monday the pitch was lively, but the fourth day was called off at 11 am, so wet were pitch and outfield.

551: *Woodfull, Australia's captain, hits Peebles for four. Duleepsinhji, Duckworth, and Hammond watch*

BRADMAN.

COMING EVENTS CAST THEIR SHADOWS AT OLD TRAFFORD OR—
— THE ENGLISH CAPTAIN SEES SOMETHING "FUNNY" ABOUT THE WICKET.

552, above: *Tom Webster's cartoon reflects England's neurosis over Bradman's domination of her bowlers. Australia's freshfaced champion for once did not trouble them in the Old Trafford Test – perhaps only because there was no second innings. 553, right: The 'old firm' – 'the two Bills' – 'Mutt and Jeff – Woodfull (left) and Ponsford open in the fourth Test*

554, above: *Peebles bowls to Fairfax at Old Trafford.* 555, left: *Leyland is bowled by McCabe for 35, one of the medium-pacer's four wickets*

1930
The Oval, August 16, 18, 19, 20, 21, 22

FIFTH TEST

England 405 (H. Sutcliffe 161, R.E.S. Wyatt 64, K.S. Duleepsinhji 50, J.B. Hobbs 47, C.V. Grimmett 4 for 135) and 251 (W.R. Hammond 60, H. Sutcliffe 54, K.S. Duleepsinhji 46, P.M. Hornibrook 7 for 92); Australia 695 (D.G. Bradman 232, W.H. Ponsford 110, A.A. Jackson 73, W.M. Woodfull 54, S.J. McCabe 54, A.G. Fairfax 53*, I.A.R. Peebles 6 for 204). Australia won by an innings and 39 runs.

Bradman did it again, taking his aggregate for the series to a (still) record 974 (average 139.14) and setting up – with the vital and courageous support of Jackson – a winning position in a match to be played to a finish. The two young New South Welshmen added 243 for the fourth wicket at a time when the ball sometimes lifted dangerously and Australia might have been overcome. Chapman was dropped – not a popular decision – and Bob Wyatt led England on his first appearance against Australia. He came in at the crisis point of 197 for 5 and settled to add 170 with Sutcliffe. Woodfull and Ponsford gave Australia a start of 159, but the Bradman-Jackson stand turned the match, the former this time making many of his runs behind the wicket, and batting 578 minutes, with one chance at 82. Peebles bowled 71 overs, and Tate (one for 153) 65.1. Larwood, who once struck Bradman painfully on the chest, took one for 132. Hobbs, in his final Test match, was bowled for nine by Fairfax, and finished with a record 3636 runs against Australia, average 54.26, with 12 centuries. Hammond ended a disappointing series with 60, last man out, the seventh of left-arm bowler Hornibrook's wickets after a blank fifth day through rain. Australia thus regained the Ashes on their captain Woodfull's 33rd birthday.

556: *A tense moment for new England captain Wyatt — his first ball, from Grimmett*

557, top, right: *A rare Sutcliffe error: the ball flies between Hornibrook and a diving McCabe.* 558, above: *Wyatt takes a superb catch to end Kippax's innings. Peebles was the bowler; Larwood is the other short leg.* 559, below: *Bradman hooks during his Oval double-century*

172

560, above: *Jackson swings a loose ball from Peebles to the leg boundary on the fourth morning of the Oval Test.* 561, left: *That evening Jack Hobbs embarked on his final Test innings, and was accorded an affectionate reception by the Australians*

562: *The end: Hobbs b Fairfax 9*

1932–33
Sydney, December 2, 3, 5, 6, 7

FIRST TEST

Australia 360 (S.J. McCabe 187*, V.Y. Richardson 49, H. Larwood 5 for 96, W. Voce 4 for 110) and 164 (J.H.W. Fingleton 40, H. Larwood 5 for 28); England 524 (H. Sutcliffe 194, W.R. Hammond 112, Nawab of Pataudi 102) and 1 for 0. England won by 10 wickets.

The 'Bodyline' tour began with one of the most heroic innings in the game's history. With Larwood and Voce (fast left-arm) bowling short-pitched balls in the direction of the batsman, with a cluster of short legs and a man or two out for the hook or top-edge, England's attack, under the unrelenting direction of captain Douglas Jardine, created unparalleled discomfort for batsmen and controversy which spread from onlookers through the sports pages into editorials and even to the music halls. Stan McCabe (22) hooked boldly and with the necessary good fortune and used his feet nimbly to get into position to cut ferociously. He hit 51 of a last-wicket stand of 55 after putting on 129 with Richardson for the fifth wicket. He hit 25 fours in his four hours, and, if anything, gave the Englishmen an argument for continuing with their policy: 'leg theory' could be hit, or so some claimed. Sutcliffe's eighth, last and highest century against Australia spanned century stands for the first three wickets: 112 with Wyatt, 188 with Hammond, and 123 with Pataudi (whose first Test it was). Sutcliffe at 43 played a ball from O'Reilly into his stumps but the bails were not dislodged. Larwood, with a strained side strapped, bowled very fast and accurately, seldom pitching short, in Australia's second innings.

563, above: *Jack Fingleton is caught by Allen in the leg-trap off Larwood. Ames is wicketkeeper and the other fielders are Jardine, Wyatt, and Hammond.* 564, right: *The slow bowling of Verity came as a kind of relief from hostilities: McCabe hits him to leg*

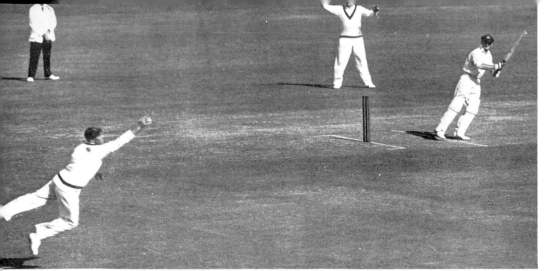

565, left: *Stan McCabe, thriving on audacity allied to quick reflexes, slashes the ball just wide of Voce at slip.* 566, below, left: *Sutcliffe plays a ball from O'Reilly into his stumps, to the mortification of McCabe and Oldfield, among others, but not himself. He went on to his highest Test score*

BOWLER	WKTS	RUNS
JARDINE		
PATAUDI		
SUTCLIFFE		
WYATT		
LEYLAND		
VERITY		15
HAMMOND	2	37
ALLEN	1	13
VOCE	1	54
LARWOOD	5	28

AUS. 1ST INGS. 360
ENG. 1ST INGS. 524

BATSMEN		
O'REILLY		7
NAGEL		21
9 FOR	164	

BATSMEN	OUT	F of W
PONSFORD	2	2
WOODFULL	0	10
McCABE	32	61
RICHARDSON	0	61
KIPPAX	19	100
OLDFIELD	1	104
FINGLETON	40	105
GRIMMETT	0	113
WALL	20	151
SUNDRIES	17	

567, left: *The Hill usually accommodates more spectators than this, but little action was expected on the final morning.* 568, above: *Nawab of Pataudi b Nagel 102 at Sydney.*

1932–33
SECOND TEST
Melbourne, December 30, 31, January 2, 3

Australia *228 (J.H.W. Fingleton 83) and 191 (D.G. Bradman 103*); England 169 (H. Sutcliffe 52, W.J. O'Reilly 5 for 63, T.W. Wall 4 for 52) and 139 (W.J. O'Reilly 5 for 66, H. Ironmonger 4 for 26). Australia won by 111 runs.*

Against the ominous portents, Australia drew level, with Bradman returning after a one-match absence to pull Bowes's first ball into his stumps, only to make a highly creditable century in the second innings, ducking and stepping across his wicket to Larwood, who sometimes had no off-side fielder in front of point. England erred in playing no slow bowler, Larwood, Voce, Allen, Hammond and Bowes carrying the attack. Fingleton's was a dour and courageous innings and McCabe and Richardson contributed valuably. Wall's pace and O'Reilly's fast-medium spinners were too much for England, who, after Bradman's grand knock (which sustained the nation's fervent faith in him), had no answer to O'Reilly again and the left-arm spin of Ironmonger. Over 200,000 watched the four days' play.

569, above: *Film sequence of Bradman's shock first-ball dismissal by Bowes; Fingleton is non-striker.* 570, below: *When the ball had to be changed soon after the start of the match, Woodfull patted the replacement back and forth with Jardine until enough shine had been taken off*

571: *Allen (out of picture) beautifully caught by Vic Richardson on the mid-wicket boundary off O'Reilly for 30 in England's first innings at Melbourne. Bowes is the not-out batsman*

1932–33
Adelaide, January 13, 14, 16, 17, 18, 19

THIRD TEST

England *341 (M. Leyland 83, R.E.S. Wyatt 78, E. Paynter 77, H. Verity 45, T.W. Wall 5 for 72) and 412 (W.R. Hammond 85, L.E.G. Ames 69, D.R. Jardine 56, R.E.S. Wyatt 49, M. Leyland 42, H. Verity 40, W.J. O'Reilly 4 for 79); Australia 222 (W.H. Ponsford 85, W.A.S. Oldfield 41 ret.ht, G.O.B. Allen 4 for 71) and 193 (W.M. Woodfull 73*, D.G. Bradman 66, G.O.B. Allen 4 for 50, H. Larwood 4 for 71).* England won by 338 runs.

The series erupted at Adelaide, where Woodfull, hit sickeningly over the heart by Larwood, who then reverted to the leg-side attack, told P.F. Warner, the MCC manager, that only one of the sides was playing cricket. Oldfield, having survived two hours, then suffered a cracked skull as he mishooked at Larwood. Mounted police lined up in readiness as the crowd's fury reached white heat. The Australian Board, who had prepared a cable of protest, sent it to Lord's, where the response several days later stated that MCC had full confidence in their team management. If an amendment to the Laws was proposed, it said, then full consideration would be given to it. Meanwhile, if Australia thought fit to cancel the rest of the tour, MCC would consent 'with great reluctance'. A further despatch was sent by the Board, reasserting that Bodyline was 'opposed to the spirit of cricket' and 'dangerous to players', but saying that cancellation was not considered necessary; a committee (Noble, Woodfull, Richardson and Hartigan) was to be set up and a report would later be submitted. A Law was adopted in November 1934 which outlawed 'direct bowling attack'. The Battle of Adelaide began with an England collapse, but Leyland, Wyatt and Paynter shored up the innings. Larwood and Allen (who refused to bowl Bodyline – and as an amateur, Australian-born at that ,was still able to hold his place) then demolished Australia, Ponsford, reinstated, bravely taking much fast stuff on the back. England built a lead laboriously, and on the fifth afternoon, after an animated innings from Bradman, the back of Australia's innings was broken, Woodfull going on valiantly to carry his bat for the second time against England.

572, above: *A victim of 'leg theory' – Bradman is caught by Allen off Larwood for 8 at Adelaide*

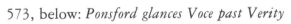

573, below: *Ponsford glances Voce past Verity*

574, top: *Woodfull hit over the heart at Adelaide by a ball from Larwood. Allen is at short leg.* 575, centre: *Hammond becomes a casualty, if less serious, as a ball from spinner Ironmonger strikes his mouth. Vic Richardson is keeping wicket in place of the injured Oldfield.* 576, bottom: *Bradman hits Verity for six (but was caught-and-bowled by the spinner's next ball)*

1932–33
Brisbane, February 10, 11, 13, 14, 15, 16

FOURTH TEST

Australia 340 (*V.Y. Richardson 83, D.G. Bradman 76, W.M. Woodfull 67, H. Larwood 4 for 101*) *and 175;* England 356 (*H. Sutcliffe 86, E. Paynter 83, D.R. Jardine 46, W.J. O'Reilly 4 for 120*) *and 162 for 4 (M. Leyland 86).* England won by 6 wickets.

Woolloongabba's first Test was fought closely on the first innings in oppressive, sultry heat, but Larwood, Allen and Verity found ways of getting rid of the home batsmen in the second innings, and a rocklike 24 from Jardine aiding Leyland's effort at No. 3 saw England to victory and the Ashes, the winning hit being a six by Paynter. Richardson and Woodfull had begun the match with a stand of 133, but apart from Bradman, who was bowled leg stump by Larwood as he tried to cut, no-one else made an impression. Jardine and Sutcliffe too began with a century stand, but a minor collapse was stemmed only when Paynter, the small Lancashire left-hander, left hospital, where he had been confined with acute tonsilitis, to make 24 before returning for another night under observation. Next day he put on a crucial 92 with Verity for the ninth wicket.

577, above: *Richardson pulls Larwood during by far the best opening stand for Australia in the series.* 578, below: *Paynter, England's sick Brisbane hero, skies O'Reilly. The wicketkeeper is 'Hammy' Love*

579, above: *McCabe cleverly caught left-handed by Jardine off Allen for 20 at Brisbane.* 580, left: *Left-hander Ernie Bromley fails to keep down a kicker from Larwood and is caught by Verity*

1932–33
Sydney, February 23, 24, 25, 27, 28

FIFTH TEST

Australia 435 (L.S. Darling 85, S.J. McCabe 73, L.P.J. O'Brien 61, W.A.S. Oldfield 52, D.G. Bradman 48, P.K. Lee 42, H. Larwood 4 for 98) and 182 (D.G. Bradman 71, W.M. Woodfull 67, H. Verity 5 for 33); England 454 (W.R. Hammond 101, H. Larwood 98, H. Sutcliffe 56, R.E.S. Wyatt 51, G.O.B. Allen 48, M. Leyland 42, P.K. Lee 4 for 111) and 168 for 2 (W.R. Hammond 75*, R.E.S. Wyatt 61*). England won by 8 wickets.

Woodfull won his fourth toss of the series, but Vic Richardson was dismissed before a run was scored – as he was in the second innings, suffering the same fate as Fingleton at Adelaide. Bradman batted with a kind of abandon, and McCabe, standing up to hit the fast bowlers, added 99 with O'Brien and 81 with Darling, both left-handers. Australia's overnight 296 for 5 was extended to 435 thanks in part to a continuation of dropped catches and near misses, and England were 159 for 2 that night after Sutcliffe and Hammond had put on 122 for the second wicket. Hammond's century owed its accomplishment to several dropped catches, but the emotive innings was Larwood's. Sent in as nightwatchman, he surprised everyone in making 98 – caught by the cumbersome Ironmonger off off-spinner Lee. For once the crowd received Larwood joyously. Australia's second innings owed almost everything to a stand of 115 between the defiant Woodfull and again a seemingly desperate Bradman. Verity used worn patches well, but Ironmonger was not so devastating when England set about getting 164. Jardine was barracked loudly as he protested when 'Bull' Alexander, Australia's squarely-built fast bowler, ran through across the batsman's area. Hammond finished the series with a six off Lee to the right of the sightscreen. Oldfield returned to the Australian XI and showed no ill-effects. Larwood, slowed down at the end of this acrimonious series by a splintered bone in the foot, finished with 33 wickets at 19.51 in the five Tests.

581, top: *Hammond's distinctive cover-drive; he scored heavily again here at Sydney, his favourite ground.* 582, centre: *Richardson takes a sharp catch at slip to dismiss Jardine – probably the wicket Australia always wanted most of all – off Ironmonger.* 583, below: *Larwood falls two short of a century, caught at mid-on*

584, left: *Conflicts now just memories, Harold Larwood (left) and Bert Oldfield share the sunshine as guests of honour in Hong Kong in 1975.* 585, below: *Hammond (left) and Wyatt leave the field at Sydney after seeing England to their fourth victory of the 1932–33 series. McCabe follows.* 586, bottom: *As The Australian Cricketer saw it*

1934
Trent Bridge, June 8, 9, 11, 12

Australia 374 (A.G. Chipperfield 99, S.J. McCabe 65, W.H. Ponsford 53, K. Farnes 5 for 102) and 273 for 8 dec (S.J. McCabe 88, W.A. Brown 73, K. Farnes 5 for 77); England 268 (E.H. Hendren 79, H. Sutcliffe 62, G. Geary 53, C.V. Grimmett 5 for 81, W.J. O'Reilly 4 for 75) and 141 (C.F. Walters 46, W.J. O'Reilly 7 for 54). Australia won by 238 runs.

Left 4¾ hours to bat, 379 in arrears, England could not withstand the spin of O'Reilly and Grimmett (who took 19 of the wickets between them), and lost with ten minutes remaining. England were led by Walters in his maiden Test against Australia, Wyatt missing the match with a broken thumb. Chipperfield, batting No. 7 in his first Test, often hit uppishly through the off, but reached 99 by lunch on the second day. He fell, however, to Farnes's third ball after the interval, caught behind by Ames. A seventh-wicket stand of 101 by Hendren and Geary saved the follow-on, and although 106 behind, England fought back to get Woodfull, Ponsford and Bradman for 69. Brown and McCabe then added 112, the latter once more batting with great flair. When Ames missed stumping the dour Brown, however, it was thought he might have done England a favour. Sutcliffe and Walters began soundly, making 51 by half an hour after lunch, but O'Reilly – into the dusty end – and Grimmett – who had Hammond stumped when he fell forward – bowled their side to victory. The tall Essex fast bowler Farnes had an impressive debut, helping for the moment to soften the loss of Larwood and Voce, who, with Jardine – for various reasons – were not playing.

587, above: *Chipperfield kills a ball from Geary at Trent Bridge. His 99 on debut brought him an odd kind of notoriety.* 588, right: *A balloon obstructs the camera view of a rival company who set up position outside the ground*

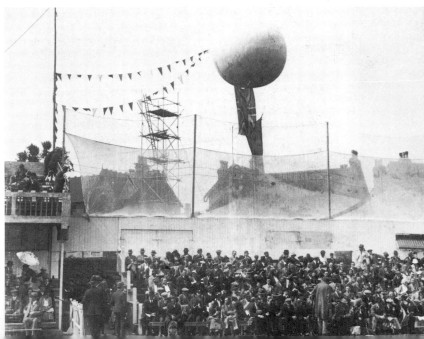

589, left: *The new firm – Sutcliffe (left) and Walters open at Trent Bridge.* 590, above: *Woodfull goes too far across to Farnes and loses his leg stump*

591, left: *Hammond st Oldfield b Grimmett 16, in England's second innings.* 592, below: *O'Reilly's hammer-blow – he has Leyland caught behind and England are eight down with 20 minutes left on the last afternoon*

1934
Lord's, June 22, 23, 25

SECOND TEST

England 440 (L.E.G. Ames 120, M. Leyland 109, C.F. Walters 82, T.W. Wall 4 for 108); Australia 284 (W.A.Brown 105, H. Verity 7 for 61) and 118 (W.M. Woodfull 43, H. Verity 8 for 43). England won by an innings and 38 runs.

'Verity's match', the first to be won by England against Australia at Lord's since 1896 and the last to the time of writing, was a triumph for rain, though in the opinion of most the Australian batting was rather too desperate at times. England were none too soundly placed after Walters's elegant innings until Leyland and Ames (the only wicketkeeper to make a century in these Tests until 1974–75) added 129 for the sixth wicket. Ames was missed by Oldfield at 96. Australia were 192 for 2 over the weekend, Brown having made a handsome 103 not out; but heavy rain left the pitch a 'slow turner' and the Yorkshire slow-medium left-arm bowler Hedley Verity used it to wonderful advantage. Farnes, Geary and Hammond were all injured, but Verity spun Australia to a follow-on by a margin of only seven runs, and returned even better figures in the second innings, when the pitch did become more difficult and only Woodfull and Chipperfield coped for any time. Verity took 14 wickets in the day.

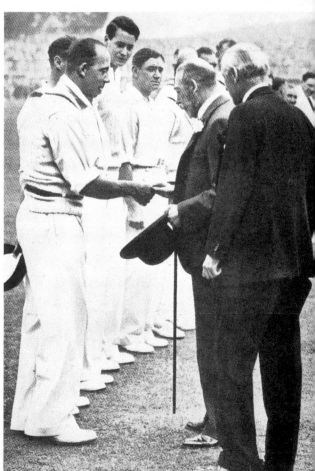

593, above, left: *Cyril Walters is caught by Bromley in O'Reilly's leg-trap for 82.* 594, above, right: *England captain Wyatt loses his aluminium finger-guard as he hooks O'Reilly.* 595, right: *A royal interest: King George V examines Wyatt's injured thumb*

596, top: *Les Ames's fine innings at Lord's ends at 120 as his opposite number, Oldfield, catches him off McCabe.* 597, centre: *Hendren holds an outstanding catch to add McCabe to Verity's heavy bag of wickets.* 598, left: *Bradman mis-hits Verity and is about to be caught by Ames in Australia's catastrophic second innings*

1934
Old Trafford, July 6, 7, 9, 10

THIRD TEST

England 627 for 9 dec (M. Leyland 153, E.H. Hendren 132, L.E.G. Ames 72, H. Sutcliffe 63, G.O.B. Allen 61, H. Verity 60*, C.F. Walters 52, W.J. O'Reilly 7 for 189) and 123 for 0 dec (H. Sutcliffe 69*, C.F. Walters 50*); Australia 491 (S.J. McCabe 137, W.M. Woodfull 73, W.A. Brown 72, H. Verity 4 for 78) and 66 for 1. Match drawn.

On a pluperfect wicket, the outcome after the first day revolved around whether Australia could avoid following on. Brown and McCabe went a long way to achieving that safety with a second-wicket stand of 196, McCabe making most of the strokes. The match is remembered as much as anything for O'Reilly's sensational spell on the first morning. With successive balls he had Walters caught at short leg, bowled Wyatt, elicited a not entirely voluntary leg glance for four by Hammond, and then bowled him. England were 72 for 3, the 'Tiger' having done the damage with a substitute ball. Hendren and Leyland added 191 for the fifth wicket, and Leyland and Ames 142 for the sixth. It was 4 pm on the second day before Wyatt declared. Australia found safe waters, but might have done so with greater comfort had not Bradman and Chipperfield been off-colour with throat infections. A talking point was Allen's first over, which contained three wides and four no-balls.

599, above: *Leyland's great rescue innings comes to an end as Ben Barnett (fielding substitute) catches him at mid-on off O'Reilly.* 600, below: *Hammond becomes O'Reilly's third victim in a sensational four balls*

601, above, left: *Allen sweeps during his innings of 61 at Old Trafford.* 602, *right: McCabe lays his bat aside for a few moments to gargle. Several of the Australians were stricken with throat infections*

1934
Headingley, July 20, 21, 23, 24

FOURTH TEST

England *200 (C.F. Walters 44, C.V. Grimmett 4 for 57) and 229 for 6 (M. Leyland 49*, C.F. Walters 45, R.E.S. Wyatt 44, E.H. Hendren 42); Australia 584 (D.G. Bradman 304, W.H. Ponsford 181, W.E. Bowes 6 for 142).* Match drawn.

After an inept England batting performance against the spinners, the match was given over to a record-smashing fourth-wicket stand of 388 between a fully fit and resolute Bradman and a masterly Ponsford. On the first evening Bowes had dislodged Brown, Oldfield and Woodfull in a runless spell, but Australia's 39 for 3 at the start of the second day had become 494 for 4 by the close, Bradman 271. He and Ponsford dealt with Bowes, Hammond, Mitchell, Verity and Hopwood in an untroubled manner, only one sharp chance from each being missed before lunch. Ponsford, who hit 19 fours in 387 minutes, was out when he trod on his stumps in hitting Verity to long-on. Next day Bradman reached his second triple-century against England with a leg snick for four off Bowes, who five minutes later bowled him. He batted 430 minutes, and hit two sixes and 43 fours. There was a minor collapse after that, but England faced arrears of 384, and were 188 for 5 on the third evening. Rain then came as the saviour.

603: *Bradman, on the way to his second triple-century against England, hooks Lancashire left-arm bowler Hopwood*

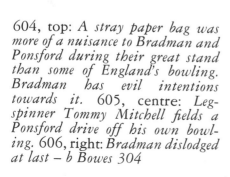

604, top: *A stray paper bag was more of a nuisance to Bradman and Ponsford during their great stand than some of England's bowling. Bradman has evil intentions towards it.* 605, centre: *Leg-spinner Tommy Mitchell fields a Ponsford drive off his own bowling.* 606, right: *Bradman dislodged at last – b Bowes 304*

607: *That sinking feeling: Hammond is run out for 20 at Leeds from a throw from square leg to Grimmett. The other batsman is Walters; Chipperfield at slip, Oldfield the wicketkeeper*

1934
The Oval, August 18, 20, 21, 22

FIFTH TEST

Australia 701 (W.H. Ponsford 266, D.G. Bradman 244, W.M. Woodfull 49, W.A.S. Oldfield 42*, W.E. Bowes 4 for 164, G.O.B. Allen 4 for 170) and 327 (D.G. Bradman 77, S.J. McCabe 70, H.I. Ebeling 41, W.E. Bowes 5 for 55, E.W. Clark 5 for 98); England 321 (M. Leyland 110, C.F. Walters 64) and 145 (W.R. Hammond 43, C.V. Grimmett 5 for 64). Australia won by 562 runs.

The enormous stand by Bradman and Ponsford in the previous Test seemed but a rehearsal, for here on a fine pitch at The Oval they put on 451 for Australia's second wicket, stretching the world Test record partnership to a figure which still stands. Bradman was in marvellous form, making his runs in 316 minutes, with a six and 32 fours. He was caught behind hooking at a Bowes bouncer. Ponsford enjoyed six reprieves during his 460 minutes and hit a five and 27 fours. Again he was out hit-wicket, this time in ducking a short ball from Allen, having seen 574 runs on the board. This was Ponsford's last Test; he had also made a century in his first. England were in at 4.55 pm on the second day, and Sutcliffe and Walters began with 104. Wickets then clattered, until Leyland was supported by Ames (who had then to drop out of the match with severe lumbago) and Allen. The Yorkshire left-hander's third century in five Test innings took 2¾ hours. Woodfull batted again and England were eventually set 708. Australia's crushing victory – their biggest in runs against England – once more occurred on captain Woodfull's birthday. Australia were not to relinquish the Ashes for 19 years. Frank Woolley, now 47, was brought back for this Test, his last, and kept wicket in Ames's absence; but he made only 4 and 0.

608: *Even Bradman tired at times. He rests on his haunches as Leyland, England's seventh bowler, places his field in the Oval Test*

609, above, left: *Bradman and Ponsford aren't finished yet – resuming their mammoth second-wicket world-record stand.* 610, above, right: *Bill Brown is bowled by 'Nobby' Clark for 10 early on the first day. Australia's next wicket fell a few minutes before close of play.* 611, right: *Bradman pulls a ball from Allen in Australia's second innings, which built on a first-innings lead of 380*

612, left: *McCabe b Allen 10: Australia 488 for 3.* 613, below: *Ponsford's second innings at The Oval was much shorter. He is caught by Hammond in Clark's leg-trap. Woolley is keeping wicket*

614: *Hammond and Sutcliffe at slip watch veteran Woolley hold a catch from Chipperfield in Australia's second innings*

1936–37
Brisbane, December 4, 5, 7, 8, 9

FIRST TEST

England 358 (M. Leyland 126, C.J. Barnett 69, J. Hardstaff 43, W.J. O'Reilly 5 for 102) and 256 (G.O.B. Allen 68, F.A. Ward 6 for 102); Australia 234 (J.H.W. Fingleton 100, S.J. McCabe 51, W. Voce 6 for 41) and 58 (G.O.B. Allen 5 for 36, W. Voce 4 for 16). England won by 322 runs.

A cliffhanger series in which several attendance records were broken began with a grand spell of fast bowling from McCormick (3 for 17), who then bowled only three overs more before being forced out by acute lumbago. Barnett and the ever-reliable Leyland added 99, and Leyland and Hardstaff 90, but Hammond's dismal form of 1934 continued with 0 and 25. Australia were 151 for 2 by the second evening, but after Fingleton's careful century Australia fell away before Voce and the new ball. Leg-spinner Ward was England's second-innings problem until Allen, the captain, paired with Hardstaff (who, as one of Oldfield's three stumping victims in the innings, enabled the Australian 'keeper to pass Lilley's record 84 dismissals in these Tests). Australia, faced with scoring 381 for victory, lost Fingleton first ball of the innings in poor light, and after overnight rain found themselves 16 for 5, 20 for 6, and soon one-down in the series as Allen and Voce bounced the ball off a distinctly unpleasant pitch. Chipperfield finished 26 not out, but Ward's nose was broken as he attempted a hook. The hook had also cost Worthington his wicket to the first ball of the match.

615, above, left: *T.W. Garrett, 78, the sole survivor from the first Test match, meets the England captain, 'Gubby' Allen, at a Sydney reception. NSW Premier B.S.B. Stevens is in the centre.* 616, right: *Maurice Leyland swings during his Brisbane century.* 517, below, left: *Sievers caught by Voce off Allen in Australia's dismal second innings.* 618, right: *Lilley's record is passed as Oldfield stumps Hardstaff*

1936–37
Sydney, December 18, 19, 21, 22

SECOND TEST

England *426 for 6 dec (W.R. Hammond 231*, C.J. Barnett 57, M. Leyland 42); Australia 80 (W. Voce 4 for 10) and 324 (S.J. McCabe 93, D.G. Bradman 82, J.H.W. Fingleton 73). England won by an innings and 22 runs.*

Bad weather was to render Bradman's second Test as captain even more unpropitious than the first. England were 279 for 3 at the end of the first day, Hammond 147; and with rain interruptions later on the second day he confirmed his return to his best, batting altogether for 458 minutes and hitting 27 fours. His sequence of Test scores at Sydney was now: 251, 112, 101, 75 not out, and 231 not out. A thunderstorm on the third morning left Australia with uneasy prospects, and Voce was soon bouncing wickedly off a length. The first three wickets fell with the score one, Bradman among them, for his second successive duck. O'Reilly (37 not out) swung at the slow bowlers later in the innings, but Allen soon had the decision whether or not to put Australia in again. He did, and that evening they were 145 for one. Fingleton and Bradman put on 124 before the former was bowled by a Sims googly next day. After Bradman's departure only McCabe offered resistance, batting enchantingly as ever until given out lbw. He may have touched the ball from Voce into his pads; but then he was within a whisker of lbw before he had scored.

619, above: *Wally Hammond's attachment to the Sydney ground is displayed again – a sweep off leg-spinner Ward during his 231 not out.* 620, right: *O'Reilly strikes with his bat for a change – a six off Verity.* 621, below: *Hardstaff hooks O'Reilly, to be dropped in the outfield. It will be seen that his off bail has fallen – a case of 'hit wicket' unobserved*

1936–37
Melbourne, January 1, 2, 4, 5, 6, 7

THIRD TEST

Australia *200 for 9 dec (S.J. McCabe 63) and 564 (D.G. Bradman 270, J.H.W. Fingleton 136, K.E. Rigg 47); England 76 for 9 dec (M.W.S. Sievers 5 for 21) and 323 (M. Leyland 111*, R.W.V. Robins 61, W.R. Hammond 51, L.O'B. Fleetwood-Smith 5 for 124).* Australia won by 365 runs.

At 130 for 6 the series seemed all but lost, but McCabe and Oldfield took the score to 183 before McCabe was caught at slip next day after rain had delayed the start. The pitch was obviously nasty, and Bradman declared for England to begin batting at 3 pm. The luck had turned. Worthington once again went without a run on the board, and apart from Hammond, whose 32 in 80 minutes was one of the finest innings of his life, only Barnett and Leyland reached double-figures as medium-pacer Sievers and O'Reilly made the ball leap. The art was in taking the bat from the ball much of the time. Darling made three catches, two of them superb. England batted on, when some thought an earlier declaration might have been worthwhile in putting Australia back in when the pitch was misbehaving. As it was, Bradman sent in O'Reilly (out for nought) and Fleetwood-Smith (who went early next day). After the fifth wicket fell at 97, Bradman joined Fingleton and saw the score to 194 that evening, and on a recovered pitch their stand climbed to a record 346 before Fingleton (386 minutes) was out. He hit only six fours. Bradman was 248 at the close, Australia 500 for 6. His innings, which was chanceless, finally closed with a catch to Allen off Verity after he had batted for 458 minutes, hitting 22 fours and as many as 110 singles. For much of his innings – which was then the highest by an Australian captain and for Australia in Australia – he was labouring under the effects of a chill. McCabe led Australia in the field for a while when England set about making 689. Their 323 was made at a happy rate, Hammond and Robins striking well as Leyland made a professional sixth century against Australia. The attendance of 350,534 over the six days is a record.

622, above, left: *Hammond's supremely skilful innings of 32 ends as Darling dives for a catch off Sievers's bowling. Sims is non-striker.* 623, right: *Leyland turns O'Reilly to leg only for Darling to pick up another lovely catch.* 624, below, left: *Walter Robins bowled by O'Reilly for 61.* 625, right: *Bradman is about to catch England's last man, Voce. Fleetwood-Smith waits to take stumps as souvenirs, while Ward runs in*

1936–37

FOURTH TEST

Adelaide, January 29, 30, February 1, 2, 3, 4

Australia 288 (S.J. McCabe 88, A.G. Chipperfield 57*, W.A. Brown 42) and 433 (D.G. Bradman 212, S.J. McCabe 55, R.G. Gregory 50, W.R. Hammond 5 for 57); England 330 (C.J. Barnett 129, L.E.G. Ames 52, M. Leyland 45, W.J. O'Reilly 4 for 51, L.O'B. Fleetwood-Smith 4 for 129) and 243 (R.E.S. Wyatt 50, J. Hardstaff 43, L.O'B. Fleetwood-Smith 6 for 110). Australia won by 148 runs.

England bowled and fielded well to dismiss Australia for only 288 on a good pitch – McCabe batted with customary skill and sparkle. Then, when a push towards command seemed there for the taking, wickets fell to the left-arm spin of Fleetwood-Smith and to the domineering O'Reilly. Barnett was 92 on the second evening after four hours, and was unusually restrained next day until he hit McCormick for four boundaries in an over. If his innings was of great value, Bradman's saved the series. Starting with 26, he batted all through the fourth day, adding 109 with McCabe and 135 with 20-year-old Gregory. When he was caught-and-bowled by Hammond, Bradman had batted 441 minutes, hitting only 14 fours, and making 99 singles in a wonderful display of concentration and skill. England faced a target of 392, and were 148 for 3 on the fifth evening. But Fleetwood-Smith spun one in from the off to bowl Hammond first thing next morning, and the remaining wickets fell steadily as the Victorian tossed and teased his way to ten in the match.

627, left: At Adelaide, Bradman (in hat) and Allen talk to a man captains always should take the trouble to consult – the head groundsman. 628, above: Bob Wyatt, mended ulna fracture still protected by a leather sheath, awaits his turn to bat

629, above, left: *Intrusion: a man with a box camera ran on to the ground and attempted to photograph Bradman (top), who turned away.* 630, left: *Charles Barnett caught by Chipperfield off Fleetwood-Smith for 21.* 631, above: *Ross Gregory (left) and Bradman resume their stand*

1936–37   FIFTH TEST
Melbourne, February 26, 27, March 1, 2, 3

Australia 604 (D.G. Bradman 169, C.L. Badcock 118, S.J. McCabe 112, R.G. Gregory 80, K. Farnes 6 for 96); England 239 (J. Hardstaff 83, T.S. Worthington 44, W.J. O'Reilly 5 for 51, L.J. Nash 4 for 70) and 165 (W.R. Hammond 56, C.J. Barnett 41). Australia won by an innings and 200 runs.

Bradman won the vital toss and demonstrated his apparent infallibility once more with a faultless innings lasting 3¾ hours. His stand with McCabe – a new Australian third-wicket record in these Tests – after two wickets had fallen for 54 amounted to 249 in only 163 minutes. McCabe, missed at 11 and 86, claimed 16 fours, many from juicy cuts. The second big stand was between the youngsters Badcock and Gregory: 161 for the fifth wicket. Australia seemed safe at 604. For England's part, admiration went out to Farnes, who bowled fast for 28.5 eight-ball overs. On the Monday England began with 33 in 17 minutes, but Barnett was then out, and later, when the key wickets of Hammond and Leyland fell, and rain deadened the pitch before it became spiteful as it dried, the result was a foregone conclusion. The last five wickets fell for three runs, and in the follow-on Hammond and Barnett's 60 was the highest stand. O'Reilly and Fleetwood-Smith took three wickets each, and the Ashes were safe in Australia's keeping – a longish-odds prospect at Christmas.

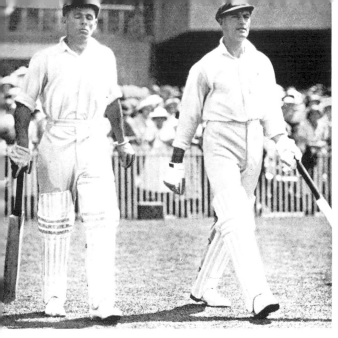

632, left: *Fingleton (left) and Keith Rigg open for Australia in the Melbourne 'decider'.* 633, above: *Bradman, at 101, almost perishes to a direct hit by Hardstaff. Bowler Farnes shouts expectantly*

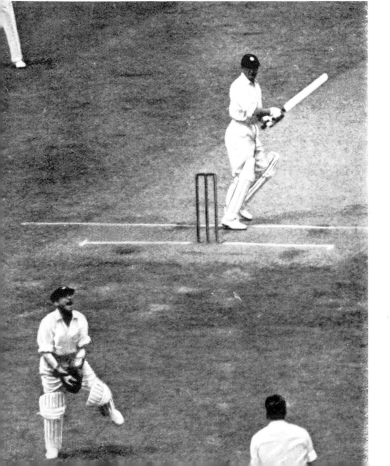

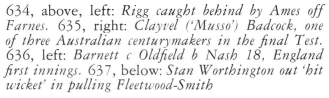

634, above, left: *Rigg caught behind by Ames off Farnes.* 635, right: *Clayvel ('Musso') Badcock, one of three Australian centurymakers in the final Test.* 636, left: *Barnett c Oldfield b Nash 18, England first innings.* 637, below: *Stan Worthington out 'hit wicket' in pulling Fleetwood-Smith*

1938
Trent Bridge, June 10, 11, 13, 14

FIRST TEST

England 658 for 8 dec (E. Paynter 216*, C.J. Barnett 126, D.C.S. Compton 102, L. Hutton 100, L.E.G. Ames 46, L.O'B. Fleetwood-Smith 4 for 153); Australia 411 (S.J. McCabe 232, D.G. Bradman 51, W.A. Brown 48, K. Farnes 4 for 106, D.V.P. Wright 4 for 153) and 427 for 6 dec (D.G. Bradman 144*, W.A. Brown 133, J.H.W. Fingleton 40). Match drawn.

Hammond won the toss, and at lunch England were 169 without loss, Barnett 98, Hutton, a fortnight from his 22nd birthday, 61 in his first Test against Australia (having played a ball onto his stumps in the third over without disturbing a bail). Barnett reached his century with an off-driven boundary first ball after the interval, and the opening stand eventually ended at 219 (in only 172 minutes, and the first double-century stand for England at home against Australia). Hutton went on to his century in 200 minutes. The next big stand was for the fifth wicket, carried overnight to a record 206 by Paynter and 20-year-old Compton (another debutant against Australia), and lasting a mere 138 minutes. Paynter, aged 36, reached his 200 in 306 minutes, and the declaration came at 3.15 on the second day. Australia at stumps were 138 for 3. The third day belonged to McCabe. Adding 69 with wicketkeeper Barnett for the seventh wicket, at the fall of which he was 105, McCabe slaughtered the bowling while shielding his tailend partners. His second hundred took only 84 minutes – the second 50 of it just 24 minutes. He was particularly severe on medium-pace leg-spin/googly bowler Wright. With more than half England's fielders on the boundary, and with last-man Fleetwood-Smith in, McCabe drove, cut and hooked 72 of Australia's last 77. That day he made 213 of the 273 scored while he batted, and altogether he hit a six and 34 fours in his 235 minutes at the crease in one of cricket's truly outstanding innings. Verity, whom Hammond was saving for the follow-on, finally had him caught at cover. Australia survived the eight hours of their second innings with little difficulty on a still-perfect pitch. Brown and Fingleton launched the innings with 89, then Bradman (365 minutes, with only five fours) put on 170 with Brown (320 minutes), and during the final day, when Verity and Wright sometimes spun sharply off the dry wicket, the captain reached his 13th century in these Tests, passing Hobbs's record.

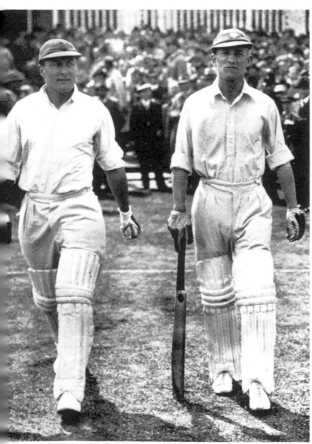

638, above, left: *Barnett and Hutton start their great opening stand at Trent Bridge.* 639, above, right: *Compton turns McCormick to long leg. Paynter is non-striker.* 640, right: *Hutton drives through mid-off*

641, left: *McCabe drives during his phenomenal innings at Trent Bridge.* 642, above: *Hassett caught by Hammond off Wright. Ames is the wicket-keeper, Hutton at short leg*

1938
Lord's, June 24, 25, 27, 28

SECOND TEST

England 494 (W.R. Hammond 240, E. Paynter 99, L.E.G. Ames 83, W.J. O'Reilly 4 for 93, E.L. McCormick 4 for 101) and 242 for 8 dec (D.C.S. Compton 76*, E. Paynter 43); Australia 422 (W.A. Brown 206*, A.L. Hassett 56, W.J. O'Reilly 42, H. Verity 4 for 103) and 204 for 6 (D.G. Bradman 102*, A.L. Hassett 42). Match drawn.

England, reduced to 31 for 3 by McCormick on a lively pitch, ran to a creditable 409 for 5 by the end of the day, Hammond 210, Ames 50. Paynter, finding touch after lunch, added a record 222 with Hammond for the fourth wicket before O'Reilly trapped him leg-before. Hammond was at his most majestic, reaching his hundred in 146 minutes, adding 186 with Ames, and batting altogether 367 minutes for his fourth double-century (and the highest score by an England captain) against Australia. He gave no chances. Bill Brown held Australia's innings together, ensuring the follow-on was avoided. The best stand was a fast 124 between him and Hassett, and in carrying his bat Brown batted two minutes longer than Hammond, and registered the 100th century for Australia v England. When Compton dropped Fleetwood-Smith at slip he deprived Farnes of a hat-trick. McCormick was again a problem to England on a damp pitch, but on the fourth day Compton and Wellard (38) saw to it that Australia's target was too distant. Nevertheless, Bradman went with customary ease to a century, the 200th in these Tests (101 for Australia), passing Hobbs's record aggregate of 3636 in England-Australia Tests.

643, below, left: *Hammond reaches his 200 at Lord's.* 644, centre: *A standing ovation for him from the members.* 645, right: *Eddie Paynter hooks during his 99*

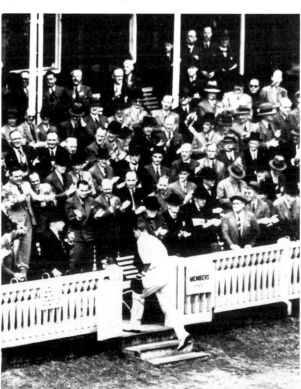

646, above, left: *Paynter lbw b O'Reilly 99, at Lord's.* 647, right: *Bradman b Verity 18*

1938
Headingley, July 22, 23, 25

THIRD TEST

England *223 (W.R. Hammond 76, W.J. O'Reilly 5 for 66) and 123 (W.J. O'Reilly 5 for 56, L.O'B. Fleetwood-Smith 4 for 34); Australia 242 (D.G. Bradman 103, B.A. Barnett 57, K. Farnes 4 for 77) and 107 for 5. Australia won by 5 wickets.*

The match set down for Old Trafford on July 8 having been abandoned because of rain without a ball being bowled, Australia seized the chance to retain the Ashes with magnificent performances by Bradman and O'Reilly. Only Hammond was unaffected for long by the pace of McCormick and the spin of O'Reilly and Fleetwood-Smith, and by the first evening Australia were 32 for one, Barnett the nightwatchman. The second day was Don Bradman's. In the gloom and on a moist pitch he manoeuvred the strike and dealt with varied bowling to put his side in the lead. In one of his finest innings he stayed three hours, striking nine boundaries. O'Reilly, attacking England's batsmen with fast-medium spinners to a packed leg-side field, then took over. He had Hammond, the key batsman, caught first ball at short leg. Left 105 for victory, Australia suffered early setbacks, and Wright, given a few more runs to bowl against, might have won it for England on his form that afternoon. The tiny Hassett, however, batted confidently for 33 after being missed at slip second ball, and the match was won before the rain came.

648, below, left: *Bradman and Hammond (in his Gloucestershire blazer) go to toss at Leeds.* 649, right: *Bill Edrich hurls his slight frame into a delivery to Bradman*

650: *Compton c Barnett (wicketkeeper) b O'Reilly 15 – England headed for defeat at Leeds*

1938
The Oval, August 20, 22, 23, 24

FOURTH TEST

England 903 *for 7 dec (L. Hutton 364, M. Leyland 187, J. Hardstaff 169*, W.R. Hammond 59, A. Wood 53); Australia 201 (W.A. Brown 69, A.L. Hassett 42, S.G. Barnes 41, W.E. Bowes 5 for 49) and 123 (B.A. Barnett 46, K. Farnes 4 for 63).* England won by an innings and 579 runs.

The course of a match whose details many an English schoolboy has been able to recite with greater ease than his multiplication tables was virtually predetermined when Hammond won the toss and batted on a grossly overprepared pitch. His instructions were for England's batsmen to conduct the innings as if no total was too high. Had Bradman and Fingleton not been injured during the innings, the match could have lasted many days more. England were 347 for one by Saturday evening, Hutton 160, Leyland 156. Hutton's century was the 100th for England against Australia. The Yorkshiremen continued their stand to 382, the highest for England in these Tests, and after Leyland was run out (having made a century in his last as well as his first Test), Hammond added 135 with Hutton, who reached 200 in 468 minutes. Paynter made nought and Compton one, but the 'collapse' was steadied by Hardstaff, who put on 215 with Hutton before the 22-year-old batsman was caught at extra-cover by Hassett off O'Reilly for 364, a score still only once exceeded in any Test. He gave only one chance – of stumping at 40 – during his 797 minutes at the wicket, having hit 35 fours and seen 770 runs recorded while he was in. 300 not out on the second evening, he took some time to overtake Bradman's record 334, but eventually square-cut Fleetwood-Smith for four to reach 336. Only Hanif Mohammad of Pakistan has batted longer in a Test innings. Hardstaff and Wood posted a fourth stand of three-figures. After the declaration at tea on the third day, Australia, having made 695 and 701 in their previous two Tests at The Oval, crumbled against the pace of Bowes and, second time round, of Farnes. Brown, first in and last out in the first innings, was on the field for the first 18½ hours of the match, as he had been in the previous Test. On a pitch perfect throughout the match O'Reilly (85-26-178-3), Fleetwood-Smith (87-11-298-1) and Waite (72-16-150-1) did a manful if unavailing job for Australia.

651, left: *With England's total around 800, Bradman put himself on to bowl – but soon fell and fractured a shinbone.* 652, right: *Hutton cuts. Wicketkeeper is Barnett, Fingleton short leg*

653, right: *A big drive by Leyland off Fleetwood-Smith during his long stand with Hutton.* 654, below: *A cut for four, and Hutton is 336.* 655, below, right: *Handshakes from Bradman and Hardstaff. (Inset: a remarkable scoreboard.)*

656, below, left: *Fellow-Yorkshiremen Verity, Bowes and Wood congratulate Hutton in the dressing-room.* 657, bottom: *England's massive victory is achieved, and Hutton leads umpire Chester, Wood, Edrich, umpire Walden, and Bowes from the field. That was it, until another world war had been started and ended*

1946–47
Brisbane, November 29, 30, December 2, 3, 4

FIRST TEST

Australia 645 (D.G. Bradman 187, A.L. Hassett 128, C.L. McCool 95, K.R. Miller 79, I.W. Johnson 47, D.V.P. Wright 5 for 167); England 141 (K.R. Miller 7 for 60) and 172 (E.R.H. Toshack 6 for 82). Australia won by an innings and 332 runs.

The last match before the Second World War having produced England's heaviest defeat ever of Australia (or any other country), the first match upon resumption produced Australia's heaviest victory over England. The home side emerged from the war with several bright prospects, whereas England, on the whole, depended on pre-war players. Only Bedser, Evans, Washbrook and Yardley, of those new to Tests against Australia, enjoyed any real success. Curiosity over the future of 38-year-old Bradman was soon settled when he overcame a nervy start and a debated 'not-out' decision to a ball caught by Ikin at slip to bat all told for 318 minutes. With Hassett, who batted over an hour longer, he added a third-wicket record of 276. Miller, a dynamic all-rounder, and McCool, both on Test debuts, each featured in further century partnerships, and by the time a demoralised England started to bat on the third day the light had deteriorated and rain interfered. England, 21 for one overnight, had a fearful day on a spiteful pitch after almost two inches of rain, and Miller was unplayable. Edrich made a courageous 16 in 1¾ hours, but after an even more torrential storm, accompanied by hail and 79 mph winds, during which the ground was submerged and the covers and stumps floated away, play was miraculously resumed on the fifth morning, and England were soon out a first time. Hutton fell to the first ball of the second innings, and left-arm medium-pacer Toshack finished off a match won almost as much by the elements.

658, above, left: *Hammond, in stormproof trilby, goes out with Bradman to inspect the pitch at Brisbane.* 659, right: *One of history's most famous disputed catches – Bradman to Ikin. It was given 'not out'.* 660, below, left: *Miller hits Wright for six. Wicketkeeper is Gibb.* 661, right: *The ground after the memorable downpour*

662: *Hammond holds his bat high to avoid one of many lifting balls on the Brisbane 'sticky'*

1946–47
Sydney, December, 13, 14, 16, 17, 18, 19

SECOND TEST

England *255 (W.J. Edrich 71, J.T. Ikin 60, I.W. Johnson 6 for 42) and 371 (W.J. Edrich 119, D.C.S. Compton 54, C. Washbrook 41, C.L. McCool 5 for 109); Australia 659 for 8 dec (S.G. Barnes 234, D.G. Bradman 234, K.R. Miller 40). Australia won by an innings and 33 runs.*

Johnson's off-spin and McCool's leg-spin spelt England's batting downfall, the batsmen usually preferring to try to play the flighted ball from the crease. Barnes batted right through the third day for 88 runs, and stayed in all for 642 minutes, putting on a record 405 with Bradman, who came in No. 6 because of a leg strain and gastric trouble. They wore down the somewhat thin bowling attack for almost all the fourth day until Bradman's 6½-hour, chanceless innings ended as he was lbw to Yardley. He had now taken part in record stands for the second, third, fourth, fifth and sixth wickets. Australia batted into the fifth day before declaring, and in 24 minutes before lunch Hutton gave a sparkling display in making 37 before his bat slipped into his wicket as he played at Miller's last ball before lunch. By close of play England were 247 for 3, and slowly next morning Edrich attained his century, batting in all for 314 minutes, hitting only seven fours and as many as 63 singles. For a time it seemed England might hold out, but 43-year-old Hammond, a shadow of his former self, failed again, and Australia were victors once more by an innings by mid-afternoon. Godfrey Evans, in his first Test against Australia, allowed no byes in Australia's huge total.

663: *Bradman and Barnes, both already past 200, come in for an interval. Yardley, Evans and Compton follow*

664, above, left: *Ikin pulls McCool during his 60 at Sydney.* 665, right: *Edrich drives McCool for four. Tribe is at forward short leg.* 666, left: *Compton cuts to Johnson at slip, from where the ball bounced to wicketkeeper Tallon, who completed the catch*

1946–47
Melbourne, January 1, 2, 3, 4, 6, 7

THIRD TEST

Australia 365 (C.L. McCool 104, D.G. Bradman 79, S.G. Barnes 45) and 536 (A.R. Morris 155, R.R. Lindwall 100, D. Tallon 92, D.G. Bradman 49, C.L. McCool 43); England 351 (W.J. Edrich 89, C. Washbrook 62, N.W.D. Yardley 61, J.T. Ikin 48, B. Dooland 4 for 69) and 310 for 7 (C. Washbrook 112, N.W.D. Yardley 53*, L. Hutton 40). Match drawn.*

England, hampered by injuries to Voce and Edrich, did well to have Australia 192 for 6, but McCool, having narrowly missed a debut century, now reached a timely hundred, hitting powerfully off the back foot. England's innings owed everything to two stands: 147 by Washbrook and Edrich, and 113 for the sixth wicket by Ikin and Yardley. Thus, with little in it on first innings, England for the first time saw a glimmer of hope. But left-hander Arthur Morris, in his third Test, batted just over six hours, hitting only eight fours, and after his dismissal at 333 for 5, though two more wickets soon fell, Tallon and Lindwall drove vigorously and made 154 in a hectic 88 minutes. The wicketkeeper batted only 104 minutes, and Lindwall, who was already making an impression as a fast bowler, 113 minutes. Set an out-of-reach 551, England had a good start (138) from Washbrook and Hutton, but wickets fell steadily until Yardley and Bedser, with a delay for rain, saw the crisis through.

667: *Hassett c Hammond b Wright 12 – Hammond's 40th catch against Australia, eclipsing W.G. Grace's record*

668, left: *The England team presented at Melbourne to the Duke and Duchess of Gloucester. The Duke was then Governor-General.* 669, below, left: *Miller c Evans b Wright 33.* 670, centre: *Hutton caught for 40 by Bradman beyond the bowler's wicket.* 671, right: *Morris's 155 is ended as he is bowled by Bedser*

1946–47   FOURTH TEST
Adelaide, January 31, February 1, 3, 4, 5, 6

England 460 (D.C.S. Compton 147, L. Hutton 94, J. Hardstaff 67, C. Washbrook 65, R.R. Lindwall 4 for 52) and 340 for 8 dec (D.C.S. Compton 103*, L. Hutton 76, W.J. Edrich 46, E.R.H. Toshack 4 for 76); Australia 487 (K.R. Miller 141*, A.R. Morris 122, A.L. Hassett 78, I.W. Johnson 52) and 215 for 1 (A.R. Morris 124*, D.G. Bradman 56*). Match drawn.

Compton and Morris provided an unusual double in each making two hundreds in the match, though Compton's second was of greatest value, coming as it did when England needed time as well as runs. Hutton and Washbrook gave England starts of 137 in the first innings and 100 in the second, avoiding the short-pitched bowling of Lindwall and Miller and sometimes hooking it convincingly. Compton and Hardstaff added 118 in the first innings to make certain of a considerable total (Lindwall bowling the last three men in four balls) yet if England were disappointed that it was passed – especially after Bedser had bowled Bradman for nought – it was because of some dour batting by Hassett and Morris, and a brilliant fourth-morning innings by Miller. The climax came on the final morning, when Evans continued to defend for 95 minutes before making the first of his ten runs. Compton farmed the strike and handled all bowlers with relative ease. At the declaration they had added 85 in 2¼ hours. In the 3¼ hours remaining Morris made his third consecutive century against England. Hammond, in his last Test against Australia, made only 18 and 22.

672, above: *Bradman is bowled by a perfect ball from Bedser.* 673, below, left: *Compton beats the field and sets off for a run during his grand double effort at Adelaide.* 674, right: *Washbrook c Tallon b Dooland 65.* 675, bottom, left: *Arthur Morris, maker of two centuries for Australia.* 676, right: *Compton hooks*

1946–47
Sydney, February 28, March 1, 3, 4, 5

FIFTH TEST

England *280 (L. Hutton 122 ret.ill, W.J. Edrich 60, R.R. Lindwall 7 for 63) and 186 (D.C.S. Compton 76, C.L. McCool 5 for 44); Australia 253 (S.G. Barnes 71, A.R. Morris 57, D.V.P. Wright 7 for 105) and 214 for 5 (D.G. Bradman 63, A.L. Hassett 47). Australia won by 5 wickets.*

Hutton and Edrich resisted some hostile early bowling on a moist pitch to add 150 for the second wicket, and England were 237 for 6 at the end of the first day. Hutton had hit only eight fours and batted five hours, but after Saturday was washed out he was stricken by tonsilitis and could not resume on Monday, when England's innings faded away. Barnes and Morris gave Australia a start of 126, but Bedser dismissed them both and in a grand piece of bowling– not as fast as usual, but with characteristic spin – Doug Wright took 7 for 105 off 29 eight-ball overs. But Lindwall had Fishlock lbw first ball of England's second innings, and McCool with leg-breaks and googlies troubled everyone but Compton. Hutton was unable to bat; Ikin made a 'pair'. Thus Australia were set only 214. Yet two wickets fell for 51, and Bradman was missed off Wright by Edrich at slip when only two. The captain and Hassett added 98, and Miller's bold strokeplay saw Australia home that evening. Yardley, having taken over from Hammond, had cause for pride in his team's fighting play.

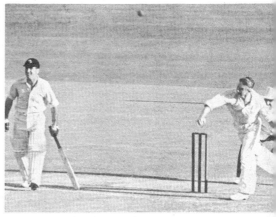

677, left: *Leg-spin/googly bowler Wright in action at Sydney. Barnes is the non-striker.* 678, above: *McCool flights one to Yardley, who was bowled by this ball. Evans backs up*

679: *Edrich at slip misses Bradman when he was two*

1948
Trent Bridge, June 10, 11, 12, 14, 15

England 165 (J.C. Laker 63, W.A. Johnston 5 for 36) and 441 (D.C.S. Compton 184, L. Hutton 74, T.G. Evans 50, J. Hardstaff 43, K.R. Miller 4 for 125, W.A. Johnston 4 for 147); Australia 509 (D.G. Bradman 138, A.L. Hassett 137, S.G. Barnes 62, R.R. Lindwall 42, J.C. Laker 4 for 138) and 98 for 2 (S.G. Barnes 64*). Australia won by 8 wickets.

Australia, led by Bradman, were to go through Britain undefeated, batting impressively into the lower depths of the order and using the 55-overs new-ball regulation to advantage, with Lindwall, Miller and Johnston a formidable pace trio. England began catastrophically, being 74 for 8 when Bedser linked with Laker to add 89. Lindwall had to retire with a strained groin, or the match might not have reached its fifth day. Laker took the first three Australian wickets, but Bradman and Hassett carefully added 120 for the fifth, and Hassett and Lindwall 107 for the eighth. Facing an enormous deficit, England, 39 for 2, were steadied by an even-time partnership of 111 by Hutton and Compton, and, weathering bad light, occasional drizzle and a lot of short-pitched bowling, Denis Compton went on to play a gallant innings lasting almost seven hours during which he had to play himself in nine times. He was out hit-wicket on the last morning in avoiding a bouncer from Miller, his 84-run stand with Evans having taken England into a small lead. The Trent Bridge crowd, remembering their own Larwood and Voce, often shouted at Miller as he struck England's batsmen or forced them to duck. Bradman now failed to score for only the fifth time against England, being caught by Hutton at backward short leg as in the first innings.

680, left: *On the fourth day Hutton and Compton resume their stand.* 681, left, below: *Hutton evades a Miller bouncer.* 682, below: *Miller's tumbling catch to dismiss Hardstaff off Johnston for 0*

683, left: *Compton's 184 is brought to a violent end as he falls into his stumps.* 684, above: *Bradman pulls during his Trent Bridge century*

1948   SECOND TEST
Lord's, June 24, 25, 26, 28, 29

Australia 350 (A.R. Morris 105, D. Tallon 53, A.L. Hassett 47, A.V. Bedser 4 for 100) and 460 for 7 dec (S.G. Barnes 141, D.G. Bradman 89, K.R. Miller 74, A.R. Morris 62); England 215 (D.C.S. Compton 53, N.W.D. Yardley 44, R.R. Lindwall 5 for 70) and 186 (E.R.H. Toshack 5 for 40). Australia won by 409 runs.

The 150th Test match between England and Australia bore the hallmark of Australia's all-round competence. England did well to have them 258 for 7 the first evening, but the tail held on, and Lindwall then breached England's innings in a fiery spell, though Miller was injured and did not bowl in the match. Lindwall's work was supplemented this time by the left-arm swing and pace-change of Johnston and the off-spin of Johnson. Barnes and Morris extended Australia's lead with an opening of 122, and Barnes and Bradman than put on 174. After Miller's virile innings the declaration came and, ironically, rain. England, facing an absurd victory demand of 596 (hastened by many dropped catches), now began the task on an enlivened pitch. In the circumstances there was no resisting Lindwall, Toshack and Johnston, especially once Compton was superbly caught by Miller at slip on the final morning.

685: *Bedser has Bradman caught by Hutton at backward square leg (out of picture) for 38*

686, above, left: *Edrich bowled middle stump for five by Lindwall at Lord's.* 687, right: *Scramble for souvenir stumps and bails at the end of the match*

1948
Old Trafford, July 8, 9, 10, 12, 13

THIRD TEST

England 363 (D.C.S. Compton 145*, R.R. Lindwall 4 for 99) and 174 for 3 dec (C. Washbrook 85*, W.J. Edrich 53); Australia 221 (A.R. Morris 51, A.V. Bedser 4 for 81) and 92 for 1 (A.R. Morris 54*). Match drawn.

Compton was again the hero in a match which was as heartening to England as it was frustrating, as rain took the fourth day and restricted the last. England were 32 for 2 when Compton had to leave the field for repairs after edging a ball from Lindwall into his brow. Stitched and with a little internal fortification, he returned at 119 for 5 and was 64 that evening. His eighth-wicket stand with Bedser was worth 121 and he batted in all for 5½ hours, having been dropped three times by Tallon behind the stumps. Towards the end of England's innings Barnes at silly mid-on was seriously injured when hit by a pull-drive by Pollard, and Australia, disrupted by his absence at the start of the innings, began badly and for once never recovered, Bedser and Pollard doing the damage with the new ball and its later replacement on an overcast day. Hutton had been dropped from the side, but his substitute, Emmett, failed a second time, and it was left to Washbrook and Edrich to build on England's lead. At 174 for 3 England nurtured daring hopes. Then came the rain.

688, left: *Compton is hit in the face by a Lindwall bouncer, which forced him to retire for treatment. Miller goes to his aid.* 689, above: *George Emmett, Hutton's replacement, is caught by Barnes off Lindwall*

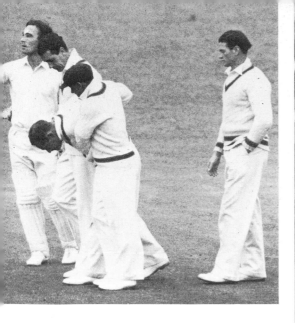

690, above: *Barnes, having been struck while fielding at close mid-on, is helped from the field by Toshack and Bradman.*
691, right: *The battered Compton raises his bat upon reaching his hundred. Tallon joins the applause*

1948
Headingley, July 22, 23, 24, 26, 27

FOURTH TEST

England 496 *(C. Washbrook 143, W.J. Edrich 111, L. Hutton 81, A.V. Bedser 79) and 365 for 8 dec (D.C.S. Compton 66, C. Washbrook 65, L. Hutton 57, W.J. Edrich 54, T.G. Evans 47*, W.A. Johnston 4 for 95); Australia 458 (R.N. Harvey 112, S.J.E. Loxton 93, R.R. Lindwall 77, K.R. Miller 58) and 404 for 3 (A.R. Morris 182, D.G. Bradman 173*). Australia won by 7 wickets.*

At one point 423 for 2, England had cause to feel disappointment at being all out for 496. Hutton, returning triumphantly, and Washbrook began with 168, following it with 129 in the second innings, and Bedser, sent in as nightwatchman, excelled himself in adding 155 with Edrich. Australia began shakily, but Harvey, aged 19 and in his first Test against England, put on 121 in 95 minutes with Miller in a whirl of contemptuous strokes and 105 with Loxton almost as quickly. Loxton hit five sixes, and Lindwall saw to it that Australia came close to England's considerable total. Yardley's team made steady progress towards a big lead, and he declared after five minutes on the last morning, hoping the roller would break up the surface of the pitch. Australia needed 404 in 344 minutes. Their victory has only once been emulated – by India, who made 406 for 4 to beat West Indies in Trinidad in 1976. Although the pitch took spin, England had to depend on Compton for the left-arm variety, and as stumping and catching chances were missed England became disheartened at the same rate as the batsmen raced to seize their unique prize. Morris and Bradman hit 301 for the second wicket in only 217 minutes, the left-hander having 33 boundaries in his 182 and Bradman 29 fours in his unbeaten 173 (which gave him 963 runs, average 192, in four Tests at Leeds). It was the Australian captain's 19th and final century against England, and took his aggregate to 5028 – still unapproached.

692, above, left: *Harvey swings a ball to leg during his debut century.* 693, right: *Bradman and Morris resume their matchwinning partnership.* 694, below, left: *Bradman doubles up after being hit by a ball from Bedser.* 695, right: *Crapp at slip misses Bradman – one of several English fielding lapses as Australia raced to an historic victory at Leeds*

1948
The Oval, August 14, 16, 17, 18

England 52 (*R.R. Lindwall 6 for 20*) and 188 (*L. Hutton 64, W.A. Johnston 4 for 40*); Australia 389 (*A.R. Morris 196, S.G. Barnes 61, W.E. Hollies 5 for 131*). Australia won by an innings and 149 runs.

Australia hammered home their superiority to finish victors 4–0 after a match remembered for England's batting humiliation and Bradman's final Test innings. Batting first on a sodden pitch, England were 29 for 4 at lunch and all out in under 2½ hours. Hutton stood firm among the wreckage and was last out, caught down the leg side by Tallon off the insatiable Lindwall for 30. That evening Australia were already 101 ahead for the loss of two wickets. Barnes and Morris opened with 117, then Bradman was bowled second ball for nought by a googly from Hollies. Hassett and Morris added 109, but it was left to the latter, who batted 6¾ hours, to carry his side to a truly decisive lead as he made his sixth century against England. Once more Len Hutton stood alone, batting 4¼ hours with a variety of partners, some of whom it was generally felt should never have been selected. Miller, bowling an exotic range of balls, got him in the end.

696: *Compton hooks Lindwall and is about to be caught by Morris (extreme right)*

697, left: *Hutton (30) is caught by Tallon down the leg side off Lindwall and England are all out for 52.* 698, above: *Bradman's Test batting career ends, bowled by Hollies for 0.* 699, right: *Miller prostrate after being stumped off Hollies for five*

1950–51
Brisbane, December 1, 2, 4, 5

FIRST TEST

Australia 228 (R.N. Harvey 74, R.R. Lindwall 41, A.V. Bedser 4 for 45) and 32 for 7 dec (T.E. Bailey 4 for 22); England 68 for 7 dec (W.A. Johnston 5 for 35) and 122 (L. Hutton 62*, J.B. Iverson 4 for 43). Australia won by 70 runs.

Hutton (8 not out and 62 not out) might have won this match for England had he not batted as low as No. 6 in the first innings and No. 8 in the second – on both occasions with the idea of utilising him when the rain-damaged pitch improved. On the last day it was heartbreakingly obvious to England that he needed only one worthwhile partner and victory would be theirs. Australia were bowled out on a good pitch on the first day, but heavy rain washed out the second and on the third batting became an evil joke as the ball leapt and turned. Twenty wickets fell that day for 130, England having no answer in the conditions to Johnston and Miller, and Australia also declaring after being overwhelmed by medium-pacers Bedser and Bailey. Moroney failed to score in either innings. By close of play England, set 193, were 30 for 6, with Hutton held back. The pitch had hardened on the fourth day, but Hutton, batting classically, was doomed to see his remaining partners all beaten. Freddie Brown, his captain, was the only other batsman to reach double-figures.

700, left: *Morris is well caught by Bailey and Australia are 0 for two wickets.* 701, above: *Hutton, England's lone batting hero, lofts Miller.* 702, below, left: *An extraordinary scoreline.* 703, below, right: *Evans catches and stumps Harvey off Bedser*

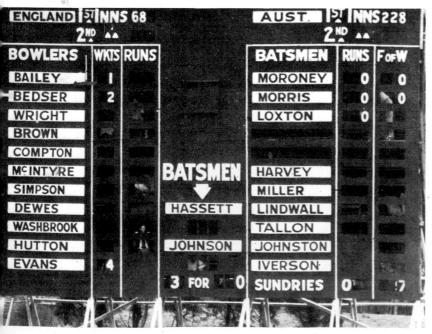

704: *Compton c Loxton b Johnston first ball – the start of a grim run of failures for him in the series*

1950–51
Melbourne, December 22, 23, 26, 27

SECOND TEST

Australia 194 (A.L. Hassett 52, R.N. Harvey 42, A.V. Bedser 4 for 37, T.E. Bailey 4 for 40) and 181 (K.A. Archer 46, F.R. Brown 4 for 26); England 197 (F.R. Brown 62, T.G. Evans 49, J.B. Iverson 4 for 37) and 150 (L. Hutton 40, W.A. Johnston 4 for 26). Australia won by 28 runs.

England showed again, with a smaller margin of defeat, that there was not a great deal between the sides. The fast-medium bowlers dismissed Australia on the opening day, but England, without Compton, seemed to have lost their chance at 61 for 6, Brian Close, at 19 years 301 days the youngest ever to play for England against Australia, failing to score. Brown, with Bailey's help, then more than doubled the score, and Evans followed with a bright 49. Iverson, the large, 35-year-old 'mystery' finger-spinner, did most damage, including the removal of Hutton (now batting at No. 4), controversially given out caught off bat and pad. A two-day break for Sunday and Christmas Day was followed by England's fightback. Bedser and Bailey again bowled admirably and Brown took four middle-order wickets, leaving England in need of 179. They were 28 that evening for the loss of Washbrook and Bailey. Hutton, upon whom everything once more depended, batted with consummate skill, but the combination of Johnston, Lindwall and Iverson was too much for the tourists.

705: *Harvey is run out by a direct hit from Washbrook (out of picture)*

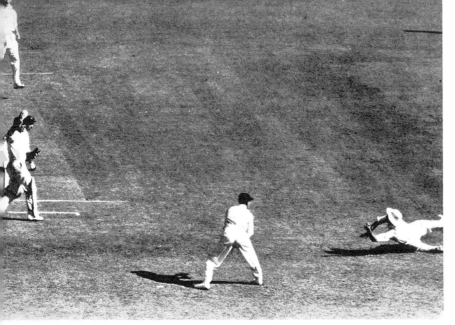

706, above, left: Bailey's brilliant full-length catch to dismiss Hassett off Brown at Melbourne. 707, above, right: Washbrook deceived and bowled by Iverson, whose grip is shown (inset). 708, left: Evans prepares to catch Johnson from out of the sun – but he was to drop it. 709, right: Hassett b Bailey 52

1950–51
Sydney, January 5, 6, 8, 9

THIRD TEST

England 290 (F.R. Brown 79, L. Hutton 62, R.T. Simpson 49, K.R. Miller 4 for 37) and 123 (J.B. Iverson 6 for 27); Australia 426 (K.R. Miller 145*, I.W. Johnson 77, A.L. Hassett 70, K.A. Archer 48, A.V. Bedser 4 for 107, F.R. Brown 4 for 153). Australia won by an innings and 13 runs.

Injuries to Bailey (thumb broken by a ball from Lindwall) and Wright (torn tendon as he was run out) left England with three main bowlers, and Bedser, 40-year-old Brown and Warr toiled through 123 eight-ball overs to take 8 for 402 between them. Brown had saved England's first innings, driving bravely, though Hutton (restored to opening) and Simpson had put on a promising 94 for the second wicket. Keith Miller, unusually circumspect, made 96 not out in over 4½ hours on the third day, and batted almost six hours altogether, hitting only six fours and a six (an off-drive off Warr). Johnson helped him add 150 for the seventh wicket. Miller thus had exerted a huge influence on the match so far, having taken three key wickets and a dazzling slip catch to dismiss Washbrook. Now Iverson, the spinner, took over, bemusing most of England's batsmen and hitting the pads repeatedly. Australia found themselves winners of the rubber with an apparent ease that surprised many who recalled the close contests at Brisbane and Melbourne.

710, above: *Brown drives Johnson during his stand with Bailey.* 711, top, right: *Bailey's thumb is broken by a ball from Lindwall. Ken Archer at slip.* 712, right: *Miller dives instinctively to catch Washbrook off Johnson*

713, left: *The perfect square-cut: Miller during his century.*
714, above: *Tallon makes a miraculous catch after the ball has rebounded from Johnson at slip, dismissing Hutton*

1950–51
Adelaide, February 2, 3, 5, 6, 7, 8

FOURTH TEST

Australia 371 (A.R. Morris 206, K.R. Miller 44, A.L. Hassett 43, R.N. Harvey 43, D.V.P. Wright 4 for 99) and 403 for 8 dec (J.W. Burke 101*, K.R. Miller 99, R.N. Harvey 68); England 272 (L. Hutton 156*) and 228 (R.T. Simpson 61, L. Hutton 45, D.S. Sheppard 41, W.A. Johnston 4 for 73). Australia won by 274 runs.

Morris, first in and last out, batted 7¾ hours for his highest Test score. He was shielded by Hassett from Bedser during the early stages after Archer had gone without a run posted, and fought his way back to form after five successive Test failures. He had stands of 95 with Hassett and 110 with Harvey, and was eventually bowled when swinging at Tattersall (who, with Statham, had been flown out to assist an injury-ridden MCC side). England's innings owed everything to Hutton. The next-highest score was Simpson's 29. Hutton became the second England player to carry his bat through the innings against Australia, and his exhibition was almost flawless. He was missed twice and stroked 11 fours in his 370 minutes. He was close to exhaustion at the end, and yet he had to field, being involved in play for the first 23¼ hours of play. Miller added 99 with Harvey for the fourth wicket and 87 with Burke before chopping his stumps with his bat just as a googly from Wright hit them when he was one short of his century. Burke, only 20 and playing his first Test, proceeded to his hundred before Hassett closed, leaving England 503 to make to win. Hutton and Washbrook started with 74, but Compton's wretched run of cheap dismissals persisted (he averaged 7.57 in eight innings), and after Simpson became Johnston's fourth victim on the last morning, Miller and Johnson took the last five wickets for seven runs, Brown not batting because of injuries sustained in a car crash.

715, above, left: *Morris out at last: b Tattersall 206.* 716, right: *Burke b Tattersall 12 – his first Test innings. He made a century in his second.* 717, below, left: *A tired Hutton leaves the field having carried his bat through the innings.* 718, right: *The Press box, Adelaide, during the fourth Test*

1950–51
FIFTH TEST
Melbourne, February 23, 24, 26, 27, 28

Australia 217 (A.L. Hassett 92, A.R. Morris 50, A.V. Bedser 5 for 46, F.R. Brown 5 for 49) and 197 (G.B. Hole 63, R.N. Harvey 52, A.L. Hassett 48, A.V. Bedser 5 for 59); England 320 (R.T. Simpson 156*, L. Hutton 79, K.R. Miller 4 for 76) and 95 for 2 (L. Hutton 60*). England won by 8 wickets.

After an interval of 12½ years and in their 15th Test since the war England at last knew what it felt like to beat Australia. Losing his fourth toss of the series, Brown must have had visions of emulating J.W.H.T. Douglas 30 years earlier in losing 5–0, for Australia were 111 for one 20 minutes before tea on the first day. Brown, bowling medium-pace, then put himself on again and took the wickets of Morris, Harvey and Miller while 12 runs were added. Hutton caught Hassett beautifully one-handed at slip, and Bedser used the second new ball to advantage, so that Australia were humbed as in the first two Tests. This time England followed up, though their lead was not as large as at one time seemed likely. Reg Simpson batted 338 minutes in a memorable display of footwork and strokeplay. He added 131 with Hutton for the second wicket, after which there was a collapse so resounding before Lindwall and Miller that at 246 for 9 Simpson was still eight short of his century. Tattersall then stayed with him while 74 precious runs were made. Simpson reached his hundred on his 31st birthday. Australia lost four wickets in erasing the deficit, Wright removing the dangerous Harvey and later bowling Hassett with a perfect leg-break. Hole, just 20, batted well in his first Test and helped set England a modest target, which was attained quite nervelessly. Alec Bedser took his haul of wickets for the series to 30, and Hutton averaged 88.83.

719, above, left: *Simpson elegantly on-drives Iverson during his century.* 720, right: *Hassett bowled by a perfect leg-break from Wright; and England glimpse victory*

721, left: *Hassett and Brown toast a good-tempered series.* 722, right: *Miller c & b Brown, for the second time in the match*

1953
Trent Bridge, June 11, 12, 13, 15, 16

Australia 249 (A.L. Hassett 115, A.R. Morris 67, K.R. Miller 55, A.V. Bedser 7 for 55) and 123 (A.R. Morris 60, A.V. Bedser 7 for 44); England 144 (L. Hutton 43, R.R. Lindwall 5 for 57) and 120 for 1 (L. Hutton 60). Match drawn.*

Fine fast-medium bowling by Bedser and a staunch century by Hassett were the features of a grimly-contested match in generally poor light and in damp conditions. The only substantial partnerships until the anticlimactic final stages were the 122 put on by Hassett and Morris for the second wicket on the opening day and 109 for the fourth by Miller and his captain. Hassett needed 5¾ hours to reach his hundred. With the third new ball Bedser and Bailey took the last six wickets for five runs. Lindwall had England 17 for 3, but Hutton and Graveney then added 59. Wickets then fell steadily to Lindwall, top-spinner Hill and left-arm swinger Davidson. Bedser routed Australia on the third day, Morris making his 60 out of 81, but a washed-out fourth day and a delayed start on the last meant England could only play out time.

723, above, left: *Hassett is bowled by Bedser for 115. The fieldsmen's expressions give some idea of how much the ball deviated.* 724, right: *Harvey cracks Bedser to leg only to be caught by Graveney.* 725, below, left: *Davidson becomes another of Bedser's 14 wickets.* 726, right: *Bedser comes in, England's 7 for 55 first-innings hero. Even better was to follow*

1953
Lord's, June 25, 26, 27, 29, 30

SECOND TEST

Australia 346 (A.L. Hassett 104, A.K. Davidson 76, R.N. Harvey 59, A.V. Bedser 5 for 105, J.H. Wardle 4 for 77) and 368 (K.R. Miller 109, A.R. Morris 89, R.R. Lindwall 50, G.B. Hole 47, F.R. Brown 4 for 82); England 372 (L. Hutton 145, T.W. Graveney 78, D.C.S. Compton 57, R.R. Lindwall 5 for 66) and 282 for 7 (W. Watson 109, T.E. Bailey 71). Match drawn.

In one of the most celebrated of matchsaving stands, Watson and Bailey came together on the final day with England 73 for 4 – 270 runs from victory – and nearly five hours remaining. They withstood the whole range of Australian bowling until Watson, in his first Test against Australia, was caught at slip at 5.50 pm. He had batted 5¾ hours, and took 201 minutes over his second fifty. Bailey soon followed, having existed for 4¼ hours. A bonny 28 from Brown (chairman of selectors this year) averted any last-minute reversal after the sterling rescue. The captains, Hassett and Hutton, made worthy centuries, Hutton's especially so after he had missed several catches, and Davidson's attacking 76 saw Australia to a solid total. Graveney supported Hutton in a second-wicket stand of 168 but was bowled by Lindwall first thing on the third morning. Compton then put on 102 with Hutton, only their second (and last) century stand together against Australia. Morris and Miller set up Australia's second innings, adding 165 for the second wicket. Miller batted almost five hours. Lindwall made England's task appreciably more difficult with a rousing half-century – and by getting Hutton and Kenyon cheaply that evening. The final day was a story of patience and determination on one side and frustration on the other.

727, above, left: *Hutton, with an injured hand, going for runs.* 728, right: *Watson hits to leg.* 729, below, left: *Graveney c Langley b Johnston 2. England in dire second-innings trouble.* 730, right: *Bailey makes a rare attacking stroke*

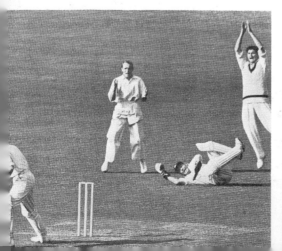

1953
THIRD TEST
Old Trafford, July 9, 10, 11, 13, 14

Australia 318 (R.N. Harvey 122, G.B. Hole 66, J.H. de Courcy 41, A.V. Bedser 5 for 115) and 35 for 8 (J.H. Wardle 4 for 7); England 276 (L. Hutton 66, D.C.S. Compton 45, T.G. Evans 44*). Match drawn.

A little less rain could have made this match a thriller. As it was, too much time – including the whole of Monday – was lost, and the pitch, though sometimes spiteful, was usually too soggy to put batsmen in peril. Harvey's century took four hours, he and Hole, who added 173 for the fourth wicket, batting on each of three days. Harvey was dropped by Evans at four and eventually caught by the wicketkeeper on the leg side standing up to Bedser. England's main resistance came in a 94-run stand by Hutton and Compton, and it was left to Simpson and Bailey, in a seventh-wicket stand of 60, to avert the follow-on on the final day. Australia then, perhaps with less application than might have been expected, were somewhat humiliated by Wardle, Bedser and Laker.

731, above, left: *Hole and Harvey resume their large stand.* 732, right: *Harvey c Evans b Bedser 122.* 733, below, left: *Archer's hostile field to Wardle.* 734, right: *de Courcy stumped during Australia's last-day debacle*

1953
Headingley, July 23, 24, 25, 27, 28

FOURTH TEST

England 167 (T.W. Graveney 55, R.R. Lindwall 5 for 54) and 275 (W.J. Edrich 64, D.C.S. Compton 61, J.C. Laker 48, K.R. Miller 4 for 63); Australia 266 (R.N. Harvey 71, G.B. Hole 53, A.V. Bedser 6 for 95) and 147 for 4. Match drawn.

Australia were frustrated – by all manner of means – by Trevor Bailey, who held an end for 262 minutes for his 38 in England's second innings and then bowled, between time-consuming adjustments, down the leg side to a negative field when Australia looked like hitting their way to the 177 required for victory in 115 minutes. Once more time was lost for rain, and on an opening day cut by 25 minutes England reached a laboured 142 for 7, Hutton having been bowled second ball by Lindwall. Australia's main stand, 84, came from Harvey and Hole. Always struggling, England managed, after wiping off the arrears, to extend their lead against a shrunken timespan remaining. Laker's 48 at No. 9 was vital.

735, above, left: *A shock for the Yorkshire crowd – Hutton b Lindwall 0.* 736, right: *Graveney well caught by Benaud for 55.* 737, below, left: *Morris puts Bedser past Evans.* 738, right: *Langley, having moved the wrong way, misses Watson off Archer*

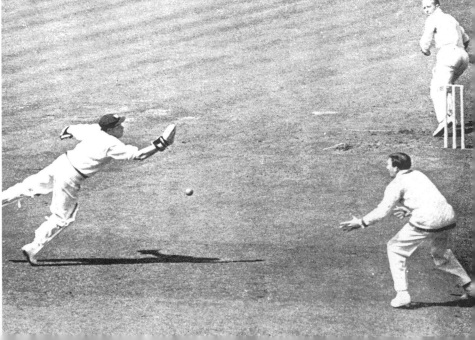

1953
The Oval, August 15, 17, 18, 19

FIFTH TEST

Australia 275 (R.R. Lindwall 62, A.L. Hassett 53, F.S. Trueman 4 for 86) and 162 (R.G. Archer 49, G.A.R. Lock 5 for 45, J.C. Laker 4 for 75); England 306 (L. Hutton 82, T.E. Bailey 64, R.R. Lindwall 4 for 70) and 132 for 2 (W.J. Edrich 55*). England won by 8 wickets.

England's cricket team, in the eventful year of achievement which accompanied the Coronation, won back the Ashes 19 years after Woodfull's 1934 Australians had appropriated them. Hassett beat Hutton at the toss for the fifth time, and though Morris soon fell to Bedser (for the 18th time in the 20 post-war Tests) and Miller scored only a single, a solid score seemed in prospect. Fred Trueman, in his initial Australian Test, finding life in a shower-freshened pitch, then had Harvey, de Courcy and Hole caught, and only a fine hard-driving innings from Lindwall saved Australia's face. Bedser finished with 39 wickets in the series – a record. Hutton, wearing his 1938 cap (which fell inches from the stumps as he avoided a short ball from Lindwall), put on 100 for the second wicket with Peter May (39), also in his first Australian Test, but the middle of the innings then fell away, and the ever-reliable and obdurate Bailey had to steer it up to, and – during a last-wicket stand of 44 with Bedser on the third morning – beyond Australia's total. A sensational afternoon ensued. On a responsive pitch Lock, left-arm spin, and Laker, off-breaks, had Australia reeling from 59 for one to 85 for 6. Archer and Davidson, one 19, the other 24, then endeavoured to hit their way out of trouble, and added 50; but Lock got them both, and soon England were faced with the task of making 132 for an emotional victory. Hutton, England's first appointed professional captain, was run out for 17 that evening, but May stayed for 64 runs with Edrich, and Compton, on the fourth afternoon, swung Morris for four to win the match and release a flood of jubilation.

739, above: *Trueman, England's fast bowling discovery, bowls to Hole with an aggressive field more typical of the Australians.* 740, left: *May, another new talent, edges past Miller*

741, above, left: *Hutton loses his composure and his cap as Lindwall digs one in.* 742, above, right: *Compton hits to the leg boundary and the Ashes are England's at last.* 743, right: *Bedser catches Ron Archer to pass Tate's record 38 wickets in an England-Australia series.* 744, below: *Len Hutton shares the pleasure of the crowd, whose enthusiasm recalled that at The Oval 27 years before*

1954–55
Brisbane, November 26, 27, 29, 30, December 1

Australia *601 for 8 dec (R.N. Harvey 162, A.R. Morris 153, R.R. Lindwall 64*, G.B. Hole 57, K.R. Miller 49); England 190 (T.E. Bailey 88, M.C. Cowdrey 40) and 257 (W.J. Edrich 88, P.B.H. May 44). Australia won by an innings and 154 runs.*

Hutton put Australia in and soon had cause to regret it as his all-speed attack failed to make much impression on a lifeless pitch. Although chances were missed in the field, Australia always seemed certain to compile a massive total, and Morris and Harvey batted with more assurance the longer they were in. The two left-handers put on 202 for the third wicket, Morris, in his final hundred against England, batting seven hours, and Harvey, who went on to add 131 with Hole, batting 380 minutes. England's woes were complete when Compton broke a finger on the pickets, and had to bat last man and virtually ineffectively. Evans was missed behind the stumps. England began horrendously, losing four for 25. Cowdrey, in his first Test match, then batted steadily, and Bailey was characteristically defiant. Edrich and May, in a stand of 124, offered the only prolonged resistance in the follow-on, and the crushing Australian victory seemed to signal that their fast attack was still a force to be feared and that the side was capable of enough high scores to win the series. Few would have been prepared to believe that there would not be another century for Australia against England for four years and 11 Tests. This was to be the final appearance against Australia of Bedser, who was discarded under Hutton's plan to depend on pace and a sedate over rate.

745, above, left: *Miller picks up a rare half-volley from Bedser and lands it for six over long-on.* 746, right: *Lindwall traps May lbw.* 747, left: *A narrow escape for Harvey as he plays Tyson just wide of Andrew*

748: *Edrich bowled for 88 by a long-hop from Bill Johnston*

1954–55
Sydney, December 17, 18, 20, 21, 22

SECOND TEST

England *154 and 296 (P.B.H. May 104, M.C. Cowdrey 54); Australia 228 (R.G. Archer 49, J.W. Burke 44, F.H. Tyson 4 for 45, T.E. Bailey 4 for 59) and 184 (R.N. Harvey 92*, F.H. Tyson 6 for 85). England won by 38 runs.*

Tyson, who cut down his run after Brisbane (where he took one for 160), bowled very fast for his ten wickets in the match, 'inspired' in the second innings after having been knocked out by a Lindwall bouncer that cracked him on the back of the head. Morris, deputising for injured Ian Johnson, put England in on a sultry morning, and Lindwall, Archer, Davidson and Johnston had them 111 for 9 before Wardle and Statham clouted 43 in the biggest stand of the innings. Bailey had early successes, and Tyson's yorkers and flyers did the rest, Statham supporting well. At 55 for 3 in their second innings England seemed doomed. Then May and Cowdrey batted very sensibly until 171. May, on the fourth morning, reached his first hundred against Australia, and batted five hours altogether. Once more there was a useful last-wicket stand, this time of 46 between Statham and Appleyard. Set 223, Australia were 72 for 2 that evening. On the final day, however, Tyson shocked his way through the batting line-up, only the masterful Harvey being able to cope. Johnston delayed the finish with a stand of 39, but the aching express bowler got him in the end.

749: *Tyson is helped from the field after being knocked cold by a Lindwall bouncer. He was never the same again – as Australia's batsmen soon discovered*

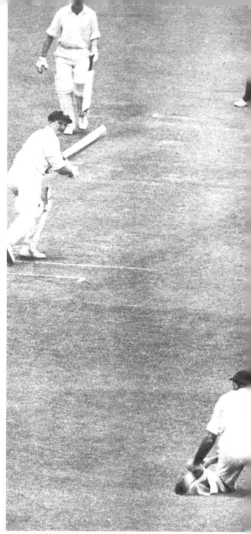

750, above, left: *Bailey b Lindwall 0 – the end of 35 minutes of concentration and torture at Sydney.* 751, right: *Favell caught low down at slip by Graveney for 26.* 752, centre: *May drives Johnston during his important stand with Cowdrey.* 753, bottom: *Evans catches Johnston off Tyson and the sides go one-all to Melbourne*

1954–55
Melbourne, December 31, January 1, 3, 4, 5

THIRD TEST

England *191 (M.C. Cowdrey 102, R.G. Archer 4 for 33) and 279 (P.B.H. May 91, L. Hutton 42, W.A. Johnston 5 for 25); Australia 231 (L.V. Maddocks 47, J.B. Statham 5 for 60) and 111 (F.H. Tyson 7 for 27).* England won by 128 runs.

Australia faced the final day in a similar position to that at Sydney: 165 from victory with eight wickets in hand. Tyson then demolished the innings on a pitch of uneven bounce, taking 6 for 16 in 51 balls, bowling at devilish speed, with Statham probing from the other end. The collapse began when Evans made a grand diving leg-side catch from Harvey – the first of eight wickets to fall for 34 runs. England were in deep trouble on the opening day, when Miller used a damp pitch well in returning figures of 9-8-5-3 before lunch. Cowdrey, just 22, then put together an immaculate century in four hours. Though stuck on 56 for 40 minutes, he showed a fine temperament in a testing situation. England had their opponents 92 for 5 on an improved pitch (which was apparently illegally watered on the rest day), but the grip was relaxed, and Australia moved into the lead. May held the second innings together with an innings of some power, and Bailey excelled himself with 24 not out in 163 minutes.

754, above, left: *Neil Harvey falls to a glorious leg-side catch by Evans, and the Australian collapse begins.*
755, right: *Benaud becomes the third of Tyson's seven victims*

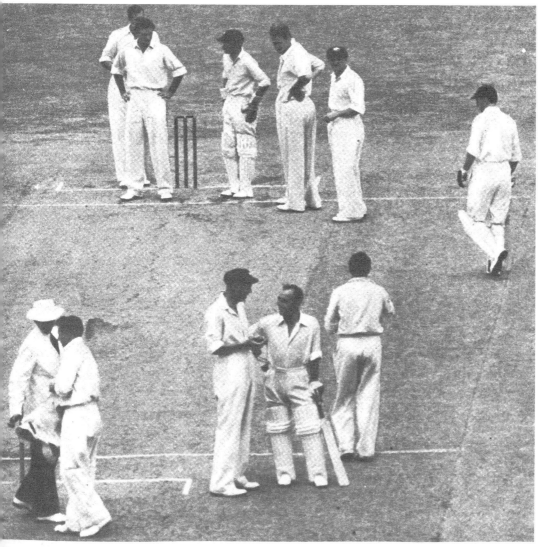

756, above: *Cowdrey's admirable century innings ends as a ball from Johnson turns a great distance to bowl him.* 757, left: *The Australian fielders examine the Melbourne pitch, which mysteriously changed its nature overnight*

1954–55
Adelaide, January 28, 29, 31, February 1, 2

FOURTH TEST

Australia 323 (L.V. Maddocks 69, C.C. McDonald 48, K.R. Miller 44, I.W. Johnson 41) and 111; England 341 (L. Hutton 80, M.C. Cowdrey 79, D.C.S. Compton 44, R. Benaud 4 for 120) and 97 for 5. England won by 5 wickets.

Set only 94 to retain the Ashes, England were dazed by Miller, who had them 18 for 3 in a fiery spell of new-ball bowling. At 49 he tumbled and caught May at cover, and it took the resolution of Compton and Bailey to see their side to 90 before the latter was out. Australia were ailing at 229 for 8 on the second day when Maddocks, Langley's replacement as wicketkeeper, put on 92 with Johnson. Tyson, Bailey and Appleyard took three wickets apiece. Hutton and Cowdrey added 99 in high heat, and there was solid batting from the middle order, and when Morris, Burke and Harvey fell to Appleyard's medium-pace off-spin on the fourth evening it looked ominous for Australia. Yet it was Statham and Tyson who did the damage next day, and once more Australia could muster no more than the miserable, mystical 111.

758, above, left: *Maddocks sweeps Wardle during his valuable 69.* 759, right: *Archer snaps up a catch from May off Benaud.* 760, below, left: *Davidson at short leg holds a reflex catch to dismiss Hutton for 80.* 761, right: *After a fright or two England have held the Ashes – Compton and Evans the batsmen in at the kill*

1954–55
FIFTH TEST
Sydney, February 25, 26, 28, March 1, 2, 3

England 371 for 7 dec (T.W. Graveney 111, D.C.S. Compton 84, P.B.H. May 79, T.E. Bailey 72); Australia 221 (C.C. McDonald 72, J.H. Wardle 5 for 79) and 118 for 6. Match drawn.

Sydney was such a wet city that play was not possible until 2 pm on the fourth day, when England batted after losing the toss. Hutton's final Test innings against Australia ended with his fourth ball, Burge at leg slip touching the ball for the first time in a Test. Graveney and May then put on 182 in 161 minutes, both batsmen, tall and classical in their strokeplay, batting delightfully. Graveney reached his century with four fours off an over by Miller, and thus became the 100th player to score a hundred in these Tests (51 for England). Cowdrey, recently down with tonsilitis, was out first ball, but after May's dismissal Compton and Bailey – slowly at first – added 134. Bailey – voluntarily – became Lindwall's 100th wicket in these Tests, and the closure was immediately applied. Australia were 82 for 2 that evening, and the draw seemed certain. It became less of a certainty next day when Australia were bemused by Wardle's flighted wrist-spin, only McDonald enduring for long. With one run needed to avoid the follow-on, Johnson was run out, and in the two hours left Wardle spun out three more Australians, and Hutton bowled Benaud with the last ball.

762, above, left: *Jack Ryder, now 65 and an Australian selector, joins in the pre-match practice at Sydney.* 763, right: *Lindwall bowls Bailey – his 100th England wicket.* 764, below, left: *Johnson is run out, and for the sake of one run Australia are obliged to follow on.* 765, right: *An oddity: Graveney takes a wicket – the prized one of McDonald, caught behind by Evans for 37*

1956
Trent Bridge, June 7, 8, 9, 11, 12

England *217 for 8 dec (P.E. Richardson 81, P.B.H. May 73, K.R. Miller 4 for 69) and 188 for 3 dec (M.C. Cowdrey 81, P.E. Richardson 73); Australia 148 (R.N. Harvey 64, J.C. Laker 4 for 58) and 120 for 3 (J.W. Burke 58*).* Match drawn.

Australia, having beaten only the Universities and lost to Surrey (the first defeat by a county since 1912), were handicapped in this match by injuries to Lindwall and Davidson. Yet England were missing Hutton (retired), Compton (knee trouble), and Tyson, Trueman and Statham (all injured). After a slow, shortened first day, and the second rained off, Richardson and May continued their partnership to 108, but Archer and Miller then cut away the middle. Australia were 19 for 2 that evening, and Laker, Lock and Appleyard had them out on a drying wicket by mid-afternoon of the fourth day. Richardson and Cowdrey made 129 that evening, and carried their opening stand to 151 on the last day, Richardson, a left-hander, completing a worthy double in his first Test. The declaration left Australia 258 to win in four hours – a prospect ruled out when three wickets fell for 41. Burke and Burge played out the last two hours.

766, right: *With the England total only six, Richardson falls after a call from Cowdrey and a run-out seems certain. The partners survived to put on 151.* 767, below, left: *Burke dropped by Watson off Lock.* 768, right: *May c Langley b Miller 73*

1956
Lord's, June 21, 22, 23, 25, 26

SECOND TEST

Australia 285 (C.C. McDonald 78, J.W. Burke 65) and 257 (R. Benaud 97, F.S. Trueman 5 for 90, T.E. Bailey 4 for 64); England 171 (P.B.H. May 63, K.R. Miller 5 for 72) and 186 (P.B.H. May 53, K.R. Miller 5 for 80, R.G. Archer 4 for 71). Australia won by 185 runs.

A good team performance by Australia brought well-earned victory. Miller, now 36, bowled 70.1 overs at a brisk speed to take ten wickets; Langley had a world Test record haul of nine dismissals (eight catches, one stumping); McDonald and Burke began with 137 in the solid, old-fashioned tradition; Benaud took a blinding catch at gully to dismiss Cowdrey, and put Australia in command with a hard-hit 97; Mackay (30), in his first Test, batted 160 minutes for 38 and 265 minutes for 31. May, though having missed several catches, showed himself to be as good a batsman as anyone in the world, Trueman as hostile a bowler, and Bailey still a brilliant close catcher. Evans made seven dismissals, so that 16 wickets fell to the wicketkeepers: indeed, Richardson's eight innings in the series were all terminated by Langley or his deputy Maddocks.

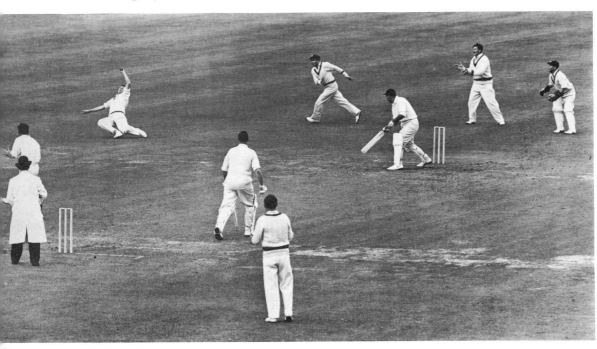

769, above, left: *Benaud's extraordinary left-hand 'self-preservation' catch in the gully to dismiss Cowdrey.* 770, right: *Benaud hooks during his 97.* 771, below, left: *May square-cuts powerfully during the Lord's Test; Langley wicketkeeper, Archer slip.* 772, right: *Miller, having taken a bail from umpire Lee's pocket, hurls it to some youngsters as he leaves the field, having taken 10 for 152 in the match*

1956
Headingley, July 12, 13, 14, 16, 17

THIRD TEST

England 325 (P.B.H. May 101, C. Washbrook 98, T.G. Evans 40); Australia 143 (J.W. Burke 41, K.R. Miller 41, J.C. Laker 5 for 58, G.A.R. Lock 4 for 41) and 140 (R.N. Harvey 69, J.C. Laker 6 for 55). England won by an innings and 42 runs.

Washbrook, now 41, was recalled by England, and, with his captain, turned the match – and the series – around. He and May took their side from the plight of 17 for 3, after Archer had used the seam alarmingly well, to 204 before May fell to a grand fine-leg catch by Lindwall. Washbrook was lbw to Benaud, but Bailey and Evans took the score past 300, and after Trueman had taken the valuable wicket of McDonald early in each innings, Laker and Lock, taking the other 18 wickets, dispatched Australia in highly professional manner, though Harvey (4½ hours) and Miller (26 in 2¼ hours) went down fighting. In depressing weather, and after having won a significant toss, England thus won against Australia for the first time at Leeds.

773, right: *May and Washbrook resume their matchsaving stand at Headingley.* 774, below, left: *Trueman knocks back McDonald's middle stump.* 775, right: *Harvey c Trueman b Lock 11, Australia's first innings*

1956
Old Trafford, July 26, 27, 28, 30, 31

FOURTH TEST

England 459 (D.S. Sheppard 113, P.E. Richardson 104, M.C. Cowdrey 80, T.G. Evans 47, P.B.H. May 43, I.W. Johnson 4 for 151); Australia 84 (J.C. Laker 9 for 37) and 205 (C.C. McDonald 89, J.C. Laker 10 for 53). England won by an innings and 170 runs.

Jim Laker, whose analyses were 16.4-4-37-9 and 51.2-23-53-10, performed the greatest bowling feat of all time in a match not without controversy. Pitch preparation was never easy in this wet summer, and patches were apparent during England's innings. The home side, all the same, proceeded steadily to their large total, Richardson and Cowdrey leading off with 174, and Sheppard, brought back to Test cricket after only four first-class innings that season, added 93 with May. England were healthily placed at 307 for 3 by the first evening, and Sheppard was out on the second afternoon after batting almost five hours – over an hour longer than Richardson. Evans made a breezy 47, and Johnson and Benaud shared 94 overs, taking 6 for 274. Laker and Lock were soon on when Australia batted, and, after changing ends, Laker struck at 48 with McDonald's wicket, caught at short leg. He bowled Harvey for nought, and at tea Australia were 62 for 2. First ball after the interval Lock took his one wicket in the match – Burke, caught at slip. The ball was turning sharply and the fieldsmen crowded in. Laker then had Craig and Mackay in one over, Miller and Benaud in another. Soon he had Archer as he tried to 'charge' him. Then Maddocks and Johnson went in one over. Australia all out 84; Laker 7 for 8 off 22 balls since tea – 9 for 16 after having begun with none for 21. The tourists had seemed to panic after the fall of the first few wickets. Following on, Australia were 53 for one that evening, McDonald retired hurt with a knee injury, and Harvey having hit his first ball, a full toss from Laker, to Cowdrey, thus 'bagging a pair'. Little play was possible on the Saturday, but Burke was lost, and Australia were now 59 for 2. Monday was wet – and windy enough for Evans's cap to be blown off – and in an hour the score advanced to 84, McDonald now returned. He and Craig batted to lunch on the final day, when Australia, 112 for 2, had just four hours to survive. Then the sun came out, and the pitch stirred. Bowling again from the Stretford end, from where he took all his wickets, Laker trapped Craig lbw: he had batted almost 4½ hours for 38. Mackay, a left-hander, then succumbed for his second duck, and Miller's scoreless innings was a quarter-hour of agony. Archer was out second ball, caught in the leg-trap, and then the sun disappeared and the pitch seemed easier. McDonald and Benaud were together at tea, but the former, after a 340-minute vigil, turned a lifter to Oakman, who held his fifth catch of the match. Benaud became Laker's 17th wicket – bowled playing, like several others, fatally back. Johnson appealed to the umpires at sawdust blowing in his eyes – a mark of Australia's despair. Laker bowled perfectly and relentlessly on. Lindwall, after making eight in 40 minutes, was caught by Lock at short leg. Then, with an hour to go, Maddocks was leg-before, and the incredible event was over. Lock, as aggressive a bowler as history has known, bowled 55 overs in the innings and finished with 0 for 69. That was almost as amazing as his Surrey partner's figures.

776, left: *the Rev. David Sheppard pulls Benaud for four during his 113.* 777, below, left: *The only wicket not taken by Laker: Burke c Cowdrey b Lock 22.* 778, right: *McDonald, caught by Lock for 32, another Laker leg-trap victim*

779, above, left: *Craig lbw b Laker 38.* 780, right: *Miller b Laker 0*

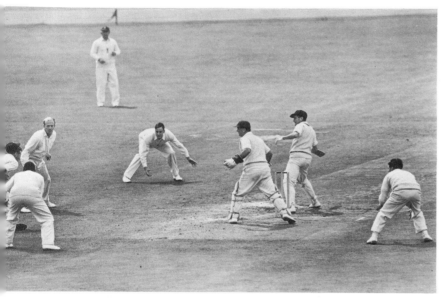

781, above, left: *Mackay c Oakman b Laker 0.* 782, right: *Archer c Oakman b Laker 0.* 783, centre: *Harvey, exasperated at having 'bagged a pair'.* 784, below, left: *Maddocks lbw b Laker 2 – the last wicket to fall (Laker's tenth in the innings and 19th of the match).* 785, right: *Laker leaves the scene of his unique triumph, enviably saddled for life with the task of discussing his 19 for 90 with eager fans*

1956
FIFTH TEST
The Oval, August 23, 24, 25, 27, 28

England 247 (D.C.S. Compton 94, P.B.H. May 83*, R.G. Archer 5 for 53, K.R. Miller 4 for 91) and 182 for 3 dec (D.S. Sheppard 62); Australia 202 (K.R. Miller 61, J.C. Laker 4 for 80) and 27 for 5. Match drawn.

Denis Compton became the third inspired comeback selection for England in the series, making a lovely 94 despite the recent loss of his right kneecap. He went in at 66 for 3 and helped May take the score to 222. Three wickets then fell at that score, and the innings subsided next day. Rain made the pitch interesting, and Laker and Lock beset many problems, reducing Australia to 47 for 5 after a now-fit Tyson had removed McDonald. Harvey (39) and Miller saved the follow-on, and with Benaud's 32 there was little in it after all. England batted confidently either side of rain interruptions, and May left Australia only two hours. Far from being a chance to level the series, it was time enough for further humiliations, and Laker took his tally for the series to a record 46 wickets at 9.60. This was the last Test appearance in England of Miller and Lindwall.

786, left: *A pull by Compton during his successful Oval comeback.* 787, below, left: *Richardson is caught behind for the seventh consecutive time in the series.* 788, right: *Australian wicketkeeper Langley, never renowned for a tidy appearance, bows to convention as Miller applies a safety pin to his split trousers*

1958–59
Brisbane, December 5, 6, 8, 9, 10

FIRST TEST

England *134 and 198 (T.E. Bailey 68, R. Benaud 4 for 66); Australia 186 (C.C. McDonald 42, P.J. Loader 4 for 56) and 147 for 2 (N.C. O'Neill 71*). Australia won by 8 wickets.*

Australia, under Richie Benaud, came back with a vengeance after the defeats of the previous two series, though this opening contest featured some pitiful cricket. Slow over rates and negative batting evoked widespread protests. Bailey's was the most outrageous display: he batted 7½ hours for 68, going in when England were 28 for one in the second innings. The pitch, greenish on the first day, did not deteriorate as half-expected, and Burke matched Bailey in batting through 51.7 eight-ball overs for 28 runs. O'Neill, aged 21, on his Test debut, injected the first real class into the match. Davidson and Meckiff took ten wickets in the match and Benaud seven – the faster men both left-arm, the second-named having an action which some observers questioned. It was not until five years later, on this ground, that Meckiff was no-balled for throwing and retired instantly. During the series the bowling actions of Rorke, Slater and Burke also came under close scrutiny by some Pressmen and opponents. With Cowdrey out to a disputed catch, the 1958–59 rubber was not off to the most harmonious of beginnings.

789, above, left: *O'Neill, on debut, drives Bailey powerfully.* 790, right: *Kline takes a stroke from Cowdrey at square leg. The verdict of 'caught' did not satisfy everyone.* 791, below, left: *May is deceived by a Benaud googly and is lbw.* 792, right: *Benaud leaps to catch Richardson off his own bowling*

1958–59
Melbourne, December 31, January 1, 2, 3, 5

England 259 (P.B.H. May 113, T.E. Bailey 48, M.C. Cowdrey 44, A.K. Davidson 6 for 64) and 87 (I. Meckiff 6 for 38); Australia 308 (R.N. Harvey 167, C.C. McDonald 47, J.B. Statham 7 for 57) and 42 for 2. Australia won by 8 wickets.

A sensational six-ball spell by Davidson, in which he captured the wickets of Richardson, Watson and Graveney, had England three down for seven on the first morning. Then Bailey, opening, took the score to 92 with May, who was then joined by Cowdrey in a stand of 118. May, whose innings began on his 29th birthday, batted in all for 5¼ hours, and his century was the first in Australia by an England captain for 57 years. The innings fell away, and when Australia's Harvey (who batted 370 minutes without giving a chance) was joined in big stands by McDonald and O'Neill, England seemed to be slipping from the picture. But Statham's gallant effort, backed by Loader, kept the match poised . . . until Meckiff ran through England's second innings, aided by some deft catching and less than admirable batsmanship. This was England's lowest score in Australia for 55 years.

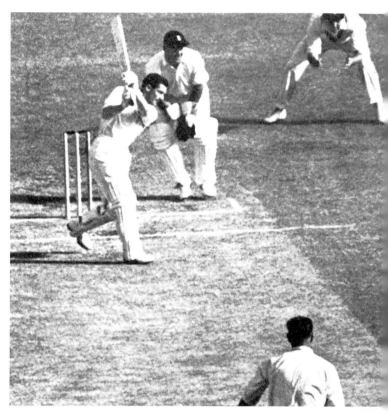

793, above, left: *Watson is bowled by Davidson in a sensational over.* 794, above, right: *Harvey steps out and drives Laker during his 167.* 795, left: *Bailey, having moved well across to Meckiff, is caught by Benaud at silly mid-on.* 796, right: *Burke, playing no stroke, is bowled by Statham*

1958–59
Sydney, January 9, 10, 12, 13, 14, 15

THIRD TEST

England 219 *(P.B.H. May 42, R. Swetman 41, R. Benaud 5 for 83) and 287 for 7 dec (M.C. Cowdrey 100*, P.B.H. May 92, R. Benaud 4 for 94); Australia 357 (N.C. O'Neill 77, A.K. Davidson 71, K.D. Mackay 57, L.E. Favell 54, C.C. McDonald 40, J.C. Laker 5 for 107, G.A.R. Lock 4 for 130) and 54 for 2*. Match drawn.

England, after a now-customary bad start, steadied with Graveney and May, then slipped, then recovered partially, Swetman, injured Evans's replacement, batting over 2½ hours. McDonald became set, in enviable contrast, and though Laker and Lock gave an idea of their greatness on an unresponsive pitch (though Lock throughout the series tended to bowl too flat and fast), O'Neill and Favell added 110 for the fourth wicket, and Mackay and Davidson a precious 115 for the seventh. England were tottering at 64 for 3 – still 74 behind – when Cowdrey joined May. The score was advanced to 246 before Burke got a ball through May's unsuspecting defence, during which time Benaud had gone on the defensive. Cowdrey's century took 362 minutes, the longest in these Tests until 1975.

797, above, left: *May and Cowdrey resume their fourth-wicket stand of 182.* 798, right: *O'Neill c Swetman b Laker 77 at Sydney.* 799, below, left: *May b Burke 92.* 800, right: *Mackay throws himself to catch Swetman (41) off Benaud*

1958–59
Adelaide, January 30, 31, February 2, 3, 4, 5

FOURTH TEST

Australia 476 (C.C. McDonald 170, J.W. Burke 66, N.C. O'Neill 56, R. Benaud 46, A.K. Davidson 43, R.N. Harvey 41, F.S. Trueman 4 for 90) and 36 for 0; England 240 (M.C. Cowdrey 84, T.W. Graveney 41, R. Benaud 5 for 91) and 270 (P.B.H. May 59, T.W. Graveney 53*, P.E. Richardson 43, W. Watson 40, R. Benaud 4 for 82). Australia won by 10 wickets.

Having won three tosses, batted and failed to make substantial first-innings totals, May this time put Australia in; but no wicket fell until 171, when Burke was caught. Australia were 200 for one by the first evening. Next day, still in fierce heat, England took wickets after lunch, when McDonald temporarily retired, Statham obtaining three good wickets. Umpire McInnes appeared to err on occasions, Mackay 'walking' after being given 'not out' to a catch by Evans, and when McDonald was given 'not out' as his runner raced for the crease *behind* the umpire, the batsman took matters into his own hands by swinging wildly and being bowled by Trueman for 170, made in 487 minutes, with 12 fours. Laker, unfit, was sorely missed. The blond giant, Rorke, dragging on his right boot several yards in delivery, broke through the centre of England's innings, and Benaud, having bowled May for 37, wrapped up the tail. Although Davidson had sprained an ankle, Australia enforced the follow-on, and Richardson (3¾ hours) and Watson began with 89. Thereafter wickets fell with regularity before Benaud, Lindwall and Rorke, and the match extended well into the sixth day only because of Graveney's disciplined innings of five hours. Australia thus had the Ashes back 5½ traumatic years after losing them.

801, above, left: *Bailey is hit on the head by a ball from Rorke. Burke has yet to show any concern.* 802, right: *The ball is on its way to Bailey, who runs out Harvey.* 803, below, left: *The lengthy 'drag' of gargantuan Australian fast bowler Rorke.* 804, right: *Favell hits the winning run and the Ashes are regained*

1958–59
Melbourne, February 13, 14, 16, 17, 18

FIFTH TEST

England 205 (P.E. Richardson 68, J.B. Mortimore 44*, R. Benaud 4 for 43) and 214 (T.W. Graveney 54, M.C. Cowdrey 46); Australia 351 (C.C. McDonald 133, A.T.W. Grout 74, R. Benaud 64, F.S. Trueman 4 for 92, J.C. Laker 4 for 93) and 69 for 1 (C.C. McDonald 51*). Australia won by 9 wickets.

Australia's fourth decisive victory of the series resulted from attacking fast bowling, probing leg-spin variations from Benaud (he finished the rubber with 31 wickets), and heavy scoring again from the tough, dependable McDonald. Australia's captain and the wicketkeeper, Grout, also took their side from an indeterminate 209 for 6 to 324 for 7. Bailey, opening for England, was twice dismissed by Lindwall without scoring, and Dexter – who had been flown out in December with Mortimore as replacements – was out first ball to Meckiff. O'Neill also went first ball, to Trueman. At 78 for 2 in the second innings, Cowdrey, having stroked a beautiful 46, was victim of a disputed run-out. In the first Test he had been considered to be unlucky to be given out 'caught' by Kline at square leg. McDonald, batting 339 minutes in the first innings and taking his aggregate for the series to 520 in the second, was Australia's batsman of the season.

805, above, left: *Trueman falls on his ear to secure a catch from Grout (74).* 806, right: *Bailey collects a 'pair' and becomes Lindwall's 217th wicket (which overtook Grimmett's Australian Test record).* 807, below, left: *McDonald hits the winning runs past Dexter.* 808, right: *Benaud and May, the captains, on the balcony at the end of the series*

1961
Edgbaston, June 8, 9, 10, 12, 13

FIRST TEST

England *195 (R. Subba Row 59, K.D. Mackay 4 for 57) and 401 for 4 (E.R. Dexter 180, R. Subba Row 112, K.F. Barrington 48*); Australia 516 (R.N. Harvey 114, N.C. O'Neill 82, R.B. Simpson 76, K.D. Mackay 64, W.M. Lawry 57).* Match drawn.

England began the final day at 106 for one, still 215 behind; but Dexter and Subba Row (who was playing in his first Test against Australia) took their stand to 109, and after Cowdrey's dismissal at 239, Barrington stayed with Dexter while 161 further matchsaving runs were made. Dexter, showing unexpected powers of concentration, batted 344 minutes and hit 31 fours. Mackay, with deceptively innocuous-looking medium-pacers, stole four good England wickets on the first day, and Harvey and O'Neill mastered the bowling of Trueman, Statham, Illingworth and Allen in a stand of 146 in 117 minutes. Rain cut the third and fourth days' play, and in the 20 minutes he batted on the penultimate day Dexter looked anything but assured, being missed at one off Davidson – a costly chance. He was stumped eventually when trying for a six off Simpson.

809, above, left: *England captain Cowdrey talks with chairman of selectors G.O. Allen during practice at Edgbaston.* 810, right: *M.J.K. Smith is caught by Lawry (out of picture) off Mackay.* 811, left: *Dexter acknowledges the applause. The bowler is Misson.* 812, below: *Mackay drives. England wicketkeeper Murray's eyebrow was injured by a ball that rebounded from a batsman's pad*

1961
Lord's, June 22, 23, 24, 26

SECOND TEST

England 206 (R. Subba Row 48, A.K. Davidson 5 for 42) and 202 (K.F. Barrington 66, G. Pullar 42, G.D. McKenzie 5 for 37); Australia 340 (W.M. Lawry 130, K.D. Mackay 54, P.J.P. Burge 46, F.S. Trueman 4 for 118) and 71 for 5. Australia won by 5 wickets.

On a responsive pitch ideal for seam bowling (there was a 'ridge' at the Nursery end) Australia disposed of a strong England XI – with May returned – and were 42 for 2 by the first evening, having lost their own first two wickets for six runs. Harvey (leading Australia in Benaud's absence through injury) and O'Neill were gone by 88, but Burge then batted stoutly with the tall left-hander, Lawry, who was playing his second Test. They added 95, and Lawry went on to a courageous hundred, batting in all for 369 minutes. Mackay stretched the lead with stands of 53 for the ninth wicket with McKenzie and 49 for the tenth with Misson. The 20-year-old McKenzie, in his first Test, plunged the ball onto a still-lively pitch and, with Davidson and Misson, left his side to make only a handful of runs for victory. The handful soon seemed a mountain as Statham and Trueman swept four wickets away for 19, and Lock touched a misjudged hook by Burge as it fell to earth. Simpson went at 58, but Burge's galvanising strokeplay saw Australia to their eighth victory at Lord's.

813, above: *Lawry mis-hooks but survives.*
814, right: *O'Neill loses his off stump to Statham*

815, left: *Barrington lbw b Davidson 66*

816, below: *Burge ends the tension by pulling Statham over midwicket for the winning runs*

1961
Headingley, July 6, 7, 8

Australia 237 (R.N. Harvey 73, C.C. McDonald 54, F.S. Trueman 5 for 58) and 120 (R.N. Harvey 53, F.S. Trueman 6 for 30); England 299 (M.C. Cowdrey 93, G. Pullar 53, A.K. Davidson 5 for 63) and 62 for 2. England won by 8 wickets.

Two extraordinary breakthroughs by Trueman on an unpredictable pitch settled the match when, in each innings, Australia showed signs of increasing command. 183 for 2 at tea on the first day, Australia tumbled to 208 for 9 as Trueman with the new ball took 5 for 16 in six overs, aided by good catches by Cowdrey and Lock. England progressed well until Davidson, cutting his pace, and McKenzie ran through the middle and later order, Lock cracking a useful 30, many off Benaud, who was troubled throughout the series by a damaged shoulder. Australia reached 99 before the third wicket fell, and then Allen had Burge lbw for nought to make it 102 for 4. Trueman then proceeded to take five wickets without conceding a run, bowling off-cutters, with 40-year-old Les Jackson, in his first Test against Australia, operating from the other end. Trueman bowled Benaud for a duck for the second time, and took 6 for 4 all told in 45 balls. Australia's last eight wickets fell in 50 minutes. England made the necessary runs that evening.

817, above: *McDonald st Murray b Lock, first innings.* 818, right: *McDonald bowled by a prodigious breakback from Jackson, second innings*

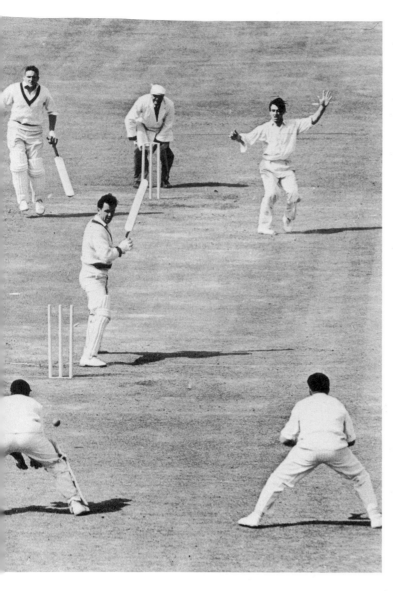

819, left: *Simpson is bowled by Trueman – the third of his five wickets for no runs.* 820, above: *Cowdrey scores off Simpson during his 93 at Leeds*

1961 FOURTH TEST
Old Trafford, July 27, 28, 29, 31, August 1

Australia *190 (W.M. Lawry 74, B.C. Booth 46, J.B. Statham 5 for 53) and 432 (W.M. Lawry 102, A.K. Davidson 77*, N.C. O'Neill 67, R.B. Simpson 51, D.A. Allen 4 for 58); England 367 (P.B.H. May 95, K.F. Barrington 78, G. Pullar 63, D.A. Allen 42, R.B. Simpson 4 for 23) and 201 (E.R. Dexter 76, R. Subba Row 49, R. Benaud 6 for 70). Australia won by 54 runs.*

On the final morning, when Allen spun out three Australians in 15 balls to make the score 334 for 9, England had the rest of the day to make 157 plus whatever the final wicket added. It added 98, Davidson taking 20 off an Allen over and persuading May to withdraw the off-spinner. McKenzie (32) gave the left-hand all-rounder staunch support, and eventually England needed 256 in 230 minutes if the series was to be left open. Pullar and Subba Row, both left-handers, began with 40, and Dexter than came in and played thrillingly for 76 in 84 minutes, apparently making certain of the match for England, who were 150 for one after 123 minutes. Having hit 14 fours and a huge six, Dexter then edged a ball that bounced and Grout took the catch. Benaud, the bowler, was coming from around the wicket, and pitching into the bowlers' rough. Second ball Peter May was bowled round his legs. Close then failed in his attempted crossbat assault, and just before tea Subba Row was yorked – another wicket to Benaud, who had 4 for 9 in 19 balls. After the interval he got Murray, Mackay trapped Barrington, and – back to over-the-wicket – Benaud had Allen brilliantly caught at slip by Simpson. The fieldsman, then daringly brought into the attack, had Trueman caught at short leg, and Davidson came back to bowl Statham, giving Australia a sensational victory with 20 minutes left. Much of the worthy cricket earlier has tended to be forgotten, but Lawry's two stout-hearted innings, Statham's use of the conditions, and May's fine 'comeback' innings all contributed to an exceptional cricket match.

821, top, left: *Lawry missed by Subba Row at slip.* 822, top, right: *Davidson hits Allen for a vital six.* 823, middle, left: *Dexter is caught by Grout – the start of the England collapse at Old Trafford.* 824, centre: *Close hits Benaud for six.* 825, right: *Subba Row b Benaud 49.* 826, below: *May b Benaud 0*

1961
The Oval, August 17, 18, 19, 21, 22

FIFTH TEST

England 256 (P.B.H. May 71, K.F. Barrington 53, A.K. Davidson 4 for 83) and 370 for 8 (R. Subba Row 137, K.F. Barrington 83, D.A. Allen 42*, J.T. Murray 40, K.D. Mackay 5 for 121); Australia 494 (P.J.P. Burge 181, N.C. O'Neill 117, B.C. Booth 71, R.B. Simpson 40, D.A. Allen 4 for 133). Match drawn.

In 104 overs on the first day England struggled to 210 for 8 after a poor start, when three wickets fell for 20. Gaunt finished with three good wickets, and only a three-hour stand of 80 by May and Barrington held the innings together. Australia began unsteadily, but O'Neill was in mighty form, and the even more strongly-built Burge added 123 with him. A delayed new ball enabled Booth to settle in, and with Burge hooking and sweeping powerfully the score advanced to 396 before Booth fell to Lock. Queenslander Burge batted chancelessly for almost seven hours, hitting 22 fours. There had been rain interruptions, and on the fourth day more time was lost, England finishing precariously at 155 for 4. Subba Row, batting with a runner because of a pulled muscle in this his final Test innings, added 172 with Barrington, and occupied the crease for 400 minutes for his 137 (having made a century in his first Test against Australia at Edgbaston). With Davidson injured, Australia hadn't the resources to come back at England in the remaining time. Benaud (51 overs) and Mackay (68 overs) bore the brunt of the second-innings work.

827, above, left: *Subba Row drives during his 137.* 828, right: *Pullar finely caught by Grout on the leg side off Mackay for 13.* 829, left: *Burge sweeps during his muscular 181.* 830, below: *O'Neill forces through the leg-trap*

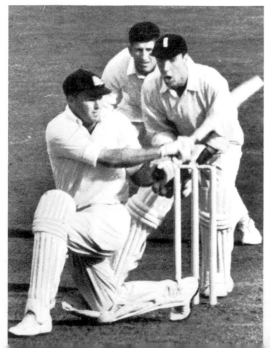

1962–63
Brisbane, November 30, December 1, 3, 4, 5

Australia 404 (B.C. Booth 112, K.D. Mackay 86*, R. Benaud 51, R.B. Simpson 50) and 362 for 4 dec (W.M. Lawry 98, R.B. Simpson 71, R.N. Harvey 57, N.C. O'Neill 56, P.J.P. Burge 47*); England 389 (P.H. Parfitt 80, K.F. Barrington 78, E.R. Dexter 70, R. Benaud 6 for 115) and 278 for 6 (E.R. Dexter 99, G. Pullar 56, D.S. Sheppard 53). Match drawn.

When Australia's sixth wicket went down for 194 a modest total seemed in prospect. The elegant Booth then added 103 with the dour Mackay, who then stayed with Benaud while 91 were put on for the eighth wicket. Booth's century lasted 217 minutes and contained not one brutal stroke. Dexter, leading England, had a fine double, batting briskly in each innings and being bowled by McKenzie for 99 when it seemed England had an outside chance on the final day. England's first innings was shored up by two four-hour innings, Parfitt's in his first Test against Australia, and Barrington's in demonstration of what a gritty and devoted player he had become. Lawry's 98 took him 260 minutes, and set up a declaration on the fourth evening that invited England to make 378 in six hours. Pullar and Sheppard started with 114, and Dexter's bold innings was the 14th half-century of the match.

831, above, left: *Centurymaker Booth glances Statham, and wicket-keeper Smith fields.* 832, right: *Parfitt lofts Benaud to be caught by Davidson at long-on for 80.* 833, below, left: *McKenzie wonderfully caught-and-bowled by Knight.* 834, right: *Dexter b McKenzie 99*

1962–63
Melbourne, December 29, 31, January 1, 2, 3

SECOND TEST

Australia 316 (W.M. Lawry 52, K.D. Mackay 49, A.K. Davidson 40, F.J. Titmus 4 for 43) and 248 (B.C. Booth 103, W.M. Lawry 57, F.S. Trueman 5 for 62); England 331 (M.C. Cowdrey 113, E.R. Dexter 93, T.W. Graveney 41, A.K. Davidson 6 for 75) and 237 for 3 (D.S. Sheppard 113, M.C. Cowdrey 58*, E.R. Dexter 52). England won by 7 wickets.

With the ball often beating the bat and occasional deliveries shooting through low, the scores would have been even more moderate but for the depth of Australia's batting and a splendid stand of 175 by Cowdrey and Dexter. Then, on the final day, Sheppard, who had failed to score in the first innings and dropped two catches, steered England to victory with a five-hour innings that included only five fours and as many as ten threes. The pitch was perhaps better than earlier, and Sheppard put on 124 with Dexter and 104 with Cowdrey before being run out with the scores level. Booth went in with Australia 69 for 4, and after Lawry (who took 275 minutes to reach 50) was out at 161, all responsibility devolved upon him. Booth batted 348 minutes, hitting only five fours, but ensuring that England were set a sizable target.

835, above, left: *Harvey run out for 10 by Trueman.* 836, right: *Dexter c Simpson b Benaud 93.* 837, below, left: *Sheppard straight-drives Benaud to reach his hundred.* 838, right: *The champagne comes out, poured by Benaud for victorious Dexter*

1962–63
Sydney, January 11, 12, 14, 15

THIRD TEST

England 279 (M.C. Cowdrey 85, G. Pullar 53, R.B. Simpson 5 for 57, A.K. Davidson 4 for 54) and 104 (A.K. Davidson 5 for 25); Australia 319 (R.B. Simpson 91, B.K. Shepherd 71*, R.N. Harvey 64, F.J. Titmus 7 for 79) and 67 for 2. Australia won by 8 wickets.

Simpson, without the accuracy of a Benaud, picked up five wickets with leg-breaks and googlies, and Davidson four with his lethal control of a new ball. Cowdrey batted 160 minutes, but Pullar existed for 3½ hours. Sheppard missed two catches during the stand of 160 between Simpson and Harvey, and with Murray off with a sprained shoulder in taking a diving catch to dismiss Lawry (Parfitt kept wicket in his place) England were in a sorry plight. Simpson batted four hours, but off-spinner Titmus brought his side back into the match with four wickets for five runs, using the breeze skilfully. Burly left-hander Shepherd hit Australia into a lead which was considered not quite enough to compensate for Australia's having to bat last, but this soon ceased to be relevant as Davidson broke open England's second innings with more fine swing bowling. McKenzie's speed, Benaud's vital dismissal of Cowdrey, and Simpson's glorious slip fielding shattered England, for whom Murray, with a painful shoulder, batted 100 minutes for three not out. Australia made the runs as rain fell; the scheduled fifth day was very wet.

839, above, left: *Murray, with an injured shoulder, drives McKenzie one-handed.* 840, right: *England 28 for 3, and the crowd on the Hill enjoying every moment.* 841, below, left: *Dexter beautifully caught by Simpson, and England hopes slump.* 842, right: *The Australian team dinner before the match*

1962-63
FOURTH TEST
Adelaide, January 25, 26, 28, 29, 30

Australia 393 (R.N. Harvey 154, N.C. O'Neill 100, A.K. Davidson 46) and 293 (B.C. Booth 77, R.B. Simpson 71, R. Benaud 48, F.S. Trueman 4 for 60); England 331 (K.F. Barrington 63, E.R. Dexter 61, F.J. Titmus 59*, G.D. McKenzie 5 for 89) and 223 for 4 (K.F. Barrington 132*). Match drawn.

Australia were 16 for 2 when Booth added 85 with Harvey, who was helped by dropped catches off successive balls from Illingworth and a missed slip catch at 26. O'Neill then entered and a transformation took place. In oppressive heat Harvey – whose century was the last of his six against England – added 194 with O'Neill in only 171 minutes, the strong, stylish O'Neill getting out as much from exhaustion as to Dexter's bowling. McKenzie led Australia's attack after Davidson pulled up with a torn hamstring in his fourth over, and gained lift from the pitch during his 33 overs. Titmus and Trueman (38) kept England within sight on the rain-shortened third day. Dexter then set about containing, and though Simpson and Booth added 133 for the third wicket, with Davidson absent, Benaud felt it necessary to bat until lunch on the last day. England's first two wickets fell for four, the fourth at 122, and Illingworth was called from a sick-bed; but Graveney saw it through with Barrington, who batted 227 minutes and reached his chanceless century with a six off Simpson. His first-innings 63 included four boundaries in four balls from Davidson – only one where it was intended – and the extra effort this provoked may have triggered the bowler's injury.

843, above: *Booth on-drives Titmus.* 844, top, right: *Statham is congratulated upon passing Bedser's all-Tests record of 236 wickets when he had Shepherd caught.* 845, bottom: *Trueman strikes Benaud for six*

846: *Harvey (11) dropped by Cowdrey at slip off Illingworth at Adelaide*

1962–63
Sydney, February 15, 16, 18, 19, 20

FIFTH TEST

England *321 (K.F. Barrington 101, E.R. Dexter 47) and 268 for 8 dec (K.F. Barrington 94, D.S. Sheppard 68, M.C. Cowdrey 53); Australia 349 (P.J.P. Burge 103, N.C. O'Neill 73, R. Benaud 57, F.J. Titmus 5 for 103) and 152 for 4 (P.J.P. Burge 52*, W.M. Lawry 45*). Match drawn.*

With all to play for, neither side was prepared to take chances, and England's innings of 321, taking 9½ hours, set the pattern. Barrington managed only four fours in his 101 (but picked up 20 twos), and fell just short of a century in each innings. He occupied the crease for 9¾ hours in the match. Australia were 74 for 3 on the second evening, but O'Neill, using his feet to get to the off-spinners Titmus and Allen, added 109 with Burge, who batted 5½ hours before being lbw attempting a sweep. He was missed at 63. Illingworth and Sheppard opened with 40 in England's second innings, Cowdrey being indisposed, and Barrington anchored the innings, adding 97 with Sheppard and 94 with Cowdrey. At lunch on the last day Dexter declared, setting Australia 241 in four hours, but four wickets fell for 70 and Lawry (four hours) and Burge played out time to the echo of the crowd's dissatisfaction. For the first time a five-match series in Australia was drawn. Neil Harvey took six catches in the match, his last for Australia, and Alan Davidson took a wicket with his final ball in Tests.

847: *Barrington pulls a short one from Benaud in the second innings. The Surrey batsman had a sturdy double of 101 and 94*

848, above: *Graveney at short mid-on has caught O'Neill (out of picture) off Allen.* 849, below: *O'Neill plays an immaculate forward defensive.* 850, right: *Harvey (left) and Davidson lead Australia out in their final Test match, followed by their captain, Richie Benaud*

1964
Trent Bridge, June 4, 5, 6, 8, 9

FIRST TEST

England *216 for 8 dec (G. Boycott 48) and 193 for 9 dec (E.R. Dexter 68, G.D. McKenzie 5 for 53); Australia 168 (R.B. Simpson 50) and 40 for 2. Match drawn.*

Rain ruined this opening contest of a frustrating series. It was the fourth morning before Dexter declared, the first day having been heavily curtailed, the second partially, and the third washed out. Boycott, in his first Test, batted cautiously, with Titmus his opening partner as John Edrich was injured before the start. Titmus was once stranded after colliding with the bowler, but Australia's wicketkeeper, Wally Grout, won much admiration by refusing to break the wicket. Bob Simpson, succeeding Benaud as Australia's captain, batting at No. 6, saved his side from a serious deficit, but Dexter, opening in place of Boycott (broken finger), thrashed 68 and a climax seemed imminent. Instead, England's run rate fell back against McKenzie, Corling and Hawke, and the closure did not come until Australia were faced with making 242 in 195 minutes. The only remaining excitement came as O'Neill hooked the first four balls of Trueman's second over to the boundary. Rain washed out play after 9.2 overs.

851, left: *Dexter drives Corling to the boundary, O'Neill following the swift passage of the ball.* 852, above: *Titmus is stranded after colliding with bowler Hawke, but Grout, the Australian wicketkeeper, nobly refrained from removing the bails*

853, above: *Booth, having just completed his stroke off Allen, is run out by Trueman from short leg.* 854, right: *Sharpe sweeps Veivers for four at Trent Bridge*

1964
Lord's, June 18, 19, 20, 22, 23

SECOND TEST

Australia *176 (T.R. Veivers 54, F.S. Trueman 5 for 48) and 168 for 4 (P.J.P. Burge 59); England 246 (J.H. Edrich 120, G.E. Corling 4 for 60).* Match drawn.

Again, something like half the match was lost through rain. Play could not begin until the third day, and Dexter then put Australia in. The sixth wicket fell at 88, but left-hander Veivers held on for 2½ hours. Dexter chipped in with the wickets of O'Neill and Burge, and Parfitt took two superlative diving catches close to the wicket. Dexter opened again, but was yorked by McKenzie second ball for two. Edrich, however, a cousin of Bill Edrich, went to a commendable hundred on his debut against Australia, batting altogether for 6¼ hours and hitting two sixes and nine fours. It was the day after his 27th birthday. Stands with Parfitt, Sharpe (35) and Titmus hauled England into the lead, but on the last day Australia withstood a pace attack, Gifford and Titmus surprisingly not being called in until well into the morning. Redpath was 53 minutes on 36 before falling to Titmus. More rain after lunch caused an abandonment at 5.20 pm.

855: *O'Neill drives handsomely at Lord's*

856, above: *Parfitt's great diving catch at short leg to dismiss Redpath (30) at Lord's.* 857, left: *Lawry bowled leg stump by Trueman
for four.* 858, below: *John Edrich comes in having made a century in
his debut innings against Australia, the first of seven*

1964
Headingley, July 2, 3, 4, 6

THIRD TEST

England 268 (*J.M. Parks 68, E.R. Dexter 66, N.J.N. Hawke 5 for 75, G.D. McKenzie 4 for 74*) *and 229 (K.F. Barrington 85); Australia 389 (P.J.P. Burge 160, W.M. Lawry 78, F.J. Titmus 4 for 69) and 111 for 3 (I.R. Redpath 58*).* Australia won by 7 wickets.

Wonderful fielding and accurate pace bowling restricted England to 268 on a good pitch, a bright innings from Dexter and valuable batting by wicketkeeper Parks saving England's face. The performance seemed adequate, nonetheless, when Australia were 178 for 7, Gifford having taken two wickets and Titmus three, bowling cleverly. Dexter then gave Trueman and Flavell the new ball. Peter Burge fed well on it, especially Trueman's persistent long-hops, and 42 runs were scored off seven overs. Burge's stand with Hawke realised 105, and the massive Queenslander had further support next morning from Grout, who added 89 with him, transforming the match. Burge batted 5¼ hours and hit – resoundingly – 24 fours. Parfitt's knuckle was broken in England's second innings, and though Edrich and Barrington resisted grimly and Dexter played untypically defensively, Australia pressed home their advantage. Flavell could not bowl, having damaged a tendon, and Titmus earned figures of 27-19-25-2 as Australia moved carefully to victory on the fourth evening.

859, above: *Burge pulls Flavell for four.* 860, below: *Grout pulls Trueman, whose short bowling was often hammered in this Test at Leeds*

861, above, left: *Barrington cuts Veivers at Leeds.* 862, right: *A powerful back-foot stroke by Burge*

1964   FOURTH TEST
Old Trafford, July 23, 24, 25, 27, 28

Australia *656 for 8 dec (R.B. Simpson 311, W.M. Lawry 106, B.C. Booth 98, N.C. O'Neill 47) and 4 for 0;* England *611 (K.F. Barrington 256, E.R. Dexter 174, J.M. Parks 60, G. Boycott 58, G.D. McKenzie 7 for 153).* Match drawn.

Winning the toss and with a perfect pitch awaiting, Simpson set about making the Ashes safe. His innings, the longest ever played against England (12 hours 42 minutes), was his first century in his 30 Tests, and contained 23 fours and a six. He was 109 at the end of the first day, when Australia were 253 for 2, and 265 at the end of the second (570 for 4). His opening stand of 201 with Lawry broke the 1909 record of Bardsley and Gregory, and he added 219 with Booth for the fifth wicket, hitting uninhibitedly on the third morning with no serious regard for the individual Test record. Rumsey, Price and Cartwright – of whom only Price had previously played Test cricket – took all seven wickets that fell to bowlers, Cartwright returning 77-32-118-2. Faced first with avoiding the follow-on, and later with only the prestige target of first-innings supremacy, England lost Edrich at 15 and Boycott at 126 before Dexter and Barrington settled down for a partnership that realised 246 in 325 minutes. The crowd at times expressed their impatience, but the normally restless Dexter set himself to the task, and Barrington, who batted all told for 685 minutes, with 26 fours, was not removed until just before tea on the final day. Both batsmen were dropped, McKenzie missing three chances, though he bowled gallantly for 60 overs. Off-spinner Veivers sent down 95.1 overs to take 3 for 155: only Ramadhin of West Indies has bowled more balls (588) in a Test innings.

863, top: *Simpson drives Mortimore for six during the later stages of his 311. 864, centre: Lawry hooks left-arm fast bowler Rumsey for six on the opening day. 865, right: Simpson out at last, hitting out at Price and being caught by wicketkeeper Parks*

866, left: *An out-of-character Dexter plays forward with restraint during England's Old Trafford marathon.*
867, right: *Barrington lbw b McKenzie 256*

1964
The Oval, August 13, 14, 15, 17, 18

FIFTH TEST

England 182 (K.F. Barrington 47, N.J.N. Hawke 6 for 47) and 381 for 4 (G. Boycott 113, M.C. Cowdrey 93*, F.J. Titmus 56, K.F. Barrington 54*); Australia 379 (W.M. Lawry 94, B.C. Booth 74, T.R. Veivers 67*, I.R. Redpath 45, F.S. Trueman 4 for 87). Match drawn.

A rained-off final day deprived England of the outside chance of squaring the series and Cowdrey, restored to the side, of a century. Boycott reached his – his first in Tests – but the outstanding incident was Trueman's dismissal of Hawke, which made him the first bowler to take 300 wickets in Test matches. McKenzie finished the series with 29 in the five matches, equalling Grimmett's Australian record for a rubber in England. Batting was least easy on the first day, and distinctly the largest stand was 44 for the first wicket. One of the few moments to lighten the proceedings was when Dexter's bat split in half as he drove Hawke, who bowled cleverly at fast-medium pace. Australia's innings was sluggish, with Titmus and Cartwright returning very tight figures and Lawry spending 5¼ hours on his 94. Veivers later brought some vigour into the batting. 255 for 4, England were then steadied by a stand of 126 between Cowdrey and Barrington, rain having the final say in a mainly unsatisfying series.

868: *Fred Trueman takes his 300th Test wicket as Hawke is safely pouched by Cowdrey at slip*

869, above: *Trueman, having taken his 300th Test wicket, hugs his accomplice, Cowdrey, and the England team share his pleasure.* 870, below, left: *Parfitt plays on to McKenzie for three and shows his chagrin.* 871, right: *Boycott comes in after making the first of his Test centuries*

1965-66
Brisbane, December 10, 11, 13, 14, 15

FIRST TEST

Australia *443 for 6 dec (W.M. Lawry 166, K.D. Walters 155, T.R. Veivers 56*); England 280 (F.J. Titmus 60, K.F. Barrington 53, J.M. Parks 52, G. Boycott 45, P.I. Philpott 5 for 90) and 186 for 3 (G. Boycott 63*). Match drawn.*

Rain permitted only 36 overs on the first day and washed out the second. Australia thus set out to raise a total sufficient to test England in the matter of a follow-on. This the tourists failed to avoid, but they saw out time without serious difficulty. Walters, not quite 20, batted 322 minutes in his first Test, showing deft footwork and a willing range of strokes. He added 187 with Lawry when Australia were 125 for 4, and then 119 with Veivers. Lawry who was to make nearly a thousand runs in Tests and other matches off M.J.K. Smith's side, batted here for seven hours. England began hesitantly but were lifted by Parks's bright innings and survived through Barrington's purposeful effort in the first innings and Boycott's in the second.

872, top, left: *Walters c Parks b Higgs 155.* 873, centre: *Walters returns after his stirring debut innings.* 874, right: *Edrich hooks Philpott for two during his 32.* 875, left: *Lawry is dropped by Barrington at slip off Titmus*

1965–66
Melbourne, December 30, 31, January 1, 3, 4

SECOND TEST

Australia *358 (R.M. Cowper 99, W.M. Lawry 88, R.B. Simpson 59, B.R. Knight 4 for 84) and 426 (P.J.P. Burge 120, K.D. Walters 115, W.M. Lawry 78, R.B. Simpson 67); England 558 (J.H. Edrich 109, M.C. Cowdrey 104, J.M. Parks 71, K.F. Barrington 63, F.J. Titmus 56*, G. Boycott 51, R.W. Barber 48, M.J.K. Smith 41, G.D. McKenzie 5 for 134) and 5 for 0.* Match drawn.

Australia seemed doomed on the last day when their fourth wicket fell at 176, when they were still 24 runs behind. Then, having edged in front, they almost lost Burge, who left his crease to play Barber, missed, and gave Parks a stumping chance which he could not consummate. Burge and Walters were not separated until their stand was worth 198 and the match was saved. Simpson, who had missed the first Test because of a broken wrist, gave his side two good starts with Lawry (93 and 120), but apart from left-hander Cowper's 200-minute innings – ended by a slip catch off Jeff Jones – there was nothing of distinction about Australia's batting until the reprieved Burge and young Walters set about frustrating England. In contrast, England's first seven batsmen all made 41 or more, and there were five sizable stands, Edrich staying over five hours in spite of much discomfort against the spinners. Cowdrey's hundred was his third at Melbourne. The stumping miss apart, England might have grasped control earlier if the brisk opening of 98 given them by Boycott and Barber had been developed. Knight, flown out as a reinforcement to the MCC side, took his four wickets in a spell in which he conceded only 18 runs.

876, above: *Lawry c Cowdrey b Allen 88.*
877, below: *Edrich caught-and-bowled by Veivers for 109*

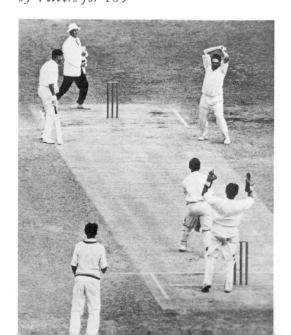

878, above: *Substitute wicketkeeper Barrington catches Simpson for 67.* 879, below: *Simpson and Lawry, Australia's reliable opening pair, about to start the first innings at Melbourne*

1965–66
Sydney, January 7, 8, 10, 11

THIRD TEST

England 488 (R.W. Barber 185, J.H. Edrich 103, G. Boycott 84, D.A. Allen 50*, N.J.N. Hawke 7 for 105); Australia 221 (R.M. Cowper 60, G. Thomas 51, D.J. Brown 5 for 63) and 174 (F.J. Titmus 4 for 40, D.A. Allen 4 for 47). England won by an innings and 93 runs.

A memorable five-hour innings by left-hander Barber set up an England victory which was made certain by Brown and Jones in a first-innings breakthrough and Titmus and Allen, the off-spinners, as the pitch became more and more helpful to the turning ball. Barber and Boycott (who was missed by Sincock at short leg when 12) opened with 93 before lunch and 234 in all (in four hours). Edrich then added 69 with Barber, but in the last session of the first day Hawke, with the new ball, took four quality wickets, and two more next morning. Edrich battled on, and reached his hundred with a six driven off leg-spinner Philpott. Allen and Jones put on 55 for the last wicket. Australia that evening were 113 for 4, and the stand of 81 between Thomas and Cowper was to be the largest of either Australian innings. Cowper stayed over four hours. Brown's taking of three wickets in an over made the follow-on fairly certain, and England's off-spinners, supported especially well by Smith, their captain, at short leg, had Australia floundering. Walters, batting for over two hours, was left 35 not out.

880, left: *Barber goes to 104 with a sweep off Cowper.* 881, above: *England captain Smith is caught behind off Hawke*

882, left: *Edrich hoists spinner Philpott to the boundary to bring up his century.* 883, right: *Burge about to be run out: Boycott throws to the far end. Lawry is the non-striker*

884, left: *Smith at short leg completes a smart catch to end Sincock's innings.* 885, right: *Boycott straight-drives McKenzie*

1965–66   FOURTH TEST
Adelaide, January 28, 29, 31, February 1

England *241 (K.F. Barrington 60, J.M. Parks 49, G.D. McKenzie 6 for 48) and 266 (K.F. Barrington 102, F.J. Titmus 53, N.J.N. Hawke 5 for 54); Australia 516 (R.B. Simpson 225, W.M. Lawry 119, G. Thomas 52, K.R. Stackpole 43, I.J. Jones 6 for 118).* Australia won by an innings and 9 runs.

Having missed the first Test through a broken wrist and the third through chickenpox, Simpson returned as Australia's captain, and reminded everyone what his side had been lacking. For just over nine hours he withstood England's pace and spin attack, hitting 18 fours and a six, and setting a new Australian first-wicket record against England with Lawry – 244. This in itself gave Australia a first-innings lead. McKenzie, originally dropped in favour of Queensland's Allan, was recalled when Allan was injured, and bowled with zest on a lively pitch in humid conditions. Cowdrey's dismissal, not for the first time, was shrouded in controversy: he had mistaken a shout from the wicketkeeper for a call by his partner, and was run out. In the second innings England were destroyed by careless batting then over-cautious batting, and persistent and skilful bowling by Hawke. Barrington hit only four boundaries in a stay of 5½ hours, and Cowdrey (35) hit only two in over 2½ hours.

886, top, left: *Lawry almost falls in hooking Jones.* 887, centre: *Simpson is congratulated on his century by partner Lawry. The Australian captain went on to 225.* 888, below: *Nightwatchman Veivers c Parks b Jones – seagulls unmoved.* 889, above: *Barrington cheerfully responds to the slow handclapping at Adelaide*

1965–66
Melbourne, February 11, 12, 14, 15, 16

FIFTH TEST

England *485 for 9 dec (K.F. Barrington 115, J.M. Parks 89, J.H. Edrich 85, M.C. Cowdrey 79, F.J. Titmus 42*, K.D. Walters 4 for 53) and 69 for 3; Australia 543 for 8 dec (R.M. Cowper 307, W.M. Lawry 108, K.D. Walters 60). Match drawn.*

The deciding match was blighted by the loss of the fourth day because of rain, a refusal to take risks, and a tedious over rate, particularly when England, with Knight replacing slow bowler Allen, were in the field. After being 41 for 2, England were steadied by an even-time stand of 178 between Edrich and Barrington, the latter reaching his hundred off only 122 balls in 147 minutes. His century came with an on-driven six off Veivers. Walters dismissed them both, as well as Smith – caught behind by Grout, whose last Test this was. Grout died two years later, having had a heart complaint for some years. Cowdrey and Parks took England into higher reaches with 138 for the sixth wicket, but there was to be no overthrowing Australia once Simpson and Thomas had been dismissed cheaply. Lawry batted over six hours, taking his tenancy of the crease against England and MCC this season to over 41 hours. He and Cowper put on 212, and Walters then stayed with Cowper while 172 were added. The likelihood of a decision faded the longer Cowper batted. He reached 100 in 310 minutes, spent a further 225 minutes getting to 200, passed Bradman's record for Australia in Australia, and when Knight bowled him for 307 he had been in for 12 hours 7 minutes, hitting 20 fours.

890, above, left: *Cowper hooks during his 307.* 891, right: *He acknowledges the applause that greeted his triple-century.* 892, below, left: *Cowper b Knight 307.* 893, right: *Barrington brings up his century with a six off Veivers*

894: *Wally Grout leads Australia out in his final Test appearance. Following are Hawke, Cowper, Thomas, Veivers, Stackpole, and McKenzie*

1968
Old Trafford, June 6, 7, 8, 10, 11

FIRST TEST

Australia *357 (A.P. Sheahan 88, W.M. Lawry 81, K.D. Walters 81, I.M. Chappell 73, J.A. Snow 4 for 97) and 220 (K.D. Walters 86, B.N. Jarman 41, P.I. Pocock 6 for 79); England 165 (J.H. Edrich 49, R.M. Cowper 4 for 48) and 253 (B.L. D'Oliveira 87*, R.W. Barber 46).* Australia won by 159 runs.

On a sporting pitch, the youngest-ever Australian side to visit England – with a very wet spring behind them – used the conditions better than the home side, whose bowling resources were thin for this match. Australia were 319 for 4 at the end of the first day, Lawry and Walters mixing watchful defence with strong attacking strokes during their stand of 144. Sheahan and Chappell then took charge with 152 for the fifth wicket. After the run-out of Chappell the innings disintegrated. Hampered by drizzle and poor light, England stuttered to 165, saving the follow-on only with the last pair together. Boycott and Edrich made 86 – more than half the total – for the first wicket. Walters' masterly handling of the bowling – especially Pocock's off-spin – ensured that Australia's lead was beyond reasonable expectation as England began the fourth innings with 9¼ hours remaining. South African-born D'Oliveira, playing his strokes late and very powerfully at times, averted a débâcle and Barber showed promise before Hawke got him. Amiss, like his opponent McKenzie, was out twice without scoring. Only 52,037 attended the match.

895, left: *Graveney caught by McKenzie at short leg off Cowper for two.* 896, opposite page, left: *Cowper bowled by Snow for 0.* 897, centre: *Sheahan, who made 88, edges a ball over Graveney at slip.* 898, right: *Walters pulls Pocock in Australia's second innings*

1968
Lord's, June 20, 21, 22, 24, 25

SECOND TEST

England 351 for 7 dec (C. Milburn 83, K.F. Barrington 75, G. Boycott 49, M.C. Cowdrey 45); Australia 78 (D.J. Brown 5 for 42) and 127 for 4 (I.R. Redpath 53). Match drawn.

The 200th Test between the two countries coincided with some bad weather, and only half the scheduled 30 hours of play was possible. The first day's play was ended at lunchtime by a prodigious hailstorm when England were 53 for the loss of Edrich to an unplayable lifter from McKenzie. Boycott and Milburn played with conspicuous courage and skill, the latter, one of the heaviest men to play Test cricket, absorbing blow after blow on his legs and body. On the second day he tore into the bowling, adding a six off Cowper (into the grandstand under the Father Time weathervane) to his previous hooked six into the Mound Stand off McKenzie. He was finally caught on the boundary off 'mystery' spinner Gleeson. Cowdrey and Barrington added 97, but the flooding had left its mark, and many were the painful knocks received: Barrington had to retire for a time and Australia's wicketkeeper, Jarman, suffered a chipped finger. Little play was possible on the third day, and Cowdrey declared on the fourth morning, when it was felt Australia might have problems. So it transpired. Lawry, the captain, was wonderfully caught by Knott, and midst a succession of catches as Snow, Brown and Knight (3 for 16) moved the ball in the air and off the pitch were three by Cowdrey at slip – taking him past Hammond's Test record of 110 – and a thrilling full-length catch by Knight at gully to dismiss Walters, who top-scored with 26. Only Gleeson, of the rest, reached double-figures. Lawry and Redpath began with 66 in the follow-on, but play was restricted by the weather to under 2½ hours on the final day. Sheahan batted 50 minutes for 0 not out. Colin Cowdrey had tossed (successfully) with a gold sovereign presented him by Sir Robert Menzies.

899: *The England team meet the Duke of Edinburgh during the 200th Test match. The Duke is about to shake hands with wicketkeeper Knott, with MCC president Arthur Gilligan following*

THE TIMES

HOW THE AUSTRALIANS WERE SKITTLED OUT AT LORD'S

England dismissed Australia for 78 in their first innings at Lord's yesterday. Good fast bowling supported by magnificent close-catching combined to put out the Australians for their lowest score in a Test match in this country since 1912. At the close of play Australia had scored 50-0 in their second innings. Report page 15.

W. M. Lawry, c. Knott, b. Brown	0
I. R. Redpath, c. Cowdrey, b. Brown	4
R. M. Cowper, c. Graveney, b. Snow	8
K. D. Walters, c. Knight, b. Brown	26
A. P. Sheahan, c. Knott, b. Knight	6
I. M. Chappell, l.b.w. b. Knight	7
G. D. McKenzie, b. Brown	5
J. W. Gleeson, c. Cowdrey, b. Brown	14
B. N. Jarman retired hurt	0
N. J. N. Hawke, c. Cowdrey, b. Knight	2
A. N. Connolly, not out	0
Extras	6
Total	78

)UND
ΈR
AY
refuses
ɜre

s is expected to
esterday's decision
omotive Engineers
rule from midnight

nich ran yesterday
o suffer widespread
n commuters, who
, face far greater
ne decision by the

ort, said yesterday
dispute. The rail-
r own and could
nent.
of the Railways
decision will com-
st be worse tomor-
that we shall find

A NOTE
ET

Correspondent

aid he could offer little
an early end to the dispute
e railwaymen demanded
se across the board.
el Thomas writes:—One
why services were not
orse affected yesterday
ply that more than two-
f the men defied their
instructions and worked
or on their rest days as
Only a handful worked
in the sense that they
out their duties in an
l way.
British Railways Board
nsider today whether to
the railwaymen's guaran-
k agreement. This would
ossible to send home men
out work by the indus-
on of others and save the
eir wages.
nry Johnson, chairman of
d, said last night that dis-
action could not be
ainst men for working to
or declining to volunteer
ime, but it could be taken
any man who refused to
itimate instructions.
proposals on train man-
issue which reached
in the productivity nego-
were sent to both unions
y with an invitation from
Railways to discuss them
Affecting some 80,000
men and guards, they
ost £2m. a year to intro-
t this would be offset by
One proposal is that
milage bonuses should be
by a flat weekly allow-
nother attempts to break
lock over the manning of
ves by men apart from

f talks take place on these
s they are unlikely to
main dispute, which is
unions' demand for an
te all-round increase with-
luctivity conditions.
rn Region cuts, page 2.

ıst act
h says

—Carlisle, June 24

e Mr. Marsh was flying to

could the question be
o Mr. Swingler, Minister
, Ministry of Transport.
in Lancashire for the day,
in the Nelson and Colne
on campaign.
ut the facts, several
entarians on both sides of
se thought Mr. Marsh had
rities wrong, for the ques-
alt with what the Ministry
"to minimize inconven-
public and industry".
armichael made a holding
nt decribing the day's
and did not allow himself
drawn into controversy
e dispute.
Castle, Secretary of State
ployment and Productivity,
10 Downing Street last
discuss the work-to-rule
Wilson, but Government
went out of their way to
ze that the discussion did
esage any possibility of
ment intervention to bring
settlement on terms that
with incomes policy. Mr.
and Mrs. Castle are said
anding firm in their view
Government's incomes
has been brought under
hallenge and they have no
n of surrendering to the
from the railway unions.
mentary report, page 14.

Gaullist
back w
ma

From CHARLES H

The victory of the Gaullist pa
in the first ballot of the Fren
parliamentary elections yesterd
could turn into a landslide in t
second vote next Sunday. Ev
on the most conservative estima
the Gaullist majority in the n
Assembly will be much more su
stantial than it was in the last.
The Government can even lo
forward to the possibility
having an absolute majority in
own right without having to r
on the qualified and critical su
port of M. Giscard d'Estain
Independent Republicans.
On the first vote the Gover
ment has recovered three-fifths
the seats it held in Parliame
with another 333 to be filled. Ve
few of its candidates have fail
to obtain the 10 per cent of vo
cast in the first ballot that th
need to remain in the second, a
a substantial number are very w
placed to win under mutual wit
drawal arrangements which w
be struck with Independent R
publican candidates.
A new development came t
night when M. Pompidou s
gested a similar arrangement
candidates of the centre—offeri
to withdraw the Gaullist candid
if the centrist had emerged in
better place in the first ballot whe
ever there was risk that a co
munist might win.
He went even further. He sa
that he was prepared to withdr

Inquiry over
bank chief's
salary

BY OUR POLITICAL STAFF

Payment of a £4,279 increase
director's remuneration to M
Jocelyn Hambros, chairman
Hambros Bank is being inves
gated by the Department
Employment and Productivi
Mr. Walker, Parliamentary Sec
tary to the Ministry, said in t
Commons yesterday.
He told Mr. Allaun, Labo
M.P. for Salford East, that t
Prices and Incomes White Pap
made it clear that the princip
of the policy applied to directo
remuneration.
"The Government expect dir
tors to show the same sense
responsibility towards these prin
ples as is being asked of wa
and salary earners", he said. "
will be keeping the question
directors' remuneration und
close review, as details becor
increasingly available through t
operation of the Companies A
1967."
Mr. Allaun said in his questi
that the chairman of Hambros h
a rise of from £20,866 to £25,
a year in the past 12 mont
besides share dividends.
Business News, page 21.

Police alerted b
strike ship

FROM OUR CORRESPONDENT

DOVER, JUNE 24

For five hours today memb
of the crew of the Israel s
Avocadocore (18,433 tons) argu
with officials as the vessel lay
anchor in the middle of the f
shrouded harbour at Dov
Police stood by on shore.
The ship, sailing to Brem
haven with a cargo of fruit w
diverted to Dover to land ei
members of the crew who w
refusing to take orders. But w
the ship was preparing to le
Dover the crew were still
board.
After immigration officers w
out by launch to board the shi
radio message asked Kent pol
to stand by. The message s
some of the seamen were arm
with knives and wire hawsers.
convoy of vehicles took police
the pierhead, but they were la
withdrawn.

13 die in Swiss
rail crash

FROM OUR CORRESPONDENT

GENEVA, JUNE 24

Thirteen people were killed a
119 injured, some seriously, wh
two trains collided head-on o
single-track stretch of the m
line from Lake Geneva to
Simplon tunnel today.
Picture, page 7.

Woman's body
near camp

FROM OUR CORRESPONDENT

GUILDFORD, JUNE 24

A murder hunt began toni
after the body of a woman in
early twenties had been fou
naked and mutilated on a tra
near the Women's Royal Ar
Corps depot at Guildford, Surr
She had been strangled and a
attacked with a blunt instrume

900, left: The Times *considered Australia's collapse for 78 worthy of front-page treatment.* 901, top: *Milburn hooks McKenzie fearlessly for four.* 902, above: *Lord's after the hailstorm; Sydney must have looked similar when the elements rebelled during the third Test of the 1884–85 series*

1968
Edgbaston, July 11, 12, 13, 15, 16

THIRD TEST

England 409 (*M.C. Cowdrey 104, T.W. Graveney 96, J.H. Edrich 88, E.W. Freeman 4 for 78*) *and 142 for 3 dec* (*J.H. Edrich 64*); *Australia 222* (*I.M. Chappell 71, R.M. Cowper 57, K.D. Walters 46*) *and 68 for 1. Match drawn.*

Further rain spoilt a contest in which England held the upper hand almost throughout. After a blank first day Boycott and Edrich began with 80, and then Cowdey, playing in his 100th Test, put on 108 with Edrich, reaching his celebratory century during a fourth-wicket stand of 93 with Graveney. Cowdrey, who also became only the second batsman (after Hammond) to make 7000 Test runs, badly pulled a leg muscle halfway to his landmark, and had Boycott as a runner. Graveney's 96, like his partner's innings, contained many fine strokes. Australia experienced a grim start, Brown bowling Redpath for nought and Snow breaking Lawry's finger; yet by the third evening they were 109 for one. After Cowper and Chappell were out, however, only Walters lasted long, and the score went from 213 for 4 to 222 all out, with Lawry unable to bat. England extended their lead at more than three runs an over (Graveney leading in Cowdrey's absence), and Australia were set 330 in 370 minutes. Heavy rain before lunch drove the players from the field, and there was no resumption.

903, below, left: *Redpath is bowled by Brown without scoring.* 904, bottom, left: *Australia's captain Lawry, out of action after a blow on the finger by Snow, catches up on his letter-writing.* 905, below, right: *Cowdrey, playing in his 100th Test, drives Gleeson to the boundary.* 906, bottom, right: *Cowdrey is congratulated by Graveney upon reaching his century*

1968
Headingley, July 25, 26, 27, 29, 30

FOURTH TEST

Australia 315 (*I.R. Redpath 92, I.M. Chappell 65, K.D. Walters 42, D.L. Underwood 4 for 41*) and 312 (*I.M. Chappell 81, K.D. Walters 56, I.R. Redpath 48, R. Illingworth 6 for 87*); England 302 (*R.M. Prideaux 64, J.H. Edrich 62, K.F. Barrington 49, D.L. Underwood 45*, A.N. Connolly 5 for 72*) and 230 for 4 (*J.H. Edrich 65, K.F. Barrington 46*, T.W. Graveney 41*). Match drawn.

Jarman and Graveney led their teams in the absence of the injured Lawry and Cowdrey, and for once there was hardly any weather interruption. Australia held the Ashes by virtue of this draw, and owed much to the young trio of batsmen, Redpath, Walters and Chappell, and the relentless attack of McKenzie and Connolly. For England, Prideaux, playing his only Test against Australia, aided Edrich in an impressive opening stand of 123, after which there was a falling away. It was left to Underwood, the last man, to put on 61 with Brown. Connolly at fast-medium moved the ball around disconcertingly. On the first day Cowper was 15 at lunch after two hours' batting. Walters and Chappell in the second innings were almost as resolute. England's eventual target was 326 at 66 an hour. The risk involved in chasing the bait was too high. Knott made three stumpings off Illingworth in the second innings, but Keith Fletcher's Test debut was unhappy: he missed three sharp slip chances and made nought and 23 not out.

907, top, left: *Prideaux swings a ball to leg only to be caught by Freeman for 64.* 908, left: *Fletcher caught by Jarman down the leg side off Connolly.* 909, above: *Ian Chappell cuts Underwood for four*

910: *Cowper, having made only five at Leeds, is stumped by Knott off Illingworth – a mode of dismissal somewhat rare in modern times*

1968
The Oval, August 22, 23, 24, 26, 27

FIFTH TEST

England 494 (*J.H. Edrich 164, B.L. D'Oliveira 158, T.W. Graveney 63*) *and 181 (A.N. Connolly 4 for 65);* Australia 324 (*W.M. Lawry 135, I.R. Redpath 67, A.A. Mallett 43**) *and 125 (R.J. Inverarity 56, D.L. Underwood 7 for 50). England won by 226 runs.*

When Australia were 65 for 5 just before lunch on the final day the match was England's. When a storm turned the field into a lake an abandonment seemed certain – yet again the elements had defied England. Then came a miraculous transformation. The ground staff, helped by volunteers from the crowd, spiked the lower outfield areas and mopped up countless gallons of water, and a resumption was possible at 4.45 pm. England then bowled to no avail for 40 minutes . . . until D'Oliveira bowled Jarman, and Underwood was put on at the pavilion end and used the drying surface to such effect that he took the wickets of Mallett, McKenzie and Gleeson, and – with time for only two more overs – Inverarity, who was on the verge of carrying his bat. Much good cricket had gone before: Edrich's 7¾-hour century (his aggregate for the series was 554), the recalled D'Oliveira's spirited 158, Lawry's stoic century, the only one for Australia in the series – begun on the second evening and ended with a disputed catch behind on the fourth morning – and Redpath's soundness, Mallett's dismissal of Cowdrey in his first over in Test cricket (and his 43 not out in over three hours), England's dash for quick second-innings runs. As Inverarity was given out lbw, each journalist had to rewrite his story.

911, below, left: *Milburn b Connolly 8.* 912, below, right: *Edrich on-drives Gleeson during his 164*

913, top, left: *The Oval outfield is flooded after the storm, but willing hands at the spikers and sacking transformed a seemingly hopeless scene.* 914, centre: *With only a few minutes remaining, Inverarity pads up to Underwood and is lbw. England, against the odds, have won.* 915, left: *23-year-old Underwood, having taken 7 for 50, gives the grateful crowd a wave.* 916, above: *D'Oliveira drives Ian Chappell on his way to 158*

1970–71   FIRST TEST
Brisbane, November 27, 28, 29, December 1, 2

Australia 433 (*K.R. Stackpole 207, K.D. Walters 112, I.M. Chappell 59, J.A. Snow 6 for 114*) *and 214
(W.M. Lawry 84, K. Shuttleworth 5 for 47*); England 464 (*J.H. Edrich 79, B.W. Luckhurst 74, A.P.E. Knott
73, B.L. D'Oliveira 57*) *and 39 for 1.* Match drawn.

Australia rode high at 372 for 2 on the second day, only to collapse against Snow and Underwood.
Indeed, the last seven wickets fell for 15 runs. Stackpole, very strong in the cut and hook, hit 25 fours
and a six, though he was lucky to survive a run-out appeal at 18, and gave two sharp chances. His robust
batting was in marked contrast with that of Lawry, his opening partner, who in the second innings held
his side together with 84 in 5½ hours. Chappell and Stackpole added 151, and Walters, sometimes
brilliant, sometimes uncomfortable, put on 209 with the double-centurion. Luckhurst batted most
convincingly for England, most of the others taking their time about their runs – time that might better
have been used chasing victory after Shuttleworth with the new ball had hurried through Australia's tail
on the last day.

*917: Stackpole receives the benefit of
a close run-out call at 18 (bowler
Shuttleworth in mid-air). The
Australian opener went on to 207*

*918: Over the top – six runs for Stack-
pole off Illingworth*

919, above, left: *Illingworth at short leg dives to pick up a catch from Redpath.* 920, right: *'Froggy' Thomson takes his only wicket of the match – Illingworth, caught by Marsh*

1970–71
Perth, December 11, 12, 13, 15, 16

SECOND TEST

England 397 (B.W. Luckhurst 131, G. Boycott 70, J.H. Edrich 47, M.C. Cowdrey 40, G.D. McKenzie 4 for 66) and 287 for 6 dec (J.H. Edrich 115*, G. Boycott 50); Australia 440 (I.R. Redpath 171, G.S. Chappell 108, I.M. Chappell 50, R.W. Marsh 44, J.A. Snow 4 for 143) and 100 for 3. Match drawn.

Perth's first Test match, well-attended, was distinguished by a debut century from Greg Chappell, who saved his side with a stand of 219 with Redpath, who made his first hundred against England. Replying to England's 397, which was founded on an opening of 171 by Boycott and Luckhurst, Australia were 107 for 5 after Snow's early breakthrough. The 22-year-old Chappell then went in and settled against the pace bowlers, stepping up the attack after tea to such an extent that 74 runs came from 10 overs. His innings lasted little more than half the time taken by Redpath. England were unhappy against Gleeson, and on the final day were in some peril, until Illingworth and then Knott stayed with Edrich. A token declaration was made when safety had been reached, and Lawry saw out the 32 overs, making 38 not out, which included his 5000th Test run and his 2000th against England.

921: *Luckhurst bowled by McKenzie after his plucky 131*

922 above: *Greg Chappell, Australia's fine discovery, during his debut century.* 923, top, right: *Knott leaps to a touch off Ian Chappell's glove, but fails to hold it.* 924, right: *A portion of Perth's population invades the pitch to let Greg Chappell know they appreciate his hundred*

1970–71
Sydney, January 9, 10, 12, 13, 14

FOURTH TEST

England *332 (G. Boycott 77, J.H. Edrich 55, A.A. Mallett 4 for 40, J.W. Gleeson 4 for 83) and 319 for 5 dec (G. Boycott 142*, B.L. D'Oliveira 56, R. Illingworth 53); Australia 236 (I.R. Redpath 64, K.D. Walters 55, D.L. Underwood 4 for 66) and 116 (W.M. Lawry 60*, J.A. Snow 7 for 40).* England won by 299 runs.

The New Year's Test at Melbourne having been washed out without a ball bowled (though the captains did toss), it was decided to stage an extra Test and to play a one-day international in Melbourne. This match at Sydney, therefore, had three to follow it; and England seized the chance to go one-up with some high-class batting and Snow's fiery bowling on a pitch which had seemed more in favour of spin. Boycott and Luckhurst began the match with 116, and the consistent Edrich again played his part. Mallett then unbalanced England with a spell of 3 for 6, but the later batsmen recovered the initiative. Only Redpath and Walters, with a stand of 99, withstood the varied England attack for long, and when the touring side went in again 96 ahead, quick runs were needed. Boycott obliged with a technically admirable innings, adding 133 with D'Oliveira after three wickets had fallen for 48. Illingworth's bowlers were then left over nine hours to dispose of Australia – who survived less than half that time in the face of Snow's devastation. Lawry carried his bat; McKenzie had his nose smashed by a lifting ball; Australia's batsmen seemed not to know which way to turn against such hostility.

925, above, left: *Knott is stumped by Marsh, his opposite number.* 926 above, right: *Lever makes a magnificent catch in the gully to end Stackpole's innings.* 927, below, left: *Mallett, caught by Knott, gives Willis his first Test wicket.* 928, below, right: *McKenzie is hit in the face by a ball from Snow; he retired hurt with blood pouring from the wound*

1970–71
Melbourne, January 21, 22, 23, 25, 26

FIFTH TEST

Australia *493 for 9 dec (I.M. Chappell 111, R.W. Marsh 92*, I.R. Redpath 72, W.M. Lawry 56, K.D. Walters 55) and 169 for 4 dec (W.M. Lawry 42)*; England *392 (B.L. D'Oliveira 117, B.W. Luckhurst 109, R. Illingworth 41) and 161 for 0 (G. Boycott 76*, J.H. Edrich 74*)*. Match drawn.

England's deplorable fielding – Cowdrey in particular had a wretched match – forced them into second place throughout a match notable for unpleasant crowd behaviour. The field was overrun when Chappell reached his century, and several items were stolen in the mêlée. Catcalling was prevalent also. Chappell and Redpath scored fast in the last session of a hot first day, which ended at 260 for one, Lawry having retired with a damaged finger. Wicketkeeper Marsh, an aggressive left-hander, dominated the second day, hitting his way to the verge of a unique (for Australia) hundred when Lawry declared. England, 88 for 3 and in serious danger, were stabilised by Luckhurst – who batted for most of his innings with a broken little finger – and D'Oliveira, who also went on to a century, driving and cutting with great force. The first-innings disparity became less than expected, but Australia were slow to capitalise, and advanced at less then four an over. Nonetheless, they had four hours in which to dismiss England. Illingworth's attitude, in return, was to decline the invitation to make 271, and to the accompaniment of clanking beer-cans England's openers played out time.

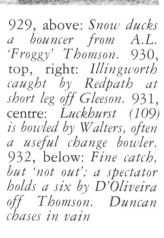

929, above: *Snow ducks a bouncer from A.L. 'Froggy' Thomson.* 930, top, right: *Illingworth caught by Redpath at short leg off Gleeson.* 931, centre: *Luckhurst (109) is bowled by Walters, often a useful change bowler.* 932, below: *Fine catch, but 'not out': a spectator holds a six by D'Oliveira off Thomson. Duncan chases in vain*

1970-71
Adelaide, January 29, 30, February 1, 2, 3

England 470 (*J.H. Edrich 130, K.W.R. Fletcher 80, G. Boycott 58, J.H. Hampshire 55, B.L. D'Oliveira 47, D.K. Lillee 5 for 84*) and 233 for 4 dec (*G. Boycott 119*, R. Illingworth 48*, J.H. Edrich 40*); Australia 235 (*K.R. Stackpole 87, P. Lever 4 for 49*) and 328 for 3 (*K.R. Stackpole 136, I.M. Chappell 104*). Match drawn.

England, with century opening stands by Boycott and Edrich in both innings, controlled this match, and though there was much debate upon Illingworth's decision not to enforce the follow-on, he was probably right, since the pitch was benevolent and his fast bowlers were engaged in four Tests in five weeks. Boycott brought much criticism down on his head from near and far by throwing his bat to the ground in annoyance after being given run-out, but the momentum of the innings was maintained with a stand of 169 between the patient Edrich and Fletcher, whose first notable Test innings this was. Solid middle batting saw England to a near-impregnable total, Lillee, in his first Test, keeping up his pace well and taking five wickets. Stackpole, with 87 out of 117, was the soul of a disappointing Australian innings, Snow, Lever, Underwood, Willis and Illingworth going about their job determinedly. Boycott was in sprightly form as England set about extending their lead, and Australia were finally left with 500 minutes and a target of 469. They began the last day at 104 for the loss of Lawry. Stackpole and Chappell put on 202 for the second wicket, the former batting almost seven hours, Chappell 5½, and at last Australia had batted for a day and a half without being dismissed.

933, above: *Stackpole b Underwood 87.* 934, centre: *Boycott, having been run out, is prompted to leave the field by Australian fieldsmen close enough to detect his reluctance.* 935, below: *Walters caught behind off Lever*

1970–71
Sydney, February 12, 13, 14, 16, 17

SEVENTH TEST

England *184 (R. Illingworth 42) and 302 (B.W. Luckhurst 59, J.H. Edrich 57, B.L. D'Oliveira 47);* Australia *264 (G.S. Chappell 65, I.R. Redpath 59, K.D. Walters 42) and 160 (K.R. Stackpole 67).* England won by 62 runs.

Ray Illingworth, in leading his side to a 2-0 victory, became the first to captain England in recapture of the Ashes in Australia since D.R. Jardine 38 years earlier. His opposing captain this time was Ian Chappell, Lawry having been dropped. The 27-year-old South Australian, grandson of V.Y. Richardson, put England in to bat, and had them out by 5.18 pm, spinners Jenner and O'Keeffe taking three wickets each. The second day was eventful. Redpath and Walters halted a collapse, but in the last session Snow cut Jenner's head with a lifting ball, was warned by umpire Rowan, and then had his shirt grabbed by an inebriated spectator on the long-leg fence. Beer-cans rained onto the ground, Illingworth sat down, as did others in his team, and soon the England captain was leading his men off the field. The umpires warned him that he would forfeit the match if he did not return, and, peace restored, Australia were ahead that evening with three wickets left. The final lead of 80 was cleared in the first-wicket stand of Edrich and Luckhurst, the Kent right-hander this time proving an able replacement for the injured Boycott. The first nine batsmen all reached double-figures, and gradually Australia were set a stiffish target. Snow bowled Eastwood, Lawry's replacement, with no run yet scored, but then broke his right forefinger running for a big hit to the long-leg pickets. This placed extra onus on Underwood and Illingworth, who carried England's hopes on the fifth-day pitch. The last day began with Australia 123 for 5 – 100 needed, Greg Chappell and Marsh in. Illingworth got the vital wicket, that of Chappell, by drifting one past his bat and having him stumped. With surprising ease the rest were accounted for, and England's 38-year-old captain was chaired by his players from the field.

936, below, left: *Jenner collapses after being struck by a lifting ball from Snow. The incident brought a warning to the bowler from umpire Rowan.* 937, below, right: *Snow's shirt is grabbed by a spectator on the Paddington Hill – another irritating moment in an inflammatory afternoon*

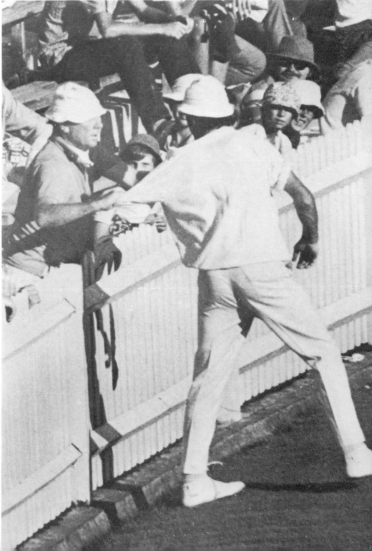

FIRST DAY COVER

London Express

938, above: *The victorious MCC side of 1970–71 record* The Ashes Song *as a permanent if unmelodic souvenir of an historic win.* 939, centre: *England's triumph coincided with a British postal strike, and a London delivery service chose what purported to be the final ball of the series as the motif on their first-day cover.* 940, below: *England did it without two key players, Snow and Boycott, seen nursing their injuries after the match*

1972
FIRST TEST
Old Trafford, June 8, 9, 10, 12, 13

England 249 (A.W. Greig 57, J.H. Edrich 49) and 234 (A.W. Greig 62, G. Boycott 47, D.K. Lillee 6 for 66); Australia 142 (K.R. Stackpole 53, J.A. Snow 4 for 41, G.G. Arnold 4 for 62) and 252 (R.W. Marsh 91, K.R. Stackpole 67, A.W. Greig 4 for 53, J.A. Snow 4 for 87). England won by 89 runs.

A poorly-attended match, marred by long periods of cold and damp weather, offered encouragement to bowlers throughout, and Snow and Arnold used the conditions best of all. Swinging and cutting the ball, they continually pressed the Australians. The fielding of both sides was not at its best, and Arnold once saw three catches go down in one of his overs. Tony Greig, South African-born, and at 6ft 7½ins the tallest cricketer to play in these Tests, had a superb Test debut, batting boldly in both innings, holding two catches, and taking five wickets. Stackpole chanced his luck in the first innings and batted 3½ hours in the second, but in contrast Ian Chappell, the captain, was out twice cheaply as he hooked. Marsh, who took five catches behind the wicket in England's second innings, thrashed 91 in a late gesture of defiance, putting Gifford four times into the crowd, but they were English conditions, and the competent home side always seemed to have a command – however tenuous – of the match. Illingworth, 40 on the opening day, had taken the chance when it offered . . . and was to be glad of it as Chappell's young side found itself as the series progressed.

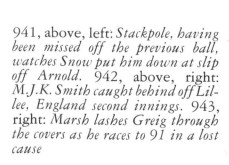

941, above, left: *Stackpole, having been missed off the previous ball, watches Snow put him down at slip off Arnold.* 942, above, right: *M.J.K. Smith caught behind off Lillee, England second innings.* 943, right: *Marsh lashes Greig through the covers as he races to 91 in a lost cause*

1972
Lord's, June 22, 23, 24, 26

SECOND TEST

England 272 (A.W. Greig 54, A.P.E. Knott 43, R.A.L. Massie 8 for 84) and 116 (R.A.L. Massie 8 for 53); Australia 308 (G.S. Chappell 131, I.M. Chappell 56, R.W. Marsh 50, J.A. Snow 5 for 57) and 81 for 2 (K.R. Stackpole 57*). Australia won by 8 wickets.

Bob Massie, a 25-year-old Western Australian (the state had four men in the Test XI for the first time), put his name on this match with an astonishing exhibition of swing bowling – mostly from around the wicket – to return analyses of 32.5-7-84-8 and 27.2-9-53-8. These are easily the best figures in a Test debut, and for Australia in any Test. He curved the ball suddenly and late, either way and to a length, and no England player could work out a reliable method of combating him. The other four wickets went to Lillee, who bowled fast and accurately. The biggest stand of England's first innings was 96 by Greig (making his third half-century in as many Test innings) and Knott. Australia began disastrously, but the Chappells steadied the innings, the upright Greg going on to a beautiful fighting century, batting in all for 6¼ hours. Marsh hit a strong 50 to gain a lead for Australia, only Snow drawing prolonged respect from the batsmen. By Saturday evening Massie had shattered England again. At 86 for 9 they were a mere 50 ahead. Massie took his 16th wicket on Monday morning, and the runs were obtained with a minimum of fuss, Stackpole hitting out in no-nonsense fashion. One-all the series stood, and if Massie had been fit for the first Test, the tourists might well have been two-up.

944, left: *The members at Lord's rise to Greg Chappell at the end of his century innings.* 945, above: *Boycott, bemused and bowled, becomes one of Massie's 16 victims in the match*

946, left: *Smith, with no answer to the violent swing of the ball, is bowled by Massie.* 947, above: *The effect of victory: Marsh, Massie, manager Steele, Lillee, Mallett, Edwards, and Hammond (seated) react to Australia's series-levelling win*

1972
Trent Bridge, July 13, 14, 15, 17, 18

THIRD TEST

Australia 315 (K.R. Stackpole 114, D.J. Colley 54, R.W. Marsh 41, J.A. Snow 5 for 92) and 324 for 4 dec (R. Edwards 170*, G.S. Chappell 72, I.M. Chappell 50); England 189 (D.K. Lillee 4 for 35, R.A.L. Massie 4 for 43) and 290 for 4 (B.W. Luckhurst 96, B.L. D'Oliveira 50*, P.H. Parfitt 46). Match drawn.

Illingworth put Australia in, assured that the pitch would become easier the longer the match went on. The ploy might have worked, but for feeble outcricket. Parfitt held four fine slip catches, but missed Stackpole when 46. The burly opener was in for 5½ hours, steering his side to a sound position. Marsh and Colley gave a boost to the tail, but had Snow had better support Australia could have been in trouble. Instead, England struggled. They took 6½ hours to make 189 – though only 88.3 overs were bowled. Luckhurst was two hours reaching double-figures. Marsh held five catches behind the stumps, and was often stretched by Lillee's bouncers and widish deliveries. Once more Massie swung the ball disconcertingly. In place of the injured Francis, Edwards opened with Stackpole, and grasped his opportunity well. He added 124 with Ian Chappell and 146 with Greg, and had been in for 5½ hours when the innings was closed. England needed 451 – a somewhat academic calculation – and had 9½ hours left. Luckhurst, in making England's highest score of the entire series, provided the base for survival, putting on 117 with Parfitt, and after a ripple of tension as three wickets fell, D'Oliveira and Greig played out time.

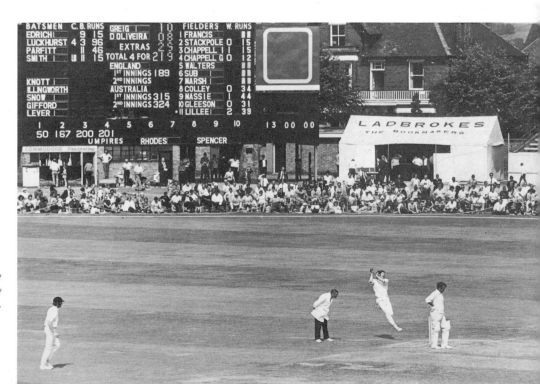

948: *Lillee bowling during the D'Oliveira-Greig stand on the final day that assured England of a draw*

949, left: *Greg Chappell b Snow 72 at Trent Bridge.* 950, above: *Edwards swings at a ball from Illingworth, taken by Knott*

1972
Headingley, July 27, 28, 29

FOURTH TEST

Australia *146 (K.R. Stackpole 52, D.L. Underwood 4 for 37) and 136 (A.P. Sheahan 41*, D.L. Underwood 6 for 45); England 263 (R. Illingworth 57, J.A. Snow 48, J.H. Edrich 45, A.A. Mallett 5 for 114) and 21 for 1. England won by 9 wickets.*

The sub-standard nature of the Leeds pitch – put down to devastation of the turf by fusarium disease when heavy rain compelled lengthy protection under covers – allowed the spinners to achieve turn even before lunch on the opening day. Australia were 79 for one at lunch, but on the bare, drying wicket they tumbled to 146 all out, Underwood using the ideal conditions to take 4 for 37 off 31 overs and Illingworth taking two wickets and two catches in the field. Edrich and Luckhurst made 43 that evening, but by lunch on the second day England were struggling at 112 for 6, Mallett, pushing through his off-breaks, having taken five quality wickets, and Inverarity, not usually a front-line bowler, mesmerising the batsmen with slow left-arm. The innings was saved by Illingworth and Snow, who made 104 for the eighth wicket, the captain batting in all for 4½ hours. Australia were given little chance against Underwood and Illingworth in their second innings: and so it transpired. After Edwards had followed his big score at Nottingham with a 'pair', and Arnold had got Ian Chappell caught behind for nought, Underwood tore through the middle in a spell of 5 for 18. The ball turned quickly and often lifted. Only Sheahan, playing straight, faced his task without the air of a condemned man. At 5.03 pm England had retained the Ashes; but some bitter discussions ensued.

951, above: *Ian Chappell caught-and-bowled by Illingworth.* 952, top, right: *Sheahan brilliantly caught by Illingworth off Underwood.* 953, centre: *Mallett dives and just misses a caught-and-bowled chance from Edrich.* 954, below: *Stackpole, already halfway through a run, receives the bad news: he is lbw to Underwood for 28 in the second innings*

1972
The Oval, August 10, 11, 12, 14, 15, 16

FIFTH TEST

England 284 (A.P.E. Knott 92, P.H. Parfitt 51, J.H. Hampshire 42, D.K. Lillee 5 for 58) and 356 (B. Wood 90, A.P.E. Knott 63, B.L. D'Oliveira 43, D.K. Lillee 5 for 123); Australia 399 (I.M. Chappell 118, G.S. Chappell 113, R. Edwards 79, D.L. Underwood 4 for 90) and 242 for 5 (K.R. Stackpole 79, A.P. Sheahan 44*, R.W. Marsh 43*). Australia won by 5 wickets.

A fine match concluded halfway through the sixth day in a result which gave much satisfaction to the Australians – and suspense and entertainment to everyone in its achievement. England were humbled on the first day by Lillee, varying his pace and using the bouncer to effect, and Mallett, now a nagging off-spinner. Knott, batting inventively and bravely, then led Arnold in a stand of 81. Australia's innings was built upon a third-wicket stand of 201 by the Chappells – the first instance of centuries by brothers in a Test match. Ian bustled, was watchful, and quick to pounce on wayward deliveries; Greg was cool and stylish and just as unemotional. They took their side within sight of the England total, and Edwards, solidly, steered Australia to a useful lead on an interrupted third day. Underwood prevented a greater deficit. Wood, in his first Test, batted fearlessly and correctly until Massie had him lbw, but it took another nimble innings from Knott to set up a sizable target for Australia. He was last out – Lillee's 31st wicket of the series: a record for Australia in England. The fast bowler sent down 56.4 overs in the match, to take 10 for 181. Set 242, Australia were 116 for one on the fifth evening, by which time Illingworth had been put out of the match with a sprained ankle. With D'Oliveira also unable to bowl and Snow with a damaged arm from a Lillee bouncer, England, now led by Edrich, made little impression. After Ian Chappell and Stackpole had added 116 for the second wicket, three wickets fell quickly, but Sheahan and Marsh in their contrasting manners gathered 71 in an unfinished stand that gave Australia – for the first time without a New South Wales player – a victory to square the series.

955, top, left: *Parfitt loses his middle stump to a quick one from Lillee.* 956, bottom: *Hampshire succumbs to a high slip catch by Ian Chappell.* 957, top, right: *D'Oliveira is victim of a smart catch by Greg Chappell.* 958, bottom: *Ian Chappell edges Illingworth through the vacant slips area to reach his century*

959, left: *Wood (90) stands up and drives Mallett for four.* 960, right: *Sheahan and Marsh hurry off after an Australian victory which marked the emergence of a strong, young side, led positively by Ian Chappell*

1974–75
Brisbane, November 29, 30, December 1, 3, 4

FIRST TEST

Australia 309 (*I.M. Chappell 90, G.S. Chappell 58, M.H.N. Walker 41*, R.G.D. Willis 4 for 56*) and 288 for 5 dec (*G.S. Chappell 71, K.D. Walters 62*, R. Edwards 53, R.W. Marsh 46**); England 265 (*A.W. Greig 110, J.H. Edrich 48, M.H.N. Walker 4 for 73*) and 166 (*J.R. Thomson 6 for 46*). Australia won by 166 runs.

Australia's new fast bowler Jeff Thomson – a strong, athletic slinger of the ball – and his opening partner Dennis Lillee, who had come back after a serious back injury, established a mastery over England which was to last until towards the end of the series, when both sustained injuries. The opening Test, on a dubious pitch hastily prepared after storms, was won as much by their bowling, backed by Walker's medium-pace, as anything else. Ian Chappell saw to it that the first Australian innings rose to some height, and his brother was watchful in both innings. England's misfortunes were compounded by Amiss's broken thumb and Edrich's broken hand – both caused by very fast balls. Greig's was the exceptional innings of the match. Willis and Lever may have been hostile at times, but the tall England batsman had to contend with the raw, sometimes wild, and lifting speed of Thomson and the deft variations of the only slightly less fast Lillee. Greig drove them and sliced them over slips with great arrogance. His century was only the second ever for England at the Woolloongabba ground. Ten for none at the start of the last day, England could not cope with Thomson until he began to tire. Using the yorker to effect, and with the support of an umbrella field that was to serve Australia exceedingly well during the series, he took 6 for 46, and Australia, one-up, seemed to be well on the way to regaining the Ashes.

961: *'Ashes to ashes, dust to dust – if Thomson don't get ya, Lillee must . . . .' Rigby's famous cartoon in the* Sydney Sunday Telegraph *which summed up the 1974–75 series*

962, left: *Greig reaches a bold century and shows his pleasure.*
963, centre: *Second-innings comedown: b Thomson 2.* 964,
right: *Thomson, having taken 6 for 46, comes in to face the
backslapping and the worship*

1974–75
Perth, December 13, 14, 15, 17

SECOND TEST

England 208 (A.P.E. Knott 51, D. Lloyd 49) and 293 (F.J. Titmus 61, C.M. Old 43, M.C. Cowdrey 41, J.R. Thomson 5 for 93); Australia 481 (R. Edwards 115, K.D. Walters 103, G.S. Chappell 62, I.R. Redpath 41, R.W. Marsh 41) and 23 for 1. Australia won by 9 wickets.

On the fast Perth pitch Australia's superiority was revealed in fast bowling, batting and fielding (17 out of 18 catches offered were held – a record seven of them by Greg Chappell). Thomson, with seven wickets in the match, created further difficulties for England by inflicting agonising blows on Luckhurst's hand and Lloyd's abdomen. Cowdrey had been flown out as a reinforcement, and found himself going out to bat only four days after arrival. He, Knott and Titmus (playing his first Test for seven years, and 42 years old, like Cowdrey) were the only England batsmen to get into the line of the bowling with consistency. Australia, having put England in, then batted solidly down the order, Edwards, strong off the back foot, adding 170 with Walters, who reached his century – and a hundred between tea and the close of the second day – by hooking a short ball from Willis, the last of the day, for six. The innings restored Walters' reputation. The pattern of the match reaffirmed that Mike Denness's side were outclassed.

965: *David Lloyd wishes he were somewhere else after taking a quick one from Thomson in the groin on the fast Perth pitch*

966, left: *Veteran Colin Cowdrey, flown out as a reinforcement, resisted bravely, then was bowled by Thomson. 967, right: Walters pulls Willis for six to reach his century – and a hundred between tea and close of play at Perth*

1974–75

Melbourne, December 26, 27, 28, 30, 31

THIRD TEST

England *242 (A.P.E. Knott 52, J.H. Edrich 49, J.R. Thomson 4 for 72) and 244 (D.L. Amiss 90, A.W. Greig 60, D. Lloyd 44, A.A. Mallett 4 for 60, J.R. Thomson 4 for 71); Australia 241 (I.R. Redpath 55, R.W. Marsh 44, R.G.D. Willis 5 for 61) and 238 for 8 (G.S. Chappell 61, R.W. Marsh 40, A.W. Greig 4 for 56).* Match drawn.

With 55 runs needed in the final hour, and four wickets in hand, Australia dithered, Marsh and Walker making only seven runs off seven overs from Titmus and Underwood. England took the new ball, and a brief batting assault took place; then Underwood bowled the penultimate over, 14 still needed. It was a model maiden. Greig bowled the last, dismissing Lillee, and the draw was played out, Australia eight runs and England two wickets short of victory. Chappell had put England in again, before 77,165 spectators on Boxing Day. Edrich and Cowdrey made 76 for the third wicket, but there was no other prolonged resistance until Knott went in. Willis, bowling shortish spells, was fast and lively, and his effort was doubly important since he lacked the support of Hendrick, who bowled 2.6 overs only before pulling a hamstring. Amiss, having batted splendidly, was caught off Mallett two runs short of R.B. Simpson's record aggregate of 1381 runs in Tests in a calendar year. He gave England a start of 115 with Lloyd, but the middle of the innings fell away in familiar fashion, only an extrovert innings by Greig, supported by Willis, seeing to it that Australia needed to make marginally the highest total of the match to win. In the event neither side was disposed to commit itself boldly enough for victory. Thomson now had 24 wickets in three Tests.

968, below, left: *Redpath c Knott b Greig 55. 969, right: Amiss drives during his 90, which left him two runs short of Simpson's calendar-year aggregate of 1381 in all Tests (passed by Viv Richards in 1976)*

970, above: *Titmus sunk by an agonising blow on the knee from Thomson.* 971, centre: *Typifying the glorious catching of the Australians, Greg Chappell ensnares Cowdrey at Mel-* bourne. 972, above: *Marsh is told the direction of the dressing-room by Greig, who has just dismissed him in Australia's second innings. Verbal exchanges were a feature of the series*

1974–75
Sydney, January 4, 5, 6, 8, 9

FOURTH TEST

Australia 405 (G.S. Chappell 84, R.B. McCosker 80, I.M. Chappell 53, G.G. Arnold 5 for 86, A.W. Greig 4 for 104) and 289 for 4 dec (G.S. Chappell 144, I.R. Redpath 105); England 295 (A.P.E. Knott 82, J.H. Edrich 50, J.R. Thomson 4 for 74) and 228 (A.W. Greig 54, A.A. Mallett 4 for 21). Australia won by 171 runs.

Australia regained the Ashes, four years after losing them on the same ground, with a decisive victory achieved with 5.3 overs in hand. Denness dropped himself for this match, Edrich taking over the captaincy, and the veteran left-hander had two ribs cracked first ball from Lillee on the last day, which forced him into the casualty ward. He returned, and held fast for 33 not out, showing that but for the accident England might reasonably have expected to play out time. McCosker had a distinguished first Test innings, opening for the first time in big cricket, and once more the Chappells contributed valuably. Lillee, Thomson and Walker again did an effective job, only Edrich, who batted 3¾ hours, and Knott, driving spiritedly, offering any real fight. Lloyd brilliantly caught Ian Chappell at leg slip as Australia's second innings got under way, but Greg Chappell and Redpath then partook of a stand of 220. The bowling was tight – especially that of Arnold – but Chappell's hundred had an inevitability about it. Redpath's took two hours longer. England were thus set 400 in 8½ hours. A thunderstorm cut 95 minutes away that evening, but having progressed to 68 without loss on the last day, England began to lose wickets to the fast bowlers and then to Mallett's off-spin. Fletcher was once hit on the head, the ball flying to cover, and Greig was stumped at the peak of the crisis. A calamitous afternoon for England; a day of unbounded joy for Australia. The attendance of 178,027 was a Sydney match record.

973, below, left: *Fletcher hit on his St George and Dragon badge by a ball from Thomson which bounced off to cover point.* 974, right: *Edrich helped off after taking his first ball, from Lillee, in the ribs; two were cracked*

975, left: *Greg Chappell hits Willis for four during his 144. 976*, right, top: *The Ashes are won, with Arnold's dismissal, and Marsh rushes to shake his captain's hand. 977*, below: *The Sydney Hill with 1975 decor. During this Test 864,000 empty beer-cans had to be cleared away*

1974–75
Adelaide, January 25, 26, 27, 29, 30

FIFTH TEST

Australia 304 (*T.J.Jenner 74, K.D. Walters 55, M.H.N. Walker 41, D.L. Underwood 7 for 113*) *and 272 for 5 dec* (*K.D. Walters 71*, R.W. Marsh 55, I.R. Redpath 52, I.M. Chappell 41, D.L. Underwood 4 for 102*); England *172* (*M.H. Denness 51, K.W.R. Fletcher 40, D.K. Lillee 4 for 49*) *and 241* (*A.P.E. Knott 106*, K.W.R. Fletcher 63, D.K. Lillee 4 for 69*). Australia won by 163 runs.

After the first day was lost through rain, Australia found themselves put in to bat by Denness, who soon had Underwood bowling on a drying pitch. Australia advanced to 52, then the left-arm spinner struck. Soon after lunch Australia were 84 for 5 – all to Underwood. It was felt by many that Titmus should have been used at the other end, but Denness's policy was to contain, and the off-spinner had only one over before lunch and seven in the innings. Walters and Jenner extricated their side by aggressive means, and as the pitch eased, Australia forgot their woes with a total of 304. England, Denness and Fletcher apart, then batted dismally. Lillee bowled at a great pace, and Thomson took three top wickets, taking his aggregate for the series to 33, a final figure since a shoulder injury when he played tennis on the rest day kept him from the rest of the series. Australia, with Willis laid low by knee damage, remorselessly enlarged their lead, Walters and Marsh accelerating to a 112-run stand before the closure, and once more England faced a target that was clearly beyond them. Amiss, Arnold and Underwood all completed 'pairs', but Knott, with the last man in with him, reached only the second century in these Test matches by a wicketkeeper.

978, left: *Greig, intimidatingly close at point, catches Redpath off Underwood. 979*, right: *Knott pulls during his century*

980, left: *Ian Chappell miscues a ball from Underwood on the first morning; the ball fell into Knott's gloves.* 981, right: *Lloyd wonderfully caught down the leg side by Marsh off Lillee at Adelaide*

1974–75
Melbourne, February 8, 9, 10, 12, 13

SIXTH TEST

Australia *152 (I.M. Chappell 65, P. Lever 6 for 38) and 373 (G.S. Chappell 102, I.R. Redpath 83, R.B. McCosker 76, I.M. Chappell 50, A.W. Greig 4 for 88); England 529 (M.H. Denness 188, K.W.R. Fletcher 146, A.W. Greig 89, J.H. Edrich 70, M.H.N. Walker 8 for 143).* England won by an innings and 4 runs.

With Thomson out of the side and Lillee retiring with a foot injury after six overs (having inflicted a third consecutive 'duck' on Amiss), England seized the opportunity to come to terms with comparatively ordinary bowling after Peter Lever had routed Australia on a humid morning, a damp patch serving as a psychological if not physical hazard (though Greg Chappell was hit in the jaw by a Lever flyer). The Lancastrian kept the ball well up, in contrast to his last Test, at Brisbane, when he took 0 for 111. He took four key wickets for five runs in one spell. Only a dogged innings by Ian Chappell spared Australia total humiliation. After having made only one century stand in the series to date, England now enjoyed three in a row: 149 by Edrich and Denness for the third wicket, 192 by Denness and Fletcher for the fourth, and 148 – taking the total to 507 – by Fletcher and Greig. Denness, missed three times, batted 8½ hours for the highest score by an England captain in Australia (passing A.E. Stoddart's 173 made 80 years before), both he and Fletcher repaying Australia's subsidiary bowlers for much torment endured during the series. Max Walker picked up five quick wickets as the tail subsided, and finished with the reward of 42.2-7-143-8, deservedly fine figures after a manful performance. Thirteen hours remained when Australia, on a good pitch, set out to resist England. Redpath batted six hours (32 in the whole series), Greg Chappell four, but the tourists kept at their task, and Greig, Arnold and Lever saw them home by 2.15 pm.

982, left: *Greg Chappell hit in the jaw by a flyer from Lever.* 983, below: *Denness's leg glance eludes Marsh and he has his century.* 984, right: *Denness c and b Walker 188 – the highest by an England captain in a Test in Australia*

1975
Edgbaston, July 10, 11, 12, 14

Australia 359 (R.W. Marsh 61, R.B. McCosker 59, R. Edwards 56, I.M. Chappell 52, J.R. Thomson 49); England 101 (D.K. Lillee 5 for 15, M.H.N. Walker 5 for 48) and 173 (K.W.R. Fletcher 51, J.R. Thomson 5 for 38). Australia won by an innings and 85 runs.

Denness, after consulting his senior players, gambled against an ominous weather forecast by putting Australia in – and lost comprehensively. Turner and McCosker took Australia to 77 without loss at lunch, and from 243 for 5 that evening the tourists progressed to 359, Marsh and Thomson hitting hard and Edwards, often playing and missing, batted four hours to ensure Australia's sound position. Fatefully, after one over of England's innings a thunderstorm drenched the ground, and after 100 minutes were lost, a new regulation added an hour to the day's play. By the close England were 83 for 7. Lillee, with his controlled ferocity, and Walker, unorthodox of action, used the favourable bowling conditions much better than some of their predecessors over the years, and England were following on half an hour into the Saturday. This time Thomson, who had been wildly erratic in the first innings, found his rhythm, length and direction. After two further rain delays, England were in ruins at 93 for 5 that evening. Further fine catching, a second 'duck' for Gooch on his Test debut, and a paralysing blow on Amiss's arm bestowed gloom upon the England camp. By mid-afternoon on the fourth day England had suffered their first defeat at Edgbaston, and Australia's dominance of the 1974–75 series was re-established.

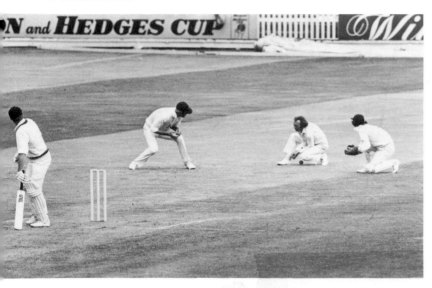

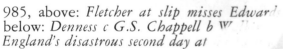

985, above: *Fletcher at slip misses Edward*
below: *Denness c G.S. Chappell b W*
England's disastrous second day at

1975
Lord's, July 31, August 1, 2, 4, 5

England 315 (A.W. Greig 96, A.P.E. Knott 69, D.S. Steele 50, D.K. Lillee 4 for 84) and 436 for 7 dec (J.H. Edrich 175, B. Wood 52, D.S. Steele 45, A.W. Greig 41); Australia 268 (R. Edwards 99, D.K. Lillee 73*, J.A. Snow 4 for 66) and 329 for 3 (I.M. Chappell 86, R.B. McCosker 79, G.S. Chappell 73*, R. Edwards 52*). Match drawn.

Spirit returned to the England XI when, after another horrendous start (49 for 4: Lillee 4 for 33), Greig, the new captain – Denness having been dropped – and Steele, prematurely grey, bespectacled, and in his first Test at 33, put on 96 for the fifth wicket to initiate a batting recovery later backed up by an inspired bowling performance. Snow matched Lillee in relentless, varied attack; but just as the doughty Steele, cavalier Greig and nimble Knott saved England's innings, so Edwards, with Thomson's help, lifted Australia from the emergency of 81 for 7, and Lillee, at No.10, clubbed three sixes and eight fours in 2¼ hours, dominating a final stand of 69 to reduce the leeway to 47. Ross Edwards, so often Australia's 'make-or-break' batsman, hit 15 fours in his 99, and fell eventually to Woolmer, lbw. First Wood then Steele stayed with Edrich while England carefully built up a sizable lead on the third day, the rugged Surrey left-hander going to his seventh – and highest – century against Australia. Greig's declaration set Australia 484 in 500 minutes, and they were 97 for one as the final day began. England's hoped-for thunderstorm arrived – but before play began. The covered pitch consequently was unharmed, and with an hour lost, Australia sedately played out time. England now needed to win both remaining matches to regain the Ashes.

989, left: *Steele, who brought character and pugnacity to England's batting, gets a ball away past Turner during his first Test innings.* 990, right: *Gooch congratulates his partner Edrich upon reaching 150*

1975
THIRD TEST
Headingley, August 14, 15, 16, 18, 19

England 288 (D.S. Steele 73, J.H. Edrich 62, A.W. Greig 51, G.J. Gilmour 6 for 85) and 291 (D.S. Steele 92, A.W. Greig 49); Australia 135 (P.H. Edmonds 5 for 28) and 220 for 3 (R.B. McCosker 95*, I.M. Chappell 62). Match drawn.

With the match interestingly poised after the fourth day – Australia needing a further 225 runs with seven wickets in hand – there was general dismay at the discovery that vandals had gouged the pitch and poured crude oil over it. They wished to draw attention to the alleged wrongful imprisonment for armed robbery of one George Davis. The match was therefore abandoned as a draw, the only comfort being that rain, which descended at noon, would have prevented victory by either side. Steele, top-scorer in both England innings, added 112 with the equally consistent Edrich for the second wicket, but, the eager Greig apart, there was little resistance to Australia's pace quartet. Gilmour, left-arm fast-medium, swung the ball late, and took nine wickets in his debut match against England. Another debutant, however, was to make an even more conspicuous mark: Phil Edmonds, tall, Zambian-born, left-arm spinner, took 5 for 17 in his first 12 overs, without maintaining faultless accuracy. He got rid of the Chappells, Edwards, Walters and Walker as Australia slid from 78 for 2 to 107 for 8. England built slowly on their lead until the fourth morning, when a concerted effort to score fast paid off. Marsh, opening the innings in this match, helped McCosker put 55 up for the first wicket, and Ian Chappell hit 50 in boundaries during the next stand, an even-time 116. Though he and his brother were out by the close, McCosker was very steady and Walters was untroubled. But a compelling final day was not to be.

994, above: Edwards, playing no stroke, is lbw to Edmonds. 995, right: Greig is run out for 51 in England's first innings

996, above: *Forensic investigators examine the damage inflicted on the Headingley pitch by vandals during the night, while Yorkshire's secretary interprets an unprecedented situation for the benefit of journalists and broadcasters.* 997, right: *How the nation's television-watchers learned of the outrage*

1975   FOURTH TEST
The Oval, August 28, 29, 30, September 1, 2, 3

Australia *532 for 9 dec (I.M. Chappell 192, R.B. McCosker 127, K.D. Walters 65, R. Edwards 44) and 40 for 2;* England *191 (J.R. Thomson 4 for 50, M.H.N. Walker 4 for 63) and 538 (R.A. Woolmer 149, J.H. Edrich 96, G.R.J. Roope 77, D.S. Steele 66, A.P.E. Knott 64, K.D. Walters 4 for 34, D.K. Lillee 4 for 91).* Match drawn.

After winning the toss, Australia made almost certain of holding their series lead by finishing the first day at 280 for one. Chappell and McCosker's stand realised 277, the ninth-highest for any wicket in England-Australia Tests. Greg Chappell's unaccountable run of failures continued with a first-ball dismissal by Old. Ian Chappell, who announced his retirement from the captaincy during this match after having led Australia 30 times, batted 442 minutes. Walters' score was his highest in a Test in England since his first, in 1968. There was a sinister change in the weather on the third day, and in poor light and intermittent drizzle England laboured to 169 for 8. Following on 341 behind, they 'set up camp' in better conditions second time round, and with Edrich and Wood grinding out 77 for the first wicket in almost three hours it was soon apparent that only concentration lapses or inspired bowling could bring about a result. Patience in abundance from the batsmen matched by growing frustration in the field saw the match creep through the fifth day – with Woolmer and Roope centre-stage for most of it – and through the sixth. Woolmer's drive to the boundary off Mallett on the final morning brought him his century in 396 minutes – the slowest ever in these Tests. His innings stretched across 495 minutes altogether, and ensured – though not until some time into the last day – that England would be safe. This was the longest cricket match ever played in England, and a further indictment of over-prepared pitches.

998, left: *Picture of a happy man: Rick McCosker acknowledges the reception given him upon reaching his first Test century.*
999, below: *Ian Chappell, captaining Australia for the 30th and final time, sweeps during his masterly innings of 192*

1000, bottom: *Bob Woolmer, who had seldom batted as high as No. 5 for his county, Kent, reaches his hundred with a drive off the back foot. Wicketkeeper Rod Marsh was behind the stumps while 1425 balls (including wides and no-balls) were sent down during the innings*

ACKNOWLEDGEMENTS

Picture sources

MCC Collection: page 1; illustrations 29, 111, 135, 153.

Radio Times Hulton Picture Library: 11, 313, 314, 476.

Illustrated London News: 27.

Ron Yeomans: 32.

New South Wales Government Printing Office: 110, 201.

David Wells: 132.

Punch: 142.

E.P. Ellison: 266.

Central Press Photos Ltd: 398, 418, 473, 475, 485, 487–9, 491–2, 494, 532, 534, 537, 540, 547–9, 554, 556–9, 588, 590–2, 614, 638–9, 642, 651–2, 657, 674, 676, 681, 683–4, 697–9, 723–4, 726, 732, 734, 739, 741–4, 746, 766–7, 786, 788, 810, 812, 821–3, 826–7, 829, 830, 848, 851, 854, 863–4, 866–71, 874–5, 877, 882, 884–5, 892, 895–8, 903–6, 911–3, 915–17, 922–3, 925, 929, 930, 932, 937, 950, 958, 963–5, 970–2, 981, 983, 985, 991.

Press Association-Reuter: 405–6, 421, 423, 688, 752, 838, 845, 949, 954–5, 959, 986.

Sport & General Press Agency Ltd: 413, 463–72, 474, 477–81, 484, 486, 519, 521, 533, 536, 539, 541–2, 544, 546, 550–1, 553, 555, 564, 570–1, 573, 575–8, 581, 593, 597–9, 606, 645, 647, 689, 690, 694, 715, 736–8, 748, 750, 754–5, 758, 760, 769, 770, 775, 778–82, 785, 813–14, 816–17, 819, 855–7, 859–62, 872, 876, 889, 893, 899, 901–2, 907, 910.

Australian News & Information Bureau: 879, 880, 887, 890–1, 894, 962, 980.

Keystone Press Agency Ltd: 886, 938, 978, 982, 984.

Times Newspapers Ltd: 900.

Australian Cricket: 918, 920–1, 924, 931, 940.

Patrick Eagar: 941, 943–6, 948, 953, 966–9, 973–7, 987–8, 992–6, 998, 999.

Ken Kelly: 952.

Sporting Pictures (UK) Ltd: 989, 990, 1000.

Marshall's Sports Service: 997.

All other illustrations are from the author's private collection of photographs, scrapbooks, postcards, cigarette-cards, books and relics. Extensive reproduction has been made from the following volumes in particular: *Famous Cricketers and Cricket Grounds* edited by C.W. Alcock (Hudson & Kearns, 1895); *The Daily Graphic*; *How We Recovered the Ashes* by P.F. Warner (Chapman & Hall, 1904); *With Bat and Ball* by George Giffen (Ward, Lock, 1898); *The Book of Cricket* edited by C.B. Fry (Newnes); *Cricket*; *Great Batsmen: Their Methods at a Glance* by George W. Bedlam and Charles B. Fry (Macmillan, 1905); *Great Bowlers and Fielders: Their Methods at a Glance* by George W. Beldam and Charles B. Fry (Macmillan, 1907); *Cricket of Today and Yesterday* Vols I & II by Percy Cross Standing (Caxton, c 1902); *Sporting Sketches*; *The Strand Magazine*; *'WG': Cricketing Reminiscences and Personal Recollections* by W.G. Grace (Bowden, 1899); *An Australian Cricketer on Tour* by Frank Laver (Chapman & Hall, 1905); *England v Australia* by P.F. Warner (Mills & Boon, 1912); *Defending the Ashes* by P.G.H. Fender (Chapman & Hall, 1921); *Mailey's Googlies* by A.A. Mailey (Graphic, 1921); *The Cricketer*; *Gilligan's Men* by M.A. Noble (Chapman & Hall, 1925); *Behind the Wicket* by W.A. Oldfield (Hutchinson, 1938); *History of the Tests* by Sydney Smith (Australasian Publishing, 1946); *The Fight for the Ashes in 1926* by P.F. Warner (Harrap, 1926); *Collins's Men* by A.E.R. Gilligan (Arrowsmith, 1926); *Those 'Ashes'* by M.A. Noble (Cassell, 1927); *The Turn of the Wheel* by P.G.H. Fender (Faber, 1929); *The Fight for the Ashes 1928–29* by M.A. Noble (Harrap, 1929); *The Tests of 1930* by P.G.H. Fender (Faber, 1930); *The Fight for the Ashes in 1930* by P.F. Warner (Harrap, 1930); *In Quest of the Ashes* by D.R. Jardine (Hutchinson, 1933); *The Fight for the Ashes 1932–33* by J.B. Hobbs (Harrap, 1933); *Ashes and Dust* by D.R. Jardine (Hutchinson, 1934); *Kissing the Rod* by P.G.H. Fender (Chapman & Hall, 1934); *1937 Australian Test Tour* by Bruce Harris (Hutchinson, 1937); *So This is Australia* by William Pollock (Barker, 1937); together with a number of post-war England v Australia tour books.

In addition, use has been made of photographs from the following newspapers: *Brisbane Courier-Mail, Sydney Morning Herald, Sydney Telegraph, Sydney Sun, Sydney Mirror, Melbourne Argus, Melbourne Age, Melbourne Herald, Adelaide Advertiser,* and *The Australasian*.

Compilation of the statistics in this book has been based principally on *England v Australia: A Compendium of Test Cricket between the Countries 1877–1968* by Ralph Barker and Irving Rosenwater (Batsford, 1969); *Wisden Cricketers' Almanack*; and *Classic Centuries in the Test Matches between England and Australia* by B.J. Wakley (Kaye, 1964).

The author wishes to record his gratitude to John Arlott for the loan of two volumes and pictorial matter previously owned by the late A.P.F. Chapman; to Patrick Eagar for his assistance in reproducing certain photographs from the period 1896 to 1898; to Stephen Green, MCC curator at Lord's, for his help in this project; and to the abovenamed authors, agencies, publishers, and other individuals.